A New New Deal

A New New Deal

*How Regional Activism Will Reshape
the American Labor Movement*

AMY B. DEAN AND DAVID B. REYNOLDS
FOREWORD BY HAROLD MEYERSON
A CENTURY FOUNDATION BOOK

ILR PRESS

AN IMPRINT OF
CORNELL UNIVERSITY PRESS
ITHACA AND LONDON

First published 2009 by Cornell University Press
First printing, Cornell Paperbacks, 2010
Printed in the United States of America

Library of Congress Cataloging-in-Publication Data

Dean, Amy B., 1962–
   A new new deal : how regional activism will reshape the American
labor movement / Amy B. Dean and David B. Reynolds ; foreword by
Harold Meyerson.
      p. cm.
   "A Century Foundation book."
   Includes bibliographical references and index.
   ISBN 978-0-8014-4838-6 (cloth : alk. paper)
   ISBN 978-0-8014-7665-5 (pbk. : alk. paper)
   1. Labor movement—United States.   2. Regionalism—United States.
3. Working class—United States.   4. Community development—
United States.   5. Coalitions—United States.   I. Reynolds, David B.,
1963– II. Title.

   HD8066.D42   2009
   331.880973—dc22

2009016723

Cornell University Press strives to use environmentally responsible
suppliers and materials to the fullest extent possible in the publishing of
its books. Such materials include vegetable-based, low-VOC inks and
acid-free papers that are recycled, totally chlorine-free, or partly composed
of nonwood fibers. For further information, visit our website at
www.cornellpress.cornell.edu.

Cloth printing   10 9 8 7 6 5 4 3 2
Paperback printing   10 9 8 7 6 5 4 3 2 1

For my mother,
Theodora "Teddie" Radove Dean
(1939–1997)
and for
Loyd Williams, Business Manager from 1993–2004,
Plumbers, Steamfitters and Refrigeration Workers Local 393

Teddie treated everyone with dignity and respect. In her world—which
can one day be our world—people were valued for who they are
and what they contribute. My life's work in the American labor
movement is a tribute to her enduring influence.
Loyd was a modern-day Walter Reuther, Sidney Hillman, and A. Phillip
Randolph. His heart was big enough to support a whole community.
We hear it beating still.
—Amy Dean

For my mother, Mary Reynolds (1923–2006), whose strong will,
questioning mind, and passionate commitment to social justice
continues to animate my life and work.
—David Reynolds

CONTENTS

Foreword by Harold Meyerson   ix

A Note from The Century Foundation by Richard C. Leone   xiii

Preface   xvii

Acknowledgments   xxiii

Introduction   1

The Birth of Regional Power Building   **19**

1. Thinking Regionally   21

2. The Regional Power-Building Model Emerges in California   39

The Three Legs of Regional Power Building   **85**

3. Developing a Regional Policy Agenda   87

4. Deep Coalitions   126

5. From Access to Governance: Building
   Aggressive Political Action   159

The Spread of Regional Power Building   **185**

6. Understanding the Spread of Regional Power Building
   across the Country   187

7. Toward a National Strategy for Spreading Regional
   Power Building   221

Notes   247

Index   261

FOREWORD

One of the happiest accidents of my life was to be in the right place at the right time to see a labor movement turn a city around. The place was Los Angeles—historically a bastion of antiunion sentiment. The time was the 1990s, when I was the political editor of the *L.A. Weekly* and when a young labor leader, Miguel Contreras, aligned the city's reawakening union movement with the burgeoning Latino immigrant community to create a progressive force that transformed L.A. into a solidly liberal city, and one that implemented policies to lessen the yawning gap between rich and poor.

Miguel was one of two California labor leaders who lit out during the '90s for this uncharted territory—building a dynamic local labor movement that tackled the growing inequality that increasingly defined America's cities. The other was Amy Dean, who headed the AFL-CIO in the community that came to symbolize American innovation and prosperity: Silicon Valley. Like their counterparts in Los Angeles, however, the workers for whom Amy spoke shared none of the storybook prosperity of the high-tech boom. The men and women who cleaned their cities' office buildings and made them glisten in the California sun worked long hours for low pay.

What Amy and Miguel confronted were the hard realities of post–New Deal America—a place where manufacturing and unions were in decline, where retail and service-sector jobs that paid little and offered no benefits were on the rise, where economic security was vanishing, and where the federal government, in the sway of Reagan-age ideologies, had no inclination to restore it. Nationally, the union movement, while struggling to grow again, remained weak and largely unable to arrest America's galloping inequality. The very idea that local collections of unions could prod their local governments to enact the kind of egalitarian policies that the federal government had once enacted—policies to raise the wages and provide benefits to workers—seemed fanciful, if not absurd.

And yet, that's what happened in Los Angeles and in San Jose and in cities up and down California and then across America. Amy and Miguel, in concert with other visionary labor leaders in their cities and in others, set up organizations that provided authoritative research on how the other half lived within their cities. They set up community alliances that pushed local governments to enact living-wage ordinances for employees of companies with municipal contracts and implemented community benefit agreements that created jobs for the residents of downtown areas where glass and steel towers rose to the sky. They established political operations that turned out the volunteers who elected politicians committed to policies of broadly shared prosperity and environmental justice.

They encountered setbacks along the way, of course. In some cities, unions proved resistant to the kind of labor-community alliance it takes to build power; in other cities, the funding base for these kinds of activities proved too narrow; and in still other cities, movements to ensure that prosperity would be broadly shared failed in the absence of sufficient prosperity to go around. But in many cities, these labor-based movements for economic justice have bettered the lot of tens of thousands of workers and their families, and mobilized whole new constituencies of progressive voters in the process.

This is the story that Amy Dean and David Reynolds of Wayne State University tell in this important book. Coming at a moment when a new president is determined to use the power of government to rebuild a middle class, when activists are looking to new forms of organizing and politics to build a better nation, when the labor movement is casting about for new ways to help working people win more secure lives, *A New New Deal* couldn't be more timely.

Even in this era of virtual reality, political movements come from places. Franklin Roosevelt's New Deal came off the sidewalks of Fiorello La Guardia's and Sidney Hillman's and FDR's own New York. Barack Obama's new new deal, if it succeeds, will be able to claim its own roots— Saul Alinsky's Chicago, of course, but also Miguel Contreras's Los Angeles and Amy Dean's San Jose.

Get a jump on the historians. Read about them here.

Harold Meyerson

Harold Meyerson is Editor at Large of the *American Prospect* and an op-ed columnist for the *Washington Post*. From 1989 through 2001, he was executive editor of the *L.A. Weekly*.

A Note from The Century Foundation

At the time of this writing, a vivid (and painful) new chapter in American and global economic history is being written. Given the scale and consequences of the present sharp financial decline, we also can be certain that it will be analyzed and reanalyzed extensively as future scholars pore over the evidence about what precipitated the collapse and what was done to halt and reverse the decline. Economics doctoral candidates yet unborn will slice and dice this history while filling bookshelves with richly detailed meta-analyses of this recession.

It is clearly hazardous, then, to venture any predictions of where the consensus about causes will wind up. Nonetheless, I will take a guess that no serious person will find that the cause was the overweening strength of labor unions in the United States. The woeful tale of union decline has been told many times. And, strikingly, even in the current crisis, the bulk of attention that unions are receiving in the press involves internecine battles, almost incomprehensible to outsiders. At the same time, it is hard to believe that the labor movement's future will not be profoundly affected by the many impacts of the recession of 2008 and beyond.

There is ample reason to believe that our economic architecture will change dramatically in the years to come. As we achieve a "new normal," we may find regulatory and tax structures altered, and compensation and accounting practices changed. Therefore, it is reasonable to ask how the relationship of workers to their employers and to one another may change. If there is constructive development as a result of the current turmoil, it seems likely that one blueprint for a revived unionism will be that described and proposed in the pages that follow. It is a model that is simply too good to ignore.

Today, labor unions often seem too small to matter, with their greatest membership being in the special case of public employees. Elsewhere, they have been ineffective in reversing the trends toward greater inequality and wage stagnation. They have lost the battle to retain defined benefit retirement plans, as defined contribution plans (where the risk is greater for workers) have become the norm—that is, for those with any retirement plan at all.

In this unpromising environment, the cases described in this book are especially interesting and extremely valuable. They relate how workers' organizations in high-growth areas such as Silicon Valley in California were able to reinvent themselves and succeed.

Their political activity has been positive, educating candidates about the goals and desires of working people. They have been active on a range of issues that affect nearly all workers. And they have grown in importance.

The Century Foundation has had a long-standing concern over the role of workers in the U.S. economy, having supported publications such as Joan Fitzgerald's *Moving Up in the New Economy: Career Ladders for U.S. Workers,* Paul Osterman's *Securing Prosperity: The American Labor Market: How It Has Changed and What to Do about It,* Simon Head's *The New Ruthless Economy: Work and Power in the Digital Age,* and the report of The Century Foundation Task Force on the Future of Unions, *What's Next for Organized Labor?*

Therefore, The Century Foundation was especially interested when Amy Dean, the former chief executive officer of the South Bay AFL-CIO Labor Council, approached us about writing a book on this important and underreported subject. She and her coauthor, David Reynolds of Wayne

State University, have given us a vivid and detailed portrait of a new brand of effective unionism in practice. On behalf of the Trustees of The Century Foundation, I commend and thank them for their work.

Richard C. Leone, *President*
The Century Foundation

PREFACE

Amy Dean

In the home where I grew up there was a picture prominently displayed of a stranger, someone nobody in my family had ever met. That stranger was Walter Reuther, president of the United Auto Workers and then the best-known labor leader in the United States. No, the Deans were not autoworkers. But my grandparents, like many others, regarded labor leaders like Walter Reuther as worthy of veneration—not because they were heads of large unions but because they were leaders of a broad movement of working people.

Reuther and similar leaders understood that the best way unions could win support from the general public was to make certain the public knew that when unions win the people win, too. That social vision was forged simultaneously in the workplace, through organizing and bargaining, and in communities, through coalition building and political action. As immigrants who came to America with few possessions except a burning desire to make a better life for themselves and their children, my grandparents found in the labor movement a champion for their deepest aspirations. I often think of that today when I see another generation of immigrants dedicating their lives to fighting not just for immigrant rights but for the rights of all workers.

Organized labor came to embody the most deeply held aspirations of my grandparents' and parents' generations. It pushed for fair and reasonable limits on working hours and for the elimination of child labor. It wanted to assure the provision of wages and benefits adequate to reduce appalling levels of poverty and deprivation. The socially popular benefits that organized labor won over time met those needs. They included the forty-hour workweek, overtime pay, health insurance, old-age pensions, and practical ways to address on-the-job grievances. By fighting and winning battles that focused on common and deeply felt human values, the organized labor movement established itself as a champion of the public good.

Building organized labor was seen as part of forging a new consensus about how our society ought to function. The labor movement played a critical role in creating many social institutions we now take for granted. These include the world's first health maintenance organization (HMO), public housing projects, cooperative businesses, and protections for civil rights and freedom of speech, as well as one of the nation's first consumer movements. Unionists like Reuther were also among the first to push for better and more accessible training and educational opportunities for the general public, a movement that culminated, in part, in the creation of thousands of community colleges across the United States.

All this, as well as my own experiences as an activist, led me to the labor movement. After college I went to work for the International Ladies Garment Workers Union in my home city of Chicago. There the classic unionized work of the city, like the steel, textile, and apparel industries, was taking a terrible beating from what was then called "foreign competition" and is now called "globalization." Working people were displaced from once secure occupations as entire industries downsized and outsourced.

In the mid-1980s the garment workers union participated in Chicago's first broad-based task force on retaining garment industry jobs. Established by the city's visionary mayor, Harold Washington, this innovative task force included leaders from the private sector, government, and labor.

I saw new relationships form among the panel members, many of whom were eager to develop programs to meet their shared concerns without having to wait for action from the state or federal government.

In 1990, already having moved from Chicago to San Francisco, I moved to San Jose, California, in the heart of Silicon Valley, to take a job with the South Bay AFL-CIO Labor Council. The region was touted as being on the cutting edge of the "new economy." But it had many similarities to industrial Chicago.

Silicon Valley was being promoted not only as the place where a new generation of high-tech products was being designed and produced but also as the birthplace of revolutionary business practices, including new relationships between employers and employees. The "new" business model emphasized "core competence," "speed to market," highly specialized labor pools, and the need for streamlined and efficient commercial operations. It was virtually the same model that had left a swath of devastated communities, decimated unions, intensified workplace exploitation, and massive job insecurity throughout the industrial Midwest.

My work with the labor movement in Silicon Valley has been devoted to putting safeguards in place that protect the quality of life for the region's working people. My experience with Mayor Washington's task force in Chicago had given me a starting point for thinking about how to do that, and led me to develop new approaches that drew together the different parts of the labor movement and the wider community of working people around a shared social vision—and a set of strategies for realizing it. I call these approaches "regional power building." The ways in which we developed regional power building in Silicon Valley, and similar experiments throughout the rest of the country, are the subject of this book.

Regional power-building efforts took a quantum jump when newly elected AFL-CIO president John Sweeney created the Central Labor Council Advisory Committee. For seven and a half years I was proud to be its leader. The committee provided the first real opportunity since the 1930s to bring together grassroots labor leaders to share best practices and to proliferate learning across regions; it also allowed us to engage national labor leaders for the first time in decades about building labor's presence in the community and in the broader region.

My work with the labor movement grew out of my own strong commitment to family and faith. My grandparents were among the millions of Jews who left Eastern Europe at the turn of the century. They escaped pogroms and arrived at Ellis Island with few possessions. But their bags were over-flowing with hopes and dreams for a better life for their children.

They brought with them a social vision that grew out of their religious faith as Jews. Part of that faith was a commitment to building commu-nal institutions to support each other. They built schools, synagogues, and trade unions. They did so as an expression of both Jewish values and the values of American democracy. From my grandparents I acquired my belief—taught to me more by example than by words—that the health of civil society is intimately linked to the health of public institutions and civic engagement, and that it is the labor movement that puts democracy into democracies.

This book grows out of my need to share the lessons of my nearly twenty years in the labor movement, both as a labor leader in Silicon Valley and as the chair of President Sweeney's Central Labor Council Advisory Committee. Through that experience I learned that our work must be deep and broad. It must be based on a new social vision; a rebuilt progressive social infrastruc-ture; a recognition of the central role of regional governance; and a new social contract that can provide the building blocks for a "new New Deal."

I hope this book contributes to a broader discussion about the future of organized labor and its contributions to the future of American democ-racy. I hope it will be of value to both practitioners and academics. Ulti-mately, I hope it contributes to addressing the problems of tens of millions of people who are working hard, playing by the rules, and nonetheless being deprived of their basic human right to a secure livelihood and a de-cent way of life. And finally I hope it will help us all take a next step toward realizing the values of that stranger whose picture my grandparents hung on their wall as an emblem of a democratic social vision.

David Reynolds

I first experienced the power of labor-community coalitions to build po-litical change as a graduate student organizer at Cornell University in the 1980s. With the leadership of then president Al Davidoff, United Auto Workers Local 2300 (which represents the university's food and building services staff) built in a series of innovative alliances, including one that supported graduate-student union organizing. The local also played an instrumental role in what at the time was known as the Tompkins-Cortland Labor Council. Working with modest resources, the council offered a model of what could be achieved in a largely rural area, such as that of upstate New York. Among their many activities, the council and Local 2300 played key roles in the election and governance of the socialist administration of Mayor Ben Nichols during the late 1980s and early 1990s in Ithaca, New York.[1] I was fortunate to be involved in both the campaigns that elected Nichols and in a governing citizen commission.

Over the past ten years I have been fortunate to do research, activism, and editing that has resulted in four books that further explored the intersection of labor and community activism with political and economic change.[2] Collectively these works have revealed the continuous and growing progressive activism found within America's grassroots. They also pointed to the need to better connect the various forms of economic activism and public policy campaigns to systematic strategies for gaining real political power. Only by knitting together separate campaigns and arenas for activism can we forge a more unified progressive movement capable of transforming America over the long term.

The regional power-building strategies presented in this book address this need. Beginning in 2002, I helped develop and coordinate a modest national network of labor educators and AFL-CIO staff dedicated to documenting and providing materials to support the emergence of the regional power building profiled in this book. Contact information and materials produced by the Regional Power Building Research Project are available on the project's website (http://www.powerbuilding.wayne.edu). Both the network and this book have the same purposes:

- To identify this current of regional labor-community organizing as a distinct model that can be discussed and debated as a coherent phenomenon. Our first step in this regard was simply to give the model a consistent name: building regional power.
- To document where the work is happening, the common strategies used by different groups, the rich adaptations to local conditions, and the various challenges and opportunities faced by regional organizers.
- To call on national leaders—in particular, those within organized labor—to see regional power building as necessary to their core revival strategies and to fully integrate this work into their strategic investments in their future.

ACKNOWLEDGMENTS

It's been said that it takes a community to raise a child; so too does it take many forms of support to write a book. It's hard to imagine that this book would have hit the high bar set by Cornell University Press but for the extensive feedback and incredibly generous support of Janice Fine. Janice, a rare individual who is respected in both the activist and academic worlds, gave so generously of her time and energy to make this book possible.

The research project that led to this book received generous support from the Carnegie Endowment for International Peace, the Century Foundation, the Nathan Cummings Foundation, the Ford Foundation, the McKay Foundation, the Ms. Foundation, the Albert Shanker Institute, and the Solidago Foundation. We are deeply grateful to those foundations and to the program officers who assisted us, including Greg Anrig, Carl Anthony, Diana Cohn, Mil Duncan, Sandra Feldman, Sara Gould, Phil Kugler, Richard Leone, Lance Lindblom, Geraldine Mannion, Rob McKay, Patricia Rosenfield, and Gloria Steinem.

We owe a deep debt of gratitude to the progressive groups and foundations that have provided support over the years to Working Partnerships USA and many of the other labor-community collaborations described in this book. These include the AFL-CIO, the California Endowment, the California Wellness Foundation, the Marguerite Casey Foundation, the Catholic Campaign for Human Development, the Nathan Cummings Foundation, the French American Charitable Trust, the Kaiser Foundation, the Charles Stewart Mott Foundation, the Needmor Foundation, the New World Foundation, the Penney Family Foundation, the Rockefeller Foundation, the Arca Foundation, the Public Welfare Foundation, the Tides Foundation, and the Unitarian Universalist Veatch Program at Shelter Rock. The leaders and program officers of these organizations gave Working Partnerships USA and other recipients the freedom to experiment and take risks so that we could contribute to the creation of a new generation of unions to assist and empower working people. Leaders who deserve special recognition include Ann Bastian, Diane Feeney, Margie Fine, Carol Guyer, Andrea Kydd, Jack Litzenberg, Catherine McFate, Victor Quintana, Frank Sanchez, and Janet Shenk. Without the resources that allowed us to create new kinds of hybrid labor-community organizations, the innovation and experimentation described in this book would not have been possible.

We offer a special acknowledgment to John Sweeney and the AFL-CIO. The Central Labor Council Advisory Committee he initiated brought together some amazing leaders who spearheaded new thinking about labor's role in the community and the work of central labor bodies. Special thanks to Bruce Colburn and Marilyn Sneiderman, the committee's staff, whose tireless efforts kept the issue of grassroots labor organization on the front burner of the American labor movement's agenda. Thanks also to the gifted group of local leaders who provided important leadership to our committee, including Stewart Acuff, the late Miguel Contreras, Ron Judd, Leslie Moody, and Bridgette Williams, and to the many others who contributed to our work along the way.

We thank the researchers from the Building Regional Power Research Project, without whose case study research and ongoing input this book could not have been written. We are especially grateful to director Hal Stack and the Labor Studies Center at Wayne State University for providing time needed to coordinate the network. The AFL-CIO repeatedly provided the crucial funding that permitted the network to conduct its research.

This book draws on the work of many researchers and labor educators within the Building Regional Power Research Project and beyond; we thank Louise Auerhahn, Monica Bielski, Jeremy Brecher, Barbara Byrd, Mike Cavanaugh, Kathleen Fernicola, Lou Jean Fleron, Larry Frank, John Goldstein, Jeff Grabelski, Jim Grossfeld, Cathy Howell, Tom Karson, David Keicher, Jim Lowe, Stephanie Luce, Linda Mulligan, Mark Nelson, Hal Plotkin, Scott Reynolds, Nari Rhee, Lorenzo Scott, Loren Stein, Kent Wong, Randy Wright, and Sarah Zimmerman. David Dobbie and David Moberg both provided interview research crucial for telling the stories of specific regions. Additional thanks are due to David Dobbie for contributing his rich knowledge on labor-community coalitions through extensive feedback and work on the manuscript.

Amy Dean's Personal Acknowledgments

Special recognition goes to Joan Emslie and the executive boards of San Jose, California's South Bay AFL-CIO, both past and present. They along with other South Bay labor leaders raised me, nurtured me, and provided the space for me and for our staff to be successful. Without Joan's leadership and the leadership of our board none of our innovative work in San Jose would have been possible. Special love and thanks go to the gifted staff that I had the privilege to work with: Cindy Chavez, Poncho Guevara, Lisa Hoyos, Anabel Ibañez, Jeanette Kjosa, John Leopold, Steve Preminger, and Christina Uribe. A special shout out to my sister and friend Phaedra Ellis Lamkins, who from day one never missed a beat in carrying forward the work of our team—she is a truly gifted leader! Special thanks also to Chris Benner for his early collaboration that helped reveal the other side of Silicon Valley, and to my dear and precious friend and confidant Bob Brownstein for teaching me political strategy, for sharing his policy chops so generously, and for turning me on to the teachings of the Buddha as well.

A special thanks to three of my "commonsense genius" assistants, Maria Escamilla, Christina Grijalva, and Jeanette Kjosa. Laboring aside these thoughtful, brilliant, and committed activists and the entire team at Working Partnerships USA has been the highlight of my professional life.

In addition, I was fortunate to receive support and advice from a number of academic leaders who have influenced my thinking as a practitioner, including Eileen Appelbaum, Tom Kochan, Ruth Milkman, Manuel Pastor, Michael Reich, Joel Rogers, and Kent Wong. The American Leadership Forum–Silicon Valley also has a special place in my heart for everything the organization has done to help shape my thinking about the relationship between labor and business. My deepest appreciation goes to Eric Benhanou, Les Denend, and Bob Saldich.

I have been blessed to have truly exceptional mentors in both work and life, including Leona Butler, Terry Cosgrove, Terry Christiansen, Susan and Phil Hammer, Esther Patt, and my special buddies Harry and Carol Saal. Thanks also to friends, associates, compatriots, and role models whom I greatly admire, including Ray Abernathy, Jerry Bukeweiz, Bruce Colburn, Miguel Contreras, Jeff Crosby, Peter and Marion Wright Edelman, Pat Lee, Rich Leib, Greg Leroy, Denise Mitchell, Jo-Ann Mort, Peter Olney, and Scott Reynolds.

Finally, hugs, kisses and deep appreciation to my wonderful family. While I ran around the world trying to make it a better place for working people, my husband, soul mate, and partner of more than twenty years, Randy Menna, made sure that the world was right for our working family. May our smart, sassy, and soulful son, Teddy, and daughter, Alix, carry on the good work of those who came before them. Thanks to my Pop, Bruce Dean—one of the hardest-working men I have ever known. And finally to my brother Jeff Dean, whose intellectual acumen and argumentative zeal forced me to refine and refine again every and all of the arguments contained within. This book could not have been written without all of you.

A New New Deal

INTRODUCTION

This book presents a strategy for building power for working people in America's metropolitan regions—and ultimately in the country as a whole. It is addressed to leaders and activists in the labor movement and their allies. Its authors have long been involved—one primarily as a leader, one primarily as a teacher and scholar—in the effort to revitalize the labor movement at the grassroots level. We believe that rebuilding labor's power at the regional level is essential for rebuilding the progressive movement as a whole—and for rebuilding American democracy. Despite the many difficulties it has faced over the past few decades, the American labor movement remains the social force with the greatest capacity to foster a broad-based movement for social and economic change. Among America's social movement organizations, unions by far enjoy the largest direct membership, staff, and other resources. In looking at who spends money on electoral politics, organized labor is the only player even remotely competing with corporate America.

This is not to say that community leaders and organizations are somehow secondary to regional power-building work. To the contrary, as we make clear throughout this book, community players have to be equal partners with unions. Indeed, to succeed over the long term, regional power building has to not only build the membership and capacity of organized labor but also help grassroots community groups grow and develop. The question is, however, who has the resources and capacity to convene a wide range of groups at the regional level? As the experiences in this book will demonstrate, organized labor has proven to be the natural anchor to pull together the many currents of progressive activism at the regional level. In other words, while meaningful change in America requires integrating the many currents of social protest, it cannot happen if the labor movement is not part of the story. In this book we examine how labor plays such a uniting role in regions across the country.

The story of the campaign for children's health care in San Jose, California, captures the significance and excitement of the regional power-building work explored in this book. In the spring of 2000, People Acting in Community Together (PACT), a faith-based community organization in Santa Clara County, surveyed the 30,000 members of its fourteen participating congregations about their health care. They discovered that in some churches more than 45 percent of families had at least one member who lacked health insurance—even though 80 percent of the families without insurance were headed by an adult who worked full-time.[1] PACT leader Maritza Maldonado called it "a wake-up call to all of us."

As PACT decided to take up the issue, it was joined by the AFL-CIO's South Bay Labor Council and its policy affiliate, Working Partnerships USA (WPUSA). Local labor councils are old but often somnolent expressions of organized labor. The South Bay Labor Council, however, was an exception. Its members had come to believe that labor needed to seek community leadership by becoming the champion of the concerns of all working families in the region—including the poor, minorities, and immigrants, and not just union members. It had set up WPUSA five years before as a "think-and-act tank" that could both provide public policy analysis and develop the community leadership and coalitions necessary to implement change.

Santa Clara County is the core of Silicon Valley, the region known at the turn of the twenty-first century as the software capital of the world.

One of the wealthiest places on Earth, Silicon Valley produced sixty new millionaires a day during the boom times of the 1990s.[2] But a highly publicized series of reports by WPUSA revealed that there were "two Silicon Valleys." Along with its wealth, Silicon Valley's "new economy" was producing poverty, inequality, and insecurity on a massive scale. A new set of policies—indeed, a new social vision based on providing for the needs of all members of the community—was required to counter this widening divide.

Unlike traditional think tanks, WPUSA was not only interested in identifying problems and proposing policies to meet them but also aimed to develop specific campaigns that would generate coalitions and begin to realize pieces of an alternative. It worked hand in hand with the labor council in this quest and took full advantage of the political clout the labor council could put behind policies it supported.

WPUSA saw an important part of its work as bringing together a cross-section of community leaders to learn about Silicon Valley's economy, form ongoing relationships with each other, and share ideas about what to do about the region's problems. When the health care campaign began, WPUSA had recently pulled together a diverse array of over three hundred stakeholders—including union organizers, housing advocates, service providers, environmentalists, and planners—in a series of roundtable discussions to establish a "community blueprint," a set of policy priorities intended to guide its work for the next several years. These stakeholders had identified affordable health care as one of their key issues and had developed an agenda for action.

Often American trade unions have approached the question of health care as something to be won for their members at the bargaining table. Some have even seen public provision of health care as undermining one of the key selling points for union membership. But when the South Bay Labor Council and WPUSA were approached by PACT, they took a very different approach. They identified children's health care as a need of workers and the community that they should be addressing. They identified PACT as a community ally that they should be working with to build broader power for working people in the region. And they recognized that a campaign for a program to provide health care for all children would be a great opportunity for strengthening their roles as leaders fighting for a better life for people in Silicon Valley.

As a result, WPUSA decided to work with PACT to launch the Children's Health Initiative (CHI). They set as their goal to make San Jose, the region's largest city and the fourth largest in California, the first city in America to guarantee health care coverage for all children.

Then the real work began. They worked out a plan to fill the gaps in existing programs, such as the exclusion of children because their family incomes were too far above the poverty line or because they couldn't prove legal immigration status. They identified potential sources of funding, including existing state and federal programs; funds allocated to local governments from the recent national tobacco lawsuit settlement; and charitable contributions. They built a support coalition whose partners ranged from the Santa Clara Family Health Plan, a major provider of health services to low-income people, to UCLA's prestigious Center for Health Policy Research, and from Santa Clara County's Health and Hospital System to, eventually, an association of big Silicon Valley tech firms. The South Bay Labor Council used its well-established ties with local political leaders and its considerable political clout to drum up support among city and county officials.

They asked San Jose mayor Ron Gonzales to commit $2 million from the city's share of the national tobacco lawsuit settlement to the program. But the mayor, pursuing other priorities, refused. Supporters responded with a series of actions, culminating with the mobilization of more than 1,000 CHI supporters at a critical meeting of the San Jose City Council. The council vote was split 5–5, with Mayor Gonzales breaking the tie with a vote against the CHI. But the confrontation only heightened public attention to the issue. "After the city council vote, the argument that tobacco money ought to be invested in healthier kids resonated throughout the community," according to PACT executive director Matt Hammer.[3]

A key theme of the South Bay Labor Council and WPUSA has been the need to treat areas like Silicon Valley not just as individual municipalities but as regions. Accordingly, the organizations moved to outflank San Jose's mayor by taking the issue to the county level. Within a week, the Board of Supervisors of Santa Clara County voted to adopt the Children's Health Initiative and fund it with $3 million of their own tobacco lawsuit settlement funds. The county's action forced the city's hand, and at a subsequent meeting the San Jose City Council voted 11–0 to fund the program.

CHI advocates had established a good working relationship with the Santa Clara County Health and Hospital System during the campaign. As the Santa Clara Family Health Plan, the Health and Hospital System, PACT, and WPUSA began designing the new program, they made sure it realized the goal of guaranteeing health care for all of Santa Clara County's 70,000 uninsured children. Run by the Family Health Plan, the program would be open to all children, regardless of immigration status; application would take a matter of minutes; and the plan would provide for all those who were ineligible for existing programs but couldn't afford to buy their own health insurance.

The new program was named Healthy Kids. According to Robert Sillen, executive director of the Santa Clara Valley Health and Hospital System, "We understood that the creation of Healthy Kids would give us the opportunity to tell working parents something we could never say before: that, no matter what your immigration status or your income, if you take the time to apply your children will be insured."[4]

On January 2, 2001, Santa Clara became the first county in the United States to offer health insurance to all of its children. Healthy Kids began reaching out to the families who needed it. For example, more than 3,000 people, mostly immigrants, gathered at Our Lady of Guadalupe Catholic Church for a kickoff event with live music, food, and programs for kids. The church became a giant enrollment center, and county workers registered more than 500 children for health insurance. Within a year, CHI was providing health care for more than 25,000 children.[5]

A 2005 study by Mathematica Policy Research has found that children enrolled in Healthy Kids are predominantly from two-parent working households that have lived in the county for at least two years. Nonetheless, two-thirds of the children enrolled did not have any health insurance coverage for six months or longer before their enrollment. Healthy Kids made a difference; as the study notes,

> Participation in Healthy Kids leads to dramatic increases in the medical care that children receive. These improvements include large gains in access to, and use of, care; sizable reductions in unmet need; and improvements in parents' confidence in, and satisfaction with, care.
>
> Participation in Healthy Kids leads to dramatic improvements in dental and vision care, including a roughly threefold increase in whether children

have a usual source of care for these services, receive a regular checkup, and receive a dental procedure such as a cavity filling or tooth extraction.[6]

CHI was wildly popular throughout California and was soon widely imitated. A poll found that 78 percent of Californians support health insurance coverage for every child in the state. By 2005, nine other counties had adopted programs similar to Healthy Kids and another twenty counties had them in the works.[7] Someday the program may be looked back on as a model—and a building block—for the national provision of health care for all.

The Children's Health Initiative, it turned out, helped the region's unions directly contribute to the interests of their members. The Service Employees International Union (SEIU), as well as other unions, had recently identified health care as a critical issue; the CHI gave them a concrete victory in pursuing it. Leaders of unions like the Hotel Employees and Restaurant Employees International Union (HERE) and the SEIU were sometimes surprised to learn how many of their own members' children were eligible for the program. And they found that public standards for what health insurance programs should include actually strengthened their hand by upping the ante at the bargaining table. More broadly, the respect and clout the labor council and WPUSA won from this and similar community leadership activities have contributed to their ability to help diverse unions in organizing, bargaining, and policy campaigns.

The CHI was also a success for the broader social and political objectives of the South Bay Labor Council and WPUSA. It successfully positioned them as community leaders. An editorial in the prestigious *San Jose Mercury News,* which had bitterly opposed previous local labor initiatives, declared CHI "an incredible success," adding, "What a credit to the initiative's visionary sponsors—Working Partnerships USA, the local labor-affiliated research group, and People Acting in Community Together (PACT), the faith-based neighborhood organizers.... Community leaders in and out of public office who've been part of this initiative should be proud of what they've accomplished—and of the example they're setting for the nation."[8]

Healthy Kids also exemplified the social vision of an inclusive community that the labor council and WPUSA were trying to impart. Their insistence that all kids who needed it should be covered regardless of financial or immigrant status served as an emblem of this vision. As the *San Jose Mercury News* editorial noted, the CHI was not just an isolated program, but one effort—among many needed—to tackle one symptom of "the growing gap between rich and poor in this county."[9]

Building Power for Working People

For some Americans, the past few decades have been the best of times. But the great majority of Americans have not shared in this prosperity. For them, the "new economy" has meant a deterioration in the quality of jobs, growing insecurity, and a squeeze between rising expenses and stagnating incomes. Their social safety net has been shredded; their basic rights as workers and simply as human beings have been eroded.

This growing polarization results from a loss of power by working people—in their unions, popular organizations, and the public sector. That loss of power is manifested in a decline in union membership, now limited to 12 percent of the workforce; a dismantling of social programs that once provided basic minimum standards for all Americans; an inability to elect political representatives who fight for the interests of working people; and a domination of political discourse by those who oppose the use of government and community institutions to provide well-being when the market doesn't.

Large corporations and the wealthy minority have managed not only to elect politicians favorable to their views but have established an entire apparatus of political alliances, think tanks, lobbyists, media, public relations flacks, and coalitions with grassroots groups that support them—despite having radically different economic interests. As a result, elite interests have established a capacity to determine the direction of society—in short, to govern.

The principal vehicles that working people have used to pursue power in the United States are the labor movement, other social movements, and the Democratic Party. How to rebuild all three has been an ongoing focus of discussion and experimentation for both activists and scholars.

There is no magic bullet. Unions, social movements, or the Democratic Party cannot rebuild worker power alone; neither can organizing, political mobilization, policy development, or infrastructure building in and of themselves. And the problem cannot be solved independently at national or local levels. Indeed, cooperation among actions in *all* of these arenas is critical to reempowering working people.

Recruiting voters for one election will not in itself reempower working people; nor will just signing up new union members. Rebuilding workers' power requires developing an independent capacity to govern a constellation of ideas, institutions, alliances, strategies, and campaigns that can successfully contest corporate domination at the local, regional, state, and national levels. In this book we examine how progressive leaders are reestablishing a capacity to govern by beginning at the regional level.

What built working people's capacity to participate in governance in the past was a social vision that motivated them to make a long-term commitment to social change. The great democratic upsurge that brought the New Deal and the empowerment of organized labor in the 1930s and '40s was the result of a vision of economic enfranchisement. It was embodied in specific policies and programs that put limits on working hours; eliminated child labor; created community colleges; instituted labor grievance procedures; and fought for adequate wages and benefits, overtime pay, health insurance and HMOs, old-age pensions, job security, housing, civil rights, civil liberties, and consumer protections. Each of these represented a partial realization of the broad vision of economic well-being and security for every family.

Revitalization of the labor movement today requires such a social vision, based on the basic values of the labor movement—and of American society at its best. That vision must embody deeply held aspirations for an inclusive society that reverses the trend toward social and economic inequality. It must represent a cultural shift toward solving problems together rather than as isolated individuals. It must be embodied in specific policies and programs that expand the social wage guaranteed by public policy and ensure adequate housing, transportation, education, health care, and employment standards for all. It must encourage a new consensus about how our society ought to function. It must envision a new social contract among business, government, and workers that puts justice for working people at the center of public policy.

Such a vision must grow organically out of local needs and struggles. It can be forged in workplaces through organizing and bargaining and, as this book explores, in communities through coalition building and political action. But at the same time it requires a deliberate process in which specific needs and objectives are synthesized into common programs.

If organized labor is to lead such a progressive revitalization, unions must be more than narrow defenders of their members' interests at work. They must become high-profile advocates for a new vision of the public good. It is by fighting and winning battles focused on common and deeply felt human values that organized labor can establish itself as a champion for the interests of the great majority of Americans.

Place-Based Labor

This process of progressive revitalization cannot occur purely at a national level. It must be place-based—that is, based in the workplaces and communities where people live, work, worship, and play. And today it must be rooted in the large metropolitan regions that are becoming increasingly crucial economic and political arenas in American life.

For organized labor to play a constructive leadership role in this process, it must first commit itself to the importance of power building at the regional level. It must aspire to being a leader of the kinds of broad-based regional movements for shared prosperity and a sustainable future profiled in this book.

The labor movement is already organized at the municipal level in central labor councils and is beginning to organize itself into larger-area labor federations. These institutions, composed of delegates from union locals in a given geographical area, have played an important role from the very beginnings of the labor movement. They bring together representatives of working people from a wide range of occupations, industries, communities, and subcultures around their common interests as workers. They often play a large role in local and regional politics. Many of the most successful current efforts at local and regional power building have been rooted in revitalized labor councils; they provide the ideal base in which labor may offer leadership and vision for the wider community.

These local institutions, however, have often been divided by conflicts among narrow interests and by political alliances that promote the interests of particular groups of workers at the expense of others or the community as a whole. Many of the cases of regional power building examined in this book begin with the story of a revitalized and reunified regional labor body led by leaders that articulate a vision of the common interests of working people in the community. Elsewhere, revitalization efforts have grown out of particular local unions or "coalitions of the willing" that hope to spark the revitalization of the regional labor movement.

The regional power-building work explored in this book involves a general model consisting of three "legs": deep coalitions, policy work, and aggressive political action.

Deep Coalitions

Even when unified, trade unionists represent only part of the population that has been impoverished and disenfranchised over recent decades. In most communities, all but a tiny elite have been hurt by the domination of American life by giant corporations and ideological conservatism. Those who have witnessed discrimination—such as immigrants, African Americans and other ethnic minorities, women, gay men, lesbians, and the transgendered—have been hurt even more.

These constituencies are represented by a new generation of organizations that have emerged in the past few years and will be reflected in the pages that follow. Some, like Strategic Concepts in Organizing and Policy Education in Los Angeles and the Association of Community Organizations for Reform Now on the national level, represent new organizing models in inner-city communities of poor people and people of color that seek labor alliances. Others represent a new generation of immigrant communities coming of age in the political process. And others, like those in the Interfaith Worker Justice and Gamaliel networks, reflect a new generation of interfaith organizing focused on social and economic justice.

Such constituencies form a potential majority coalition that could become the governing force in America's cities, towns, and regions. What is necessary for the emergence of such a governing force? It requires effective organizations, broad popular mobilization, a shared vision, practical policy proposals to implement that vision, and a political strategy that can change the direction of government. Labor can be a central part of such a force, but it needs a whole community of allies in order to acquire the necessary power. How can the labor movement help nurture such a community of allies?

In most communities there are already a wide range of campaigns by particular groups—labor and otherwise—around particular issues. These often grow into coalitions that bring together groups from diverse sectors of the community. But these links often fade away once the immediate issue has passed. The regional power-building model examined in this book seeks to overcome this pattern to establish long-standing connections rooted in a common effort to build governing capacity over time.

Such deep coalition building requires building a cross-community leadership team—a body of leaders with shared understandings who can think in terms of the movement as a whole. It requires the development of a common understanding of the problems of the community and a common vision of what needs to be done for the common good. It requires building a willingness to support each others' objectives. And it involves a willingness at times to put the concerns of other coalition partners first in the interest of the coalition as a whole. Such deep coalition building can make a community of allies be more than just the sum of its parts. The results, as we will see, can represent both the specific interests of workers and more general values: democracy, fairness, opportunity, and solidarity.

Policy Work

Business is organized to govern from the regional to national levels through its organizations, think tanks, lobbyists, alliances, and control of political parties, candidates, and officeholders. It develops its own agendas and implements them. To be effective, labor and its allies must develop their own public policy agenda for working families, independent of business or politicians. They must redefine the public debate by putting the focus on issues that can unify workers and community allies, such as job security, affordable housing, health care, public safety, education, and transportation.

This requires a research and policy capacity to define concrete steps toward a new social vision. To meet that need, regional labor groups have initiated "think-and-act tanks," research and policy action organizations that typically include not only labor representatives but also community activists, religious leaders, and community-oriented academics on their boards. These organizations develop and propagate a broad vision of what's wrong and what to do about it. Their research reports often reveal the "dark side" of how regional economies are affecting their residents—a story often concealed by business-oriented local boosters. They monitor how government and other local institutions are actually working—or not working. They draft concrete proposals for new programs and regulations. They help see that these are properly implemented and that those responsible for them are held accountable over time.

Unlike conventional think tanks, however, these think-and-act tanks develop their approaches in constant interaction with the grassroots labor and community organizations these policies are intended to serve—and whose action is necessary to implement them. They often initiate new labor-community coalitions and provide the ammunition for their campaigns. Fostering relationships and coalitions is central to their work, which creates a unifying and achievable public policy agenda that serves as a focus both for grassroots organizations and for labor-friendly candidates and officeholders.

Aggressive Political Action

Gaining power in the political arena is an obvious way to implement such proposals. But in local and regional arenas, many organizations—unions and community organizations among them—often pursue narrow objectives that may benefit some of their members but are useless or even harmful for other workers, potential allies, and the broader public.

Efforts to build regional power for working people therefore often start with attempts to overcome divisions within labor, and between labor and its allies. For example, new leadership in regional labor councils has often created new procedures that allow labor as a whole, rather than just individual unions, to endorse and campaign for political candidates. They have organized joint campaign and voter turnout operations that pool the efforts of all local unions. They have developed common labor platforms that provide an agenda for working people as a whole rather than just one or another particular union.

This process can't stop with organized labor, however. Building a force capable of governing requires that labor develops a similar process of political cooperation and mobilization with all those who share common interests. The goal is to build a sustained neighborhood and workplace infrastructure of activists who will bring out their neighbors on an ongoing basis for elections, referendums, or support for a strike or community campaign.

As the cases covered in this book illustrate, political power building involves far more than just endorsing candidates and getting out the vote. It involves educating candidates about the labor movement and the needs and goals of working people. It involves recruiting, training, and promoting "labor champions" who will fight for labor's agenda—and for its allies. It means fighting those who ignore, oppose, or turn against labor's agenda—even if they have been political allies in the past or are members of the same party as labor's champions. And it means participating in governance after elections are over—for example, by providing regular briefings for office holders and mobilizing support for progressive proposals.

The result is that labor and its allies have an impact on how regions are actually governed. Such power building has led governments to adopt a comprehensive high-road economic development strategy, raise labor market standards, support union organizing, train and hire local residents for jobs, improve health care access, require community benefit standards for developers, and defend immigrant workers. Each such achievement represents a partial realization of the broad vision of economic well-being and security for every family, as well as representing the beginning of a shift in the direction society is going—a shift in governance. And such achievements lay the groundwork through which an increasing number of individuals and groups may identify the constellation of labor and its allies as a vehicle with which they can work to meet their needs.

Why It Matters

From the perspective of progressives, liberals, the Left, and all those who seek more democracy and equality in America, the three-legged power-building approach explored in this book provides a concrete and tested strategy for moving our society in that direction. Of course, it needs to be complemented by action at the state, national, and even global levels. But if the labor movement is prepared to stand for broad social interests, all advocates of greater democracy and equality have an interest in supporting it.

From the point of view of organized labor, such a strategy provides a way to help meet the needs of its members along with all other working people. Well-connected and respected regional coalitions can be critical for organizing, especially in the public sector and in those many industries dependent on regional public decisions. Such coalitions have directly supported union organizing efforts; they have also won labor peace agreements, living wage ordinances, and other policies that have encouraged the recruitment of thousands of workers. They provide a way to address contingent and other difficult-to-organize workers. They present labor as a strong, smart champion of working people's values—and therefore worthy of support.

More broadly, greater union density is likely to be a by-product of other developments—not just recruiting. Labor is unlikely to revive without becoming part of a larger social awakening that aims to put the nation on a different course. Labor must prove that it and its allies can develop an alternative vision and deploy the power to implement it. Therefore, social vision and political action are necessary for union growth. Increasing union membership in the workplace is not an alternative to organizing at the regional level; they must reinforce each other, or neither will succeed.

Rebuilding our civic infrastructure with strong, permanent grassroots organizations that provide working people the power to govern at a regional level is a worthwhile end in itself. But it is also part of a national strategy. These power-building configurations are spreading to a greater number of locations around the country. They are forming state and national networks. They have the potential to serve as the regional building blocks for a new pattern of governance at the state and national levels, and there is no shortcut that will circumvent the need for those building blocks. Ultimately they contain the seeds of a "new New Deal." They deserve the support not only of people in communities and regions around the country but also of national groups that have an interest in a decentralized strategy to establish popular governance in America.

An Overview of the Book

In the first part of this book we examine regional power building's origins. In many ways, labor and its allies are catching up with the regional thinking that has already developed among key elements of the business community. Chapter 1 examines intellectual foundations of this regional perspective and explores how changes within the national AFL-CIO have created a space in which organized labor can experiment with progressive regional strategies. Chapter 2 explores regional power building's incubation in California. It takes up in detail the experience of author Amy Dean in forging a labor-led progressive regional movement in Silicon Valley. We then compare this experience to the pioneering work in Los Angeles and the subsequent spread of power building work elsewhere in the state and country.

In the second part of the book we explore each of the three "legs" critical to forging an effective regional movement for progressive change. Chapters 3 through 5 detail agenda and policy development, deep coalition building, and aggressive political action.

The last two chapters examine the issues involved in further spreading the regional power-building model. Chapter 6 explores the emergence—or lack thereof—of the model in six different regions across the country. These experiences highlight the importance of leadership from organized labor, foundation funding, adjusting strategies to the regional economic context, and peer-to-peer support. These factors point to the role national leaders and organizations can play in regional power building's further spread. We close in chapter 7 with a discussion of what needs to be done to move regional power building from the margins to the center of progressive strategizing for reclaiming the country. In particular, we argue that organized labor as a national movement must develop a greater appreciation of the importance of regional power-building work and integrate it more fully into its planning and investments for a better future.

Vision and Power: A Lesson from American Labor History

At the end of 1936, a relatively small group of autoworkers sat down in several plants owned by General Motors, then the world's largest corporation, to win company recognition of their union. In the eighteen months following this stunning victory, over three million American workers organized themselves into unions. The modern industrial labor movement had been born!

How did a single organizing victory at one corporation prove to be the spark for a worker-organizing wave that transformed entire industries and the nation? This question cuts to the crux of the challenge facing organized labor today. In 2005, when the Change to Win federation split off from the AFL-CIO, both sides agreed that union density cannot increase at a significant scale when unions simply organize one isolated workplace at a time. However, even aggressive and large-scale industry-based organizing by specific unions is not sufficient to turn organized labor's fortunes around. Historically, labor's rebound as a movement has not come from incremental increases in membership by individual unions but from intense periods of social awakening that see workers joining unions in large numbers. So, how can the labor movement build toward such a decisive wave today?

Organized labor's rebirth in the 1930s grew from a transforming social vision that had been forged through both workplace and community activism. (We use the term community activism in a broad sense that includes electoral organizing, but which reaches well beyond simply election campaigns.) Obviously, this work did not occur in a vacuum, but in the context of the social and economic crisis of the Great Depression. We should note, however, that throughout the first half of the Depression decade, economic collapse and the threat of unemployment provided a powerful weapon with which management fought unions. Indeed, in the early 1930s many commentators inside and outside organized labor predicted that the Depression would see the final death of organized labor—not its rebirth.

The turnaround came from key changes in strategy on the part of organized labor at both the workplace and community levels. In the workplace, the new Congress of Industrial Organizations (CIO) broke with the American Federation of Labor's (AFL) exclusive focus on organizing only skilled workers by craft (typically white, U.S.-born men) to organize the entire workforce (including women, minorities, and immigrants) in whole industries. The CIO also brought to America militant sit-down tactics in which workers effectively seized workplaces to prevent management from operating via the use of strikebreakers. In the community, the CIO abandoned the AFL's hostility toward "radicals" and embraced many of the left-wing activists organizing not just in workplaces but also in neighborhoods.

Organizationally, the labor movement became intertwined with grassroots groups such as councils of the unemployed, consumer cooperatives, communities of faith, women's auxiliaries, ethnic and immigrant organizations, and civil rights networks. These connections delivered the community support key to countering employer and government violence and winning many organizing battles. Finally, the AFL had practiced a nonaligned electoral politics that "rewarded their friends and punished their enemies" and sought narrow instrumental policy action rather than broad social reform. The CIO unions did not simply ally with the Democratic Party, but embraced the vision of social change symbolized by the New Deal and the legal recognition of the right to organize. Through CIO political structures, the new industrial labor movement attempted to push the New Deal to its maximum potential and to intimately connect workplace organizing to calls for industrial democracy and social reform.

The connections among workplace organizing, community work, political activism, and social vision came together to turn the famous 1936–37 General Motors sit-down strike from yet another lost cause into a victory that sparked a broad-based organizing wave. The years prior to 1936 had seen GM defeat a series of organizing attempts. The company had done its workplace and community work; it spent millions on building an extensive workplace spy network that allowed management to purge "troublemakers" and to resort to physical force to maintain control of plants in the event of a strike. GM's extensive community outreach gained it favorable media coverage and allowed it to build such antistrike worker groups as the Flint Alliance. Through political work, GM enjoyed the support of sympathetic judges who would issue injunctions against striking workers and allow state authorities to use the National Guard as a last resort to "restore order."

The 1936 GM strike was won only because organized labor countered GM at both the workplace and community levels. Worker-to-worker organizing by United Auto Workers (UAW) supporters at GM had established an underground network in several key plants. However, GM's spying efforts and fear campaign meant that workers in only a few plants actually engaged in the sit-down strike. With only a minority of plants down, workers had to rely on community support to provision them, provide moral support, gain positive media coverage, and fend off GM attempts to use the Flint, Michigan, police force to recapture occupied plants.

In the end, after a month and a half, it was a battle against company thugs and the police by UAW members and their community supporters that successfully shut down a key engine plant and finally forced GM management to recognize the union. This decisive victory would have been canceled out completely had the CIO and the nascent UAW not engaged in successful political action prior to the strike to elect a Democratic governor (Frank Murphy) who pledged not to use the Michigan Guard to violently expel striking workers. The political work had not just changed the personnel in key government posts but placed issues of industrial democracy and the right to organize into community discussion.

The same synergy that won union recognition at GM helps explain the massive organizing wave that followed. Key segments of the community in Michigan and elsewhere rallied behind striking GM workers because the battle was not just about justice for the autoworkers but also about turning the nation in a new direction. If workers could win union recognition at GM, the world's largest corporation, then workers could organize any industrial firm. And building unions in industry after industry would become a central vehicle for addressing the central social crisis of the era by redistributing wealth and power in America.

Because the social vision forged through workplace and community work had taken root across the country, union organizers did not have to convince laborers, workplace by workplace, of the virtues of joining a union. The social vision had been established, and the victory at GM had demonstrated that workers could win. Visible and often militant community support discouraged employer and government violence—creating "union towns" and giving workers the physical safety in which to organize. Thus, three million workers organized into unions in the next year and a half, often not waiting for official union organizers to launch the effort. As a case study of steel industry organizing in Pennsylvania during the 1930s suggests, labor's independent community and political organizing often predated and set the stage for workplace organizing success.[10]

To reestablish itself as a growing social and visionary force in America today, the labor movement must engage effectively in both workplace and community organizing. Indeed, historically in the United States and today in many parts of the world, to speak of the "labor movement" is to speak in terms of two rather than one set of social institutions. One set—labor unions—organizes laborers at the workplace level. The other set—labor-based left-wing political parties in many countries and the political structures of union federations in the United States and the regional efforts profiled in this book—organizes workers in their communities. The broadly shared alternative vision and sense of grassroots movement momentum—so key during the eras of the labor movement's institutional revival—arise out of the synergy between workplace and community activism.

The Birth of Regional Power Building

1

Thinking Regionally

When labor and its allies begin to build power at the regional level they are often catching up to the thinking found among important segments of the business community. Many communities have an employer-oriented group, or even several groups, that will think and plan at a regional level. These initiatives can take the form of civic-employer alliances—such as the MetroHartford Alliance in Connecticut or the Joint Venture–Silicon Valley Network in California. They can also operate more as industry-based groups that think regionally—such as the Silicon Valley Leaders Group, an association of manufacturers. Regardless of their form, these regional employer groups seek to foster business success by planning and influencing public policy at the regional level. The MetroHartford Alliance, for example, defines its work as fulfilling a vision "to compete aggressively and successfully for jobs, talent and capital for the Hartford Region and to ensure that the Hartford Region is a premier place for all people to live, work, play and raise a family."[1]

In an age of "globalization" in which the global wanderings of "foot-loose" corporations fill the news, why do significant sectors of the corporate community give time, attention, and resources to regional thinking? In the first half of this chapter we explore the motivations for this regional focus. We will then turn to the changes within the AFL-CIO in the 1990s that helped create space for innovative local labor leaders to pursue regional-based work.

Why Think Regionally?

Many scholars have documented the link between central cities and their suburbs. While postwar suburban growth often came at the expense of central cities, research over the past two decades has suggested that the fate of much of suburbia is linked to the fate of the core city. For example, in examining eighty-five large metropolitan areas between 1988 and 1991, William Barnes and Larry Ledebur found that regions with high income disparities between city and suburbs had lower or negative employment growth, while those with the strongest employment growth had relatively low disparities.[2] Dan Luria and Joel Rogers have documented how the large-scale manufacturing decline experienced by Detroit and Milwaukee also hit the inner ring suburbs hard (and in Detroit the outer ring as well).[3]

More recently, scholars of "new regionalism" have moved beyond questions of suburb versus central city to identify the metropolitan region as the basic unit of economic geography.[4] Barnes and Ledebur define economic regions as open systems linked to other regions through the national and global economies rather than as isolated or self-sufficient, and point out five basic tenets:

1. The economic region is the basic building block of the economy.
2. It is a single, integrated, and interdependent regional economy overlaid by political jurisdictions of cities, suburbs, and surrounding non-metropolitan areas.
3. Economic regions are centered around, or polarized to, one or more urban or metropolitan areas. The fulcrum of the local economic region is the metropolitan area, not "the city" or any governmental jurisdiction.

4. These metropolitan centers are the sources of new ideas, new technologies, and innovations that drive economic growth and development within the region.... It is the metropolitan centers of the economic regions, rather than the core cities alone, that are the source of creativity and innovation.

5. Economic regions, therefore, are an essential resource in the economic growth process. They are generators or engines of growth in the national economic system.[5]

The existence of a regional economy helps explain why business investment simply does not go entirely to low-wage, low-regulation locations. "If low labor costs and unfettered opportunities for business were the only issues that mattered, Haiti would be one of the most rapidly expanding economies in the world," argue Manuel Pastor, Peter Dreier, J. Eugene Grigsby, and Marta López-Garza. "What actually attracts business is the entire geographically based infrastructure of skills, markets, and expertise. These are the assets that make it worthwhile for business to accept higher labor and community standards in return for access to an educated, skilled and enthusiastic pool of workers, supportive business suppliers, and the 'intangibles' of sound public policy."[6] Barnes and Ledebur describe these factors as a "regional economic commons" whose development or neglect significantly impacts business prosperity. Seen from the perspective of business, the regional economic commons includes the following factors:

1. *Labor Markets.* Firms must have workers. The regional labor market is not simply about low labor costs. Whether regions provide the right workers, with the right skills and at the right levels of supply, heavily shapes management and investment decisions. Equally important, firms that draw a significant part of their workforce nationally depend upon the region's quality of life to attract skilled workers.

2. *Customers.* Much of the service economy is based on regional firms selling to regional customers. Industries such as health care, education, retail, entertainment, building services, construction, and the like have to be near their customers. Similarly, companies that contract to other firms enjoy distinct advantages by locating near their corporate customers. Even for firms that sell nationally or internationally the region's transportation infrastructure will nevertheless raise or lower costs.

3. *Supply and Input Markets.* Growing out of the industrial revolution were regional concentrations based on an industry's need for raw materials and energy. In addition, today most firms depend upon material or service inputs produced by other firms. While a company's supply chain can span the world, face-to-face relationships still offer huge advantages for doing business.

4. *Peer Firms.* Despite competing with each other at one level, businesses may also enjoy many advantages in locating near similar firms. Despite modern communication and travel capacities, face-to-face relationships—which include rich interactions outside work hours—still offer great value. Annalee Saxenian notes that "'geographic proximity promotes the repeated interaction and mutual trust needed to sustain collaboration.'" Pastor and colleagues add that "collaboration, in turn, leads to joint efforts and the continual transmission of new technologies and industrial innovation. It can lead to a generalized sense of the 'common,' and therefore a recognition of the need to provide public goods and infrastructure that can lower costs for all businesses."[7]

The corporate restructuring of the last several decades includes core patterns that enhance the importance of these four factors. For example, the basic corporate model has moved from the giant vertically integrated corporation of the early and mid-twentieth century to a "leaner" corporation with a smaller internal core connected to a complex web of suppliers and supporting firms. Corporate restructuring has broken many career ladders and led to steady increases in contingent employment relations (part-time work, independent contracting, and temporary employment). As fewer employees stay at a single firm, but instead move between jobs, employers become more dependent on the qualities of regional labor markets and the ability of regions to attract and retain skilled workers.

All of the above factors depend upon public policy decisions. Policy areas include education (K–12, vocational, and college), transportation, economic development, public-private partnerships, land-use planning, and measures that impact the quality of life (housing affordability, social services, parks and recreational opportunities, arts and entertainment, congestion, etc.). The devolution of responsibility for social well-being over the last few decades from federal to state to local levels (often without accompanying resources) has also increased the importance of regional public decision making.

The Fragmentation of Regional Governance

The problem for business as well as for labor and its allies is that while public policy is important for regional economic and social well-being, the actual governing structure in the United States fragments along smaller jurisdictional boundaries of city, village, township, and so forth.

While historically urbanization in America proceeded through the steady annexation by cities of surrounding growth areas, this process gave way to the establishment of suburbs that hemmed in city growth and fragmented public policy among many smaller governments. The degree of fragmentation varies enormously across the country. Michigan, for example, is particularly notorious: Detroit ranked ninth out of 361 regions rated by the metropolitan power diffusion index formulated by David Miller at the University of Pittsburgh.[8] Public authority in the region is divided among 375 distinct governmental bodies. In eighth place is Los Angeles, whose regional planning has to incorporate 539 local bodies. By contrast, Albuquerque, New Mexico, has managed to expand its city boundaries to incorporate almost all population and economic growth—but such a pattern is far less common.

Whether severe or moderate, municipal fragmentation in the United States undermines regional economies. Myron Orfield and David Rusk have detailed the problems in ways that incorporate both business and economic justice concerns.[9] Public resources that could go to developing a region as a whole become divided among many little boxes of local villages, townships, cities, exurbs, and school districts. Regions spend huge amounts of local, state, and even federal public resources building whole new layers of public infrastructure for the latest suburban ring while similar infrastructure in already established cities and older suburbs decays. Residents and businesses are forced into increasingly longer commutes across a more greatly dispersed urban area. Rather than promoting the region as a whole and attracting new investment to the area, most planning efforts in the little municipal boxes compete with each other and a region's major city to steal away the largest share of those existing regional properties that deliver the greatest net public revenue: office space and other business centers, retail complexes, and upscale housing.

In terms of both regional business prosperity and social justice, most municipalities lose in this fragmented free-for-all. Many inner-ring suburbs have suffered, or are at risk of suffering, the same urban decay that has savaged so many parts of our nation's older central cities. Fragmented regions witness concentrations in poverty and racial segregation that undermine economic vitality as well as equity. At the same time, many fast-growing bedroom communities do not have the public resources to accommodate or plan well for growth. According to Orfield, only a small number of affluent job centers (about 11 percent of the total urban communities found nationwide) actually prosper in the current fragmented game through success in attracting offices, retail centers, and upscale homes.[10]

County governments offer a level of public authority that encompasses the smaller municipal units. However, they are limited in their ability to serve as a kind of regional government by several factors. Metropolitan economic regions often span more than one county. Furthermore, the main authority of county governments that is consistent across the United States revolves around social service functions. By contrast, county authority around such crucial issues as land use and economic development planning varies depending upon the state. Incorporated areas (cities and towns) generally control these matters within their own boundaries. In states such as California, the county has authority over unincorporated areas. In "home rule" states (such as Michigan), however, all local jurisdictions are incorporated—thus, township governments have land use and economic development authority over areas not in cities or towns. Even in cases where counties have control over unincorporated areas, these jurisdictions tend to have less population and include the wealthier "exurbs," which are not a good starting point constituency for regional power building work.

Thus, the common government structures found regionally in America jurisdictionally separate the very functions of land use planning, economic development programs, and social services that effective regional work needs to integrate. The rare examples of effective regional public planning have had to overcome this limitation either by intensive and successful work to build alliances among the many fragmented structures of government within a region (for example, Grand Rapids, Michigan) or have enjoyed or obtained state legislation to foster regional planning (such as the state-created regional governing structures in Oregon or the regional tax revenue sharing program in Minnesota).[11]

The growing importance of the regional level for business practices combines with current regional fragmentation in public authority to produce a leading edge of business-driven regional thinking and reforms. As organized labor and other progressive movements seek to recover community-based geographical strength they must seek to parallel this regional effort. Power building in California and elsewhere reflects this new regional reality. Although we may use a major city as a shorthand reference for an overall urban area, the strategies described in this book are not about building power in the cities of San Jose, California, or Denver, but in the South Bay region or the greater Denver metropolitan area as a whole.

We should note that the above factors help explain not simply the growth of regional thinking among business players but also why some currents of employer-oriented regional thinking include equity considerations and goals that may seem to parallel what labor and its allies want to see. These overlaps can provide ground for tactical cooperation. However, as we will detail in chapter 3, business-oriented economic development thinking is traditionally weak on social justice concerns and employer regionalism will rarely see the growth of strong membership-based labor and community organization as a core part of its regional solutions. As Manuel Pastor, Chris Benner, and Martha Matsuoka have argued, while a case can be made that regional equity is good for business, "there also needs to be a set of constituencies and institutions with 'skin in the game'—folks that have a critical stake in keeping equity on the regional agenda and that see the regional agenda as a new way to fulfill long standing demands for fairness in American society."[12] Keeping or inserting social justice concerns into regional planning requires labor and its allies to understand and break into the game of governing a region.

Toward a New Regional Governance Regime

In studying urban politics, scholars have come to realize that simply looking at who holds elected office and what their agenda is does not provide a full look at the local power structure.[13] Indeed, conservative cries of "big government" aside, public authority in the United States is often quite limited, especially at the local level. In the words of Clarence Stone, "Even though the institutions of local government bear most of the formal responsibility for governing, they lack the resources and the scope of authority to govern without the active support and cooperation of significant private interests."[14]

The body of "regime theory" scholarship can help us understand both what regional employer-oriented groups are attempting to accomplish and what labor and community groups need to do to build real power. While this literature originally developed in reference mainly to big city governance, its insights apply equally well to regional thinking.

According to regime theory, if those in charge of local government want to seriously influence the overall direction of their community they must ally with private groups that offer the resources and capacity to implement an agenda. The term *regime* has come to characterize the informal webs that bring together various public and private interests in a coherent way that allows them to govern. These relations revolve around a core group of "shakers and movers." They provide ways for public and private players to cross over their particular institutional boundary lines. Through frequent interaction in leadership development programs, issue forums, policy groups, and social networks, members of a regime develop a common identity and language.

Functioning regimes do not necessarily control all aspects of government, but they do set the framework for overall government planning and direction. Regime players share a common understanding of what the problems are and, in general terms, how they should be addressed. Regime players may not always agree, but they resolve their conflicts within the assumptions and framework provided by the regime. This common understanding shapes the public debate in terms of what issues get attention and how they are discussed.

Urban regimes are not static, but allow members to adapt to changing circumstances in ways that maintain an overall power structure. Individual groups may be incorporated or pushed out of a governing regime without fundamentally altering the regime itself.

In the United States, nearly all urban regimes revolve around linking public authority to private business. Under normal circumstances in a capitalist society employers quite simply have the most to offer public authorities. Economic development cannot happen without private investment. Business location and relocation decisions can make or break a community. Furthermore, municipal budgets depend on borrowing from private financial markets, especially for large-scale development projects.

Business also has much greater capacity to access information than government. By funding think tanks, research groups, and their own internal capacity, employers often have a far greater ability than does local government to understand the details of a regional economy and to develop concrete policy. Large businesses can often act relatively quickly and can command the resources and expertise needed for big, complex development projects. In short, if you are a government official and want to accomplish some form of "community improvement," joining forces with local business authorities provides the most readily available path to success.

While their details may vary, for the past half century most urban regimes have taken the form of a "growth coalition."[15] These regimes unite public figures with those large business interests that have the greatest fixed investments. Such regime partners include real estate developers, banks and financial institutions, utilities, newspapers, professionals such as lawyers and architects that gain fees from development projects, some corporations with downtown headquarters, and—if there is a healthy commercial district—major downtown retailers, restaurants, and hospitality interests.

Growth coalitions generally share common approaches and goals. They focus on downtown redevelopment, typically through large-scale corporate projects. Their postindustrial vision is rooted in the service economy. Traditionally, growth coalitions have been relatively unconcerned with suburban sprawl. Their agendas tend toward spatial divisions among downtown office and entertainment space, suburban residential communities, and the inner-city ghettoes sandwiched in between.

The public energy for growth coalitions tends to reside in the executive branch. Government planning and implementation take place through the mayoral offices, public-private commissions, and administrative departments that tend to be insulated from public view. Growth regimes gravitate toward supply-side solutions in which private business leads and public authority follows. Growth politics are big on tax abatements and public subsidies and weak on public oversight and accountability. Public funds typically are used for those development costs that promise few financial returns, while profitable investment opportunities are left for business. In other words, the public assumes many costs and risks, while private business enjoys much of the direct gain.

Growth regimes can also include groups and populations that builders of labor-community regional power will want to bring into their coalitions. For example, many traditional regimes incorporate organized labor, especially the building trades and public sector unions. Unions often gain construction jobs as a result of electoral support for regime politicians and alliances with commercial developers. Similarly, political support for incumbent politicians can deliver organizing and contract gains in the public sector. Not surprisingly, central labor council leadership has traditionally come from the building trades and/or public sector unions. The first wave of power-building innovations came primarily from those urban areas in which the local labor movement was relatively less incorporated into the governing regime. As urban populations have become more black and brown, urban growth regimes have sought with varying degrees of success to incorporate key middle-class and business interests from African American, Latino, and immigrant communities. Thus, cities such as Detroit, Atlanta, Los Angeles, and Gary, Indiana, have been able to transition to having black mayors while keeping the basic outlines of the growth regime intact. However, the incorporation of interests from labor and communities of color always represents a tension, since such players are at best junior partners in the regime.

Regime theory provides a basic framework for understanding what employer-oriented regional groups are attempting to do: to establish a more sophisticated and regional-oriented growth regime that can use coordinated public policy to promote a healthy regional economic commons upon which they depend.

Similarly, the ultimate goal of the regional work covered in this book is to establish a governing regional regime that includes labor and community groups as equal partners, focuses on measures of social well-being and not just business success, and provides a laboratory for progressive public policy ideas. Seen in this way, it becomes clear that simply mobilizing a progressive voting base to elect "nice people" is not enough. While politicians need votes to win, they need more than votes to govern. Since local governments do not alone have the resources, expertise, or authority to adequately tackle major regional problems, they must seek alliances with outside forces. If progressives do not build an alternative source of alliances and capacity, even committed progressive government officials will be compelled to work with key elements of the business establishment, and on that establishment's terms.

Thus, progressive power building must build the elements of a regional regime. This is why all the elements outlined in this book are necessary for building real power: deep coalitions, leadership development, policy work, applied research, candidate development, and aggressive political action. Election-by-election mobilization alone is not nearly enough. Like business, labor and allied groups need to develop the capacity to understand the regional economy, develop policy alternatives, and offer the year-round grassroots mobilizing ability that delivers community support as a means of backing up politician allies while holding them accountable when they drift off course.

History confirms that what happens at the local and regional level can have a much broader effect. Thanks to our nation's federal system, state governments enjoy a great deal of actual and potential authority over basic social and economic policies.[16] The electoral bases of both state legislative seats and the U.S. House of Representatives are rooted in local districts. Regional progressive regimes can lead to progressive voices in state legislatures and in Congress. Thus, "regional" organizing is not simply about municipal governments and regional economies but building a base for state (and ultimately national) governing regimes.

Different Kinds of Regionalism

The notion of changing the governing regime helps to distinguish between different forms of regional thinking and action. In their excellent book on grassroots regional organizing, *This Could Be the Start of Something Big,* Pastor, Benner, and Matsuoka distinguish among several forms of equity-oriented regionalism.[17] *Community development regionalism* has grown out of the struggle of community development corporations to address the poverty found in the communities in which these corporations are based. Attempts to intervene in regional policy develop out of the limitations of neighborhood-based work buffeted by powerful regional forces and decisions. Pastor, Benner, and Matsuoka point out, however, that such community development regionalism can be limited by a community development corporation's need to maintain relationships with investors, local officials, and foundations as well as the organization's ultimate mission, which remains locally based. *Policy reform regionalism* grows out of a range of "policy entrepreneurs"—nonprofit and for-profit policy experts and consulting groups—who advocate for regional reforms that may or may not include an equity perspective. While helping policymakers develop regional perspectives, such advocates can be limited by their need to "mainstream" their thinking and by a basic orientation that leans more toward "elite persuasion" rather than organizing broad constituencies. Neither community development nor policy reform regionalisms look toward fundamental change in a region's governing regime.

The *social movement regionalism* that is the focus of *This Could Be the Start of Something Big,* however, aims in one way or another to contribute to regime change. It grows out of emerging regional thinking by grassroots organizations oriented on building a just, equitable, and sustainable society. As the authors argue, for these groups "the region is not only a new level for understanding problems and proposing solutions, it is also a new, fundamental, and strategic scale for building a broad-based social movement for justice."[18] Because it defines social movement regional organizing broadly, Pastor, Benner, and Matsuoka's book covers a wide range, from the work of many single organizations or coalitions to the kind of broad and integrated regional power-building programs explored in the present volume. Many of the authors' examples grow out of the diverse currents of community organizing. Some of these community groups, such as Strategic Concepts in Organizing and Policy Education in Los Angeles, are key partners in the regional power-building work described herein. Pastor, Benner, and Matsuoka's insight that the region is not simply a site in which to pass specific policy reforms but a distinct space for growing grassroots capacity is especially relevant to the power building work we examine in this book.

Organized Labor Returns to the Regional Community

Since its birth, the American labor movement has always included geographically based organizations that unite workers across unions. The role and influence of such local and regional bodies, however, has varied considerably over time. The work to build regional power intertwines with efforts to rebuild and grow the role of cross-union labor structures. We finish this chapter by exploring the historical decline of such regional bodies and the recent national opening to revive such bodies since 1995.

The Decline of Regional Cross-Union Structures

Soon after the birth of the United States, workers like printers, molders, shoemakers, and tailors began to form trade unions. While building organizations in their occupations, workers also began to form structures that represented all unions in each city. These rapidly became what labor historian David Montgomery has called "the main center of labor activity in the Age of Jackson."[19]

By the end of the Civil War, such cross-union bodies had been established in cities from Boston to San Francisco. In Chicago, for example, thirty-three local unions participated in the Chicago Trades Assembly, which raised money to aid strikers, helped arbitrate disputes with employers, and stigmatized and boycotted union-busting employers. It propounded its own election platform, asked candidates to support it, and endorsed pro-labor candidates. In 1866, aldermen from seven of Chicago's sixteen wards pledged to support the Trades Assembly's proposed municipal ordinance providing the eight-hour workday for city employees, and the next month it was passed.

The first efforts to form national labor organizations emerged from these local labor councils.[20] They played a critical role in the Knights of Labor, which became America's predominant labor organization in the 1870s and '80s. The Knights operated as a political club and community organization as much as an instrument for collective bargaining. The community work was especially key for uniting a labor movement that would otherwise have been divided at the workplace level. What gave the Knights strength was the diversity of workers it encompassed, from ship carpenters to railway workers to textile plant employees. However, these workers operated in occupations and went to workplaces that divided them by skill, gender, race, and whether U.S.- or foreign-born. At the level of workplace bargaining many of these workers could easily have seen each other as enemies or competitors as much as they could friends. The solidarity that united better-off white, male, U.S.-born and skilled craft workers with the often foreign-born unskilled working poor was forged in the Knights' community and political work.

The Knights of Labor fought not just for collective bargaining agreements but also raised early calls for the elimination of child labor, the eight-hour workday, equal pay for equal work, and the graduated income tax. The same regions in which the Knights built significant bargaining strength also saw workers mount a series of contests for governing power.[21]

When a few national craft unions split off in 1886 to form what would prove the successor to the Knights of Labor, the American Federation of Labor (AFL), the role of local labor assemblies radically changed.[22] AFL doctrine placed all significant authority with national unions, and not with central labor bodies at the local level. Basic powers like setting dues, authorizing strikes, and negotiating with employers were all centralized at the national level within each union. Local assemblies continued but gradually became subordinate.

Local cross-union initiatives played an important role in the organizing of industrial unions during the 1930s and '40s. Central labor councils often served as the organizing base for workers and mobilized massive support behind their strikes, for example. But the newly formed Congress of Industrial Organizations (CIO) continued the AFL policy of subordinating local labor councils to separate national unions—and the same policy continued when the AFL and the CIO merged in 1955. When a group of unions withdrew from the AFL-CIO in 2005 to form the Change to Win federation, their new strategy for aggressive organizing did not include a new role for local labor councils. (A subsequent agreement for Solidarity Charters did, however, allow locals of Change to Win unions to rejoin regional AFL-CIO bodies.)

Of course, national unions have continued to have locals—some of them large and powerful. But these locals have generally pursued their own policies and those of their national unions. The most important funding for local activities, endorsements for local electoral candidates, and support for strikes and organizing comes primarily from national unions and their local affiliates, not from local labor councils.

Indeed, many local councils have traditionally focused less on the broad interests of area unions and workers as a whole than on playing insider politics on behalf of particular union locals. Leaders of many labor councils have long focused on union construction work, support for public sector unions, and other benefits for specific affiliates won through close personal relationships with political establishment figures. This tradition often placed them in a position hostile to progressive forces among local unions and the broader community. By the 1980s, the roughly six hundred central labor councils around the country had largely declined into weak, unambitious organizations. If they couldn't pay the electric bill and had to close, no one would notice, secretary-treasurer William Lucy of the American Federation of State, County and Municipal Employees told a group of labor council leaders in the mid-1990s.

Creating Space for Innovation

When John Sweeney ran for president of the AFL-CIO in 1995, his campaign strategists realized that the votes from the central labor council delegates could prove crucial in a close convention floor fight against Tom Donahue, who had moved up to president when Lane Kirkland retired. So they organized central labor council leaders, even paying for some officers from smaller cities to attend the convention in New York. Donahue, on the other hand, sent a letter to every central labor council warning leaders that they shouldn't be involved in the decision about who should lead the labor movement and should leave such important matters to the international unions. The move by Sweeney's New Voices team won them widespread support from central labor council leaders and tapped an enthusiasm among many to play a larger role in the labor movement.

Despite the general decline of regional labor bodies, some councils had experimented with innovation in the early 1990s, carving out central roles in coalition building and political action, and organizing support. Meeting the year before the Sweeney election and again during the convention, four council leaders—Stewart Acuff from Atlanta, Ron Judd from Seattle, Bruce Colburn from Milwaukee, and Amy Dean from San Jose, California—decided to form an organization and develop a common strategy. In the past, central labor councils had typically approached the AFL-CIO about funding issues, such as trying to mandate full affiliation of all local unions, but this new group started with ideas about new programs, figuring that if they built stronger central labor council agendas they would eventually get the resources.

Sweeney was willing to work with the new local leaders who could help implement new AFL-CIO programs, especially because it seemed easier to begin transforming central labor councils than state federations. In January 1996, Dean began acting as chair of a labor council advisory committee that would educate the national union affiliates about the potential of central labor councils. The new leaders emphasized the need to have strong grassroots mobilization and solidarity on the regional level to support the expanded organizing that the New Voices campaign advocated. They also promoted the value of coordinated political endorsements at the regional level to make clearer to politicians what was expected of them for labor backing.

In July 1996 the advisory committee organized the first formal convention of central labor councils in the federation's history (previously, Lane Kirkland had periodically met only with about thirty of the biggest councils). At that Denver meeting, participants talked about how to create a new culture of mobilizing workers that could spark a renaissance of organizing by local and national unions. A new official advisory committee on the future of labor councils met after the convention—with the assistance of the AFL-CIO Field Mobilization Department—to develop the themes that would eventually form the basis for the AFL-CIO Union Cities program.

The committee began by identifying the best practices of successful central labor councils. It then put together a framework for action on organizing, politics, economic development, and making the local labor movement leadership more accurately mirror the workforce. In order to qualify as Union City participants, central labor councils had to pledge to take eight actions:

1. Make organizing the top priority and promote the national AFL-CIO's call for unions to place 30 percent of their resources into organizing.
2. Mobilize members and allies against antiunion employers by establishing a "street heat" network that will get at least 1 percent of regional union members to become active volunteers.
3. Build political power through active political action committees and community alliances.
4. Promote, with community allies, regional economic growth that serves the needs of workers and their communities.
5. Offer popular education on economic issues by sponsoring the AFL-CIO's Common Sense Economics program.
6. Support worker organizing by persuading municipal governments to pass resolutions supporting the right to organize. Councils should help to build support for the right to organize as a condition of labor's candidate endorsements.

7. Encourage diversity within council executive boards, committees, officers, and delegate bodies so that these structures reflect the diversity represented by affiliate unions.

8. Increase the number of regional union members by aiming for a 3 percent union growth rate within the region by the turn of the millennium.

A little more than one-fourth of the six hundred central labor councils (the councils representing more than half of overall AFL-CIO membership) participated in the Union Cities program. However, there were probably thirty to forty councils that were most active, and many of those would have been active even without Union Cities. Yet, AFL-CIO surveys indicated that Union Cities participants, especially smaller labor councils, were far more active than councils that had not participated. For example, 90 percent of Union Cities participants reported some mobilization of members, compared with only 55 percent of councils that did not participate. On the other hand, few if any councils met specific goals such as mobilizing 1 percent of members to become volunteers every year.

The AFL-CIO initially did not push the international unions to support Union Cities, and it focused on building up its national staff more than regional organizations. As the AFL-CIO ramped up its new political work in 1996, the national political staff created ad hoc structures for the specific elections rather than rely on strengthening state and local organizations. In truth, it would have been impossible to rely on many such bodies, but as we explore further in chapter 5, the money spent on that election—and elections that followed—failed to build a lasting regional political infrastructure that could mobilize for both national elections and for regional power.

By 2000, the central labor council advisory committee wanted to move work with local councils to a new stage, developing better ways to control local politics, steer economic development, build coalitions, and define what it meant for politicians to be labor candidates. However, the AFL-CIO was mainly interested in mobilizing for national politics, especially the 2000 presidential race, and not in using its vast political spending to simultaneously build lasting local political infrastructure. George W. Bush's narrow election, with its clear antilabor agenda, created a new sense of urgency and discontent among affiliates, thus pushing Union Cities into the background. There was an increased focus at the federation on tactics for short-term success, not the often time-consuming process of rebuilding substantial regional institutions, and the AFL-CIO effectively abandoned Union Cities.

Nonetheless, as we will see, labor councils have been central players in most successful cases of regional power building. As the only major regional cross-union labor body, a reinvigorated council is a natural leader in power building innovations. Furthermore, when power building work does not include a regional labor council transformation, it suffers from weakness in the core third leg—aggressive and unified political action on the part of labor.

Despite its mixed results and eventual move into the background, the Union Cities program did encourage and support the labor council experimentation that produced and helped spread the regional power-building model. The stage had been set to consolidate the model in California and to spread it elsewhere in the country. The New Voices administration and the Union Cities initiative lent legitimacy to central labor council innovation. Unlike in the past, regional leaders who wished to experiment with power building strategies could pursue work that was officially endorsed by the AFL-CIO and the national labor movement. Although the labor movement as a whole could hardly be said to have embraced and steered resources to Union Cities work on the ground, council leaders could draw on technical support from sympathetic AFL-CIO staff and link up with other innovative leaders through the work of the central labor council advisory committee. Although the particular Union Cities initiative collapsed, we will explore in chapter 7 how newer programs such as the New Alliance and the Leadership Institute continue AFL-CIO work to revitalize regional and state labor bodies in ways informed by the regional power-building model.

2

THE REGIONAL POWER-BUILDING MODEL
EMERGES IN CALIFORNIA

Two metropolitan areas in California produced the first experiments of what would become the regional power-building model: San Jose and Los Angeles. We explore San Jose first in order to draw on the intimate participant knowledge of author Amy Dean. Using this rich case study as a reference point, we turn to the emergence of the same basic model along a slightly different path in Los Angeles, and power building's subsequent spread to other parts of the state.

Both regions have ended up with strong labor councils and key affiliates working closely with community groups through a closely linked 501(c)3 organization on issue campaigns, political action, and union organizing; however, they developed from somewhat different starting points. In San Jose, power building grew directly out of a revitalized labor council that formed a nonprofit "think-and-act tank." In Los Angeles, power building grew through a more organic process as a core group of activists founded a think-and-act tank, transformed the Los Angeles County AFL-CIO, and enhanced the mobilization and educational capacity of several other key players. These experiences show that there is no single path to follow in developing the three legs of the power building model, but that all three elements are necessary and must reinforce each other.

Power Building in Silicon Valley

With its core city of San Jose, the Santa Clara Valley (or Silicon Valley) is known as a highly integrated and prosperous economic region with nearly two million residents.[1] This continuously growing population is diverse, with about 44 percent of Santa Clara County's residents being non-Hispanic whites, roughly 25 percent Asian American, and 24 percent Mexican American.[2] The region is known for its dense concentration of electronics and computer companies. Manufacturing provides the largest employment, at 22 percent of the workforce, with professional and business services holding second place at 19 percent.[3]

With a population of close to one million, the city of San Jose has figured prominently in regional work due to its size, access to resources, and historically moderate-to-liberal governing coalition. In the early 1970s, a white middle-class revolt led by feminists and environmentalists displaced the long-standing growth alliance between city hall and real estate developers. However, while Silicon Valley generally tends to be a Democratic Party stronghold, its liberalism around social and growth management issues upholds a strong free-market ethos. While the Santa Clara County Chamber of Commerce tends to represent smaller business interests, two other business bodies help articulate larger employer interests in regional development decisions: the Silicon Valley Leaders Group (an association of manufacturers) and Joint Venture–Silicon Valley Network (a public-private consortium). Both these groups focus on enhancing the region's long-term competitiveness through "smart growth," information technology infrastructure, education, and an ability to attract elite workers.

Organized labor was historically marginal to regional policy debates. Union membership in the metropolitan region's private workforce hovered around 9 percent in the late 1980s and early 1990s before falling to 7.6 percent by 2006.[4] Most notably, the now dominant high-tech industry has managed to grow while remaining mostly union free. Despite these limitations, due to the region's demographic size the South Bay AFL-CIO has enjoyed a resource base of over 100,000 members.[5] However, by the mid-1980s the South Bay Labor Council (SBLC) had severely divided into factions.[6] Taking over the helm in 1985, Rick Sawyer succeeded in bridging the council's left-right divide, including the establishment of a new procedure for producing unified electoral endorsements. Affiliates agreed not to endorse candidates before the council process and then to follow the jointly agreed-upon endorsement afterward. Sawyer built this unity through a great deal of "homework" and one-on-one outreach to affiliate leaders.

Sawyer hired Amy Dean as political director in 1991. When selected to take over from Sawyer in 1994, Dean enjoyed a reunified council open to rethinking organized labor's role in Silicon Valley. Through a long-term planning process, key affiliate leaders decided to create a new identity for organized labor and for the SBLC. They wanted the community to see the labor movement as a strong, smart, and powerful champion of working-peoples' values, and they wanted local opinion leaders to conclude that organized labor was at least as capable and credible a steward of the local economy as was business. A survey of approximately four hundred union members measured rank-and-file hopes for the future. Some members viewed larger societal issues as either impervious "forces of nature" and/ or something outside of organized labor's core concerns. Yet, many others said that their own priorities were the same as those of the nonunion general public, including concerns over home ownership, job security, health care, public safety, and good education for their children. The survey revealed that a new council-led program to articulate a broad social agenda would likely draw sufficient rank-and-file support.

Establishing the Three Legs of Regional Power Building

The South Bay Labor Council developed three synergistic elements to develop and put a new social vision into practice. These are the three necessary legs for any regional power-building program. After detailing each element we will then show how they were integrated together to produce a rich series of policy and issue campaigns.

Research and Policy Development Capacity   The earliest new policy battles around taxes and business subsidies showed SBLC and affiliate leaders that they needed accurate, local public policy research and solid data to back up their arguments. In 1995 the council launched Working Partnerships USA as a 501(c)3 to provide crucial capacity for regional research, policy development, and coalition building. A 501(c)3 is a special designation made by the U.S. Internal Revenue Service that exempts nonprofit organizations from certain taxes. Such organizations cannot directly engage in electoral politics, and are restricted in their level of lobbying work. They can, however, engage in extensive educational and research work that supports policy campaigns.

This new nonprofit organization allowed the SBLC to accomplish several goals in addition to its explicit research, policy development, and coalition building capacities. Recruiting diverse individuals to serve on its board of directors allowed Working Partnerships' leadership to reflect the broad range of labor and community groups that the regional work hoped to link together.

The creation of Working Partnerships USA also allowed the SBLC to attract foundation resources and in turn build significant capacity. Typically, union-led work rarely attracts foundation attention. When it does, the most common form is support for the narrow job services and workforce training of social-service-oriented nonprofit programs traditionally affiliated with labor councils. Working Partnerships, however, represented something radically different. As Diana Cohn, formerly of the Solidago Foundation—A Working Partnerships funder—explains, "Working Partnerships USA was unique at the time. It developed capacities for research, advocacy, and coalition building that the labor movement doesn't normally have. Even where the labor movement has such capacities, they are typically spread among different organizations; Working Partnerships synthesized them."[7]

Foundation support from both national and California sources translated into sizable capacity. While under Dean's leadership the SBLC expanded its staff from two to eight by 2003, and Working Partnerships USA's staff grew to more than twenty members, with a budget that exceeded $2 million by 2002.

At an immediate instrumental level, the nonprofit provided local unions with new levels of support. For example, the organization's staff came to intimately know the budgets of government agencies at the municipal and county levels and could track the fiscal and economic development decision-making process. As a result, Working Partnerships could alert local unions and help them shape policy decisions at an early stage rather than reacting from a weak position later in the process. More strategically, however, this growing proactive capacity allowed the labor movement to become a regional player that could initiate and promote its own policy approaches. As we will see, these proposals would both unite leaders and activists within the house of labor and draw in many community players.

The starting point toward this larger agenda began with research that established a progressive labor-community perspective on Silicon Valley's economy—one that differed dramatically from official wisdom. Shortly after its launch in 1993, Joint Venture issued a highly optimistic report implying that the regional economy was thriving to the benefit of everyone. In response to this and other similarly glowing accounts, Working Partnerships USA conducted framing research that painted a very different picture simply by viewing the Silicon Valley economy through the lens of working families.

Working Partnerships' first report, *Shock Absorbers in the Flexible Economy,* published in May 1996, showed how the regional economy increasingly relied on part-time, temporary, and contracted work.[8] It found that temporary-agency employment was growing in Silicon Valley at three times the national average. Over a decade, contingent jobs had accounted for most employment growth, with employers displacing many full-time, permanent positions with jobs paying a fraction of previous salaries and rarely providing health benefits. The report's impact was heightened by the Service Employee International Union's Justice for Janitors campaign, which scored its first local victories organizing subcontracted janitors cleaning the buildings of major local corporations. This first report raised two related questions that have remained central concerns for the regional power building initiative: As the economy grows, what is the quality of jobs being created? And what is the relationship between this business success and the economic well-being of the community? The demonstrated failure of thriving businesses to create good jobs raised troubling questions about how to evaluate—and manage—this new economy.

Two years later, as part of a successful living wage campaign, Working Partnerships released a second framing report titled *Growing Together or Drifting Apart? Working Families and Business in the New Economy.*[9] The study, which received national media attention, further shocked believers in the Silicon Valley shared-success myth by revealing how the high-tech boom was actually deepening economic, racial, and ethnic inequality. For example, it showed that only the top 10 percent of regional workers were earning more in real terms than they had ten years earlier. During the same period, workers in the bottom quarter, disproportionately nonwhite and with a high school education or less, had lost 13 percent of their earning power—making minimal self-sufficiency nearly impossible for many of them.

Subsequent Working Partnerships reports focused on growing economic insecurity, lack of affordable housing, the middle-class squeeze, failed economic development policies, the need for health care, problems of immigrants, and the persistent hardships experienced by working families following the dot-com bust of 2000. *Sacramento Bee* columnist Peter Schrag wrote that Working Partnerships USA reports "reinforced the growing evidence that beneath the much-celebrated boom in California's high-tech economy—behind each of those baby-faced Silicon Valley millionaires and every billion dollar initial public offering—there are a hundred low-paid contingent workers with no job security, no benefits and only the most uncertain future."[10]

The broad framing research did more than puncture the prevailing myth of widespread prosperity; it gave legitimacy to the South Bay Labor Council and Working Partnerships' leading roles in developing a regional movement for progressive power. While Working Partnerships' more detailed research helped develop concrete policy reforms, the organization's staff and the SBLC would play leading roles in building the coalitions that put ideas into practice.

Building Enduring Relationships and Deep Coalitions   Central to the SBLC's regional strategy was an understanding that the regional labor movement was most likely to grow and succeed if it operated with strong allies. The policy campaigns, which we will describe later, all involved often broad and diverse coalitions of labor, community, and even employer groups. Amid this broad coalition work, however, the council and Working Partnerships sought to develop deeper and more ongoing partnerships between organized labor and key community groups. These deeper partnerships have helped drive the broader coalition campaigns.

The SBLC's relationship with the Association of Community Organizations for Reform Now (ACORN) offers an illustrative example of such deeper partnerships. The local ACORN chapter has been a critical labor ally for electoral mobilizations and policy campaigns around regional development, housing, and tenant rights. Seeing a growing ACORN chapter as providing key capacities for building regional power, the SBLC has actively supported its growth and development. For example, it made the strategic decision to focus its housing work on an ACORN-sponsored proposal to protect tenants against evictions, even though the issue was not a top labor priority. The two groups strategized together and jointly canvassed target neighborhoods. The labor council emphasized its relationship with ACORN in part because they shared a vision of building power as grassroots, membership-based organizations. "[The council] had a vision for what [it] wanted to get done in San Jose, really grow power for the labor movement," explains ACORN organizer Jon Eller. "We could understand that and we wanted to build power for our membership. It's kind of rare to have that kind of relationship where both sides of the table, both community and labor, are speaking the same language about power."[11] Reflecting the deep partnership, ACORN lead organizer Dereka Mehrens also sat on the board of Working Partnerships USA before becoming staff.

The ongoing cooperation between the SBLC and People Acting in Community Together (PACT) represents a different form of enduring relationship. Affiliated with the national Pacific Institute for Community Organizing network of faith-based community organizations, PACT is a two-decades-old organization whose base of congregations encompasses 35,000 families, and it was a lead ally of the SBLC in its campaign to use tobacco lawsuit funds for the new Children's Health Initiative. PACT held meetings with city council members and members of the board of supervisors and mobilized supporters for community meetings to support funding for CHI. They also participated in planning the details of the Healthy Kids program. PACT and the council also took part in an ultimately unsuccessful attempt to build the Housing for All coalition to push housing reforms.[12] Coalitions between labor and community groups like PACT often involve tensions around different organizational styles. Unions are formal organizations with legally established governance procedures that can take formal decisions that bind the organization.

Community groups like PACT emphasize the participation and development of "volunteer leaders" (with a potentially slower decision-making
process) and the organization follows an outsider strategy that precludes
political endorsements and carefully protects its federal 501(c)3 status
against charges of electioneering. Thus, the work between the council
and PACT has focused more on specific policy issues rather than overall
political programs. Yet, the relationship remains an ongoing one. Lead
organizer Matt Hammer explains PACT's continued looking forward to
working on projects with labor and the council as working with "important allies in the community."[13]

The Interfaith Council (IFC) on Race, Religion, Economic and Social Justice represents yet another form of deep relationship. The IFC
was jump-started and nurtured by the SBLC in 1997 to create a structure
through which activist, liberal clergy could work on labor issues. Early
in its history, for example, the IFC worked closely with the SBLC on the
living wage campaign, the Children's Health Initiative, and immigrant issues. While still receiving staff support from the South Bay AFL-CIO, the
IFC has more recently moved toward greater independence—developing
its own religious framework for driving the pursuit of specific campaigns,
rather than simply responding to labor calls for assistance.[14]

While practical campaign work helps develop deep relationships among
core partners, Working Partnerships USA and the SBLC also teamed up
with San Jose State University to establish a formal relationship-building
mechanism, the Labor/Community Leadership Institute. Inspired by regional leadership development and networking initiatives conducted by
business, the program sought to create a diverse cross-constituency, cross-
campaign leadership team. The "students" are specially targeted and recruited for the institute. Before the program was first launched, Working
Partnerships conducted a "power survey" to identify five hundred of the
most influential Silicon Valley leaders who were either sympathetic or
might be made sympathetic to a regional labor-progressive agenda. It then
invited participants from among these civic leaders, unionists, community
activists, clergy, and elected officials to a nine-week course that examined
the Silicon Valley economy through a social justice lens, identified the public decisions that influence it, and discussed the role of labor, community,
and political organizing in steering this economy in more equitable and
sustainable directions.

The program proved successful from the outset, with its first round sparking intense discussions about new alliances, campaigns, and political action. "Participants get much more than solid, local economic information in the Working Partnerships' classes," explains Father Bill Leininger, who as an IFC leader has been both a student and teacher. "They also get a sense of what is possible, what they and their fellow classmates, and all those who have come before them, could accomplish by working together."[15] The Leadership Institute has helped build ties between white working-class communities and people of color, an alliance that proved decisive in several recent elections. It has also spawned other complementary study and action groups. The Neighborhood Community Institute, for example, specializes in educating and building relationships among leaders of neighborhood groups. The Faith in Action series of educational meetings on policy and the economy brought in the religious community by highlighting the links between labor's work and traditional social concerns of faith groups.

The Leadership Institute has helped labor be proactive in its community outreach. Rather than waiting until unions were in the middle of a campaign to seek allies, the program has established a permanent network that can respond proactively to both injustices and opportunities. It has strengthened local leaders' understanding of how to ground their organizational strategies in a shared analysis of the regional economy; provided a common framework and language to discuss issues; developed relationships that cut across class, race, ethnicity, and occupational divisions in Silicon Valley's fragmented economy; and helped the labor movement form and deepen relationships with organizations that were key partners in subsequent coalitions.

Fostering More Unified and Aggressive Political Action   Whether innovative coalitions can win concrete changes in public policy ultimately depends on the ability of labor and its allies to impact a region's political balance of power. Beginning in the mid-1980s, the South Bay AFL-CIO undertook a series of campaigns to strengthen the labor movement's political clout. By the end of the decade labor-endorsed candidates were a majority on the San Jose City Council. Despite these advances, labor saw many Democrats (running for local government in nonpartisan elections) as excessively sympathetic to business and not fully understanding or sharing labor's priorities once in office. Working through several steps that closely integrated with other power building work, the labor council sought to move labor's political presence in Silicon Valley from one of access to officeholders to one of becoming a participant in the governing fabric.

As a first step, the SBLC strengthened its unified endorsement process. Traditionally, many unions had made their own candidate endorsements. The endorsements of unions with greater members and money often carried more clout than those of the SBLC. By contrast, council affiliates now participate in a unified council-driven process that emphasizes public policies that serve all of labor. Endorsements go to candidates with a track record of fighting for the common interests of all branches of the labor movement. According to interviews conducted with local labor leaders by Barbara Byrd and Nari Rhee, while individual unions may disagree during the process, it is rare for them to break ranks once a choice has been made.

A council endorsement not only brings unified union support but coordinates a growing electoral mobilization capacity. With modest staff of its own, the SBLC draws on staff and rank-and-file volunteers from affiliate unions to provide the nucleus for a well-oiled get-out-the-vote and precinct-walking program. For example, as many as forty union staff might be paid by their locals to work on the election team for several weeks leading up to an election, giving a capacity to mobilize six hundred or more volunteer precinct walkers in a single day.[16]

What most distinguishes power-building politics from traditional labor political work, however, is the way in which efforts made during the election season integrate with the ongoing coalition building and policy development work. Rather than present candidates with a laundry list of issues provided by each individual union and community ally, the SBLC offers a unified program often rooted in Working Partnerships USA's research and the shared social vision uniting key labor and community players. To help officeholders understand this agenda on a concrete level, the council now briefs candidates through weekend meetings, explaining the rationale for its policies and defining what it means for candidates to stand with the labor movement. Preparing for the briefings also brings unions together to better understand their common agenda and how best to advocate it. The ongoing policy and coalition work also allows the SBLC to recruit candidates drawn from the community that unions and Working

Partnerships had nurtured. The Leadership Institute has proved to be an excellent source of such candidates.

In addition to the general elections, labor has used its political capacity to fight for prolabor candidates in Democratic primaries. For example, in the March 2000 primary election in a solidly Democratic state assembly district, Manny Diaz, a city council member who supported the council-led living wage campaign, faced probusiness Democrat Tony West. According to Working Partnerships' policy director, Bob Brownstein, West had powerful allies, including "the state attorney general, the mayor of San Francisco, and a number of statewide business interests."[17] West outspent Diaz two to one, pouring his money into a blizzard of negative mailings. But Diaz campaigned as a labor Democrat with plans to introduce a living wage bill in the state legislature, and the labor movement contributed ten thousand volunteer hours for its voter mobilization effort, producing a 53 percent victory for Diaz. Silicon Valley's *Metro* weekly reported the outcome with the headline, "Labor-Backed Candidates Stomp Big Business Boys in Legislative Races."[18]

By 2002, labor's power-building-linked electoral work had led to what the *San Jose Mercury News* called "a showdown between the city's most powerful political interests, labor and business."[19] Labor-backed candidates faced and defeated probusiness candidates for six city council districts. The stakes were especially high in District Seven, where two Democrats—Ed Voss, heavily backed by business, and Terry Gregory, labor's candidate—squared off. When Gregory and other candidates won, the newspaper reported that SBLC Amy Dean was "the most powerful woman in San Jose. And the union organization she leads dominates the South Bay's political landscape."[20]

Since this time, labor and its allies have continued to win victories on policy initiatives with the same formula of research, coalition-building, and political action, but the balance of power has shifted. The fights have been less fractious, and some labor-promoted policies—such as expanding the scope of the living wage ordinance or establishing criteria for publicly supported development—are now more readily accepted.

With San Jose encompassing roughly half of Silicon Valley's population, the building of labor's political program has logically been focused there. However, shifting regional development requires a capacity to push policy in jurisdictions beyond the main city. The region's second-largest city,

Sunnyvale, provided the next logical step for expanding the council-led electoral program. The council also pushed the regional Democratic state and congressional delegations toward a more progressive, labor-oriented perspective.[21] Far from detracting from organizing for national elections, the regional strategy created a strong base from which to affect them.

Because labor's growing electoral capacity integrated with its other elements for building regional power, organized labor essentially put the political structure on notice that the ballot box was the beginning—not the end—of labor's involvement in politics. Unions, the council, and their allies expected to be actively involved in governance after an election. Many candidates responded favorably to the shift and proved eager to work with a group that could analyze policy, crunch numbers, and turn out hundreds of people on short notice. The labor council instituted regular policy briefings for city council members, anticipating issues and informing legislators of labor's expectations. That presence made the labor movement and its allies an integral part of the governing process, guaranteeing that the interests of working people and their communities were not ignored as decisions were made. As Chris Block, executive director of the Charities Housing Development Corporation, explains, "because Working Partnerships and the labor council are always at the table, it means that in Santa Clara County the progressive agenda is always part of the debate."[22]

Toward a New Social Contract: Moving Concrete Campaigns

Integrated together, the three power-building elements provided the capacity to move a progressive policy and organizing agenda that began to shift the debates and direction of Silicon Valley's future development.

Tax Subsidies   A successful 1995 campaign to reform how Santa Clara County granted business tax subsidies marked the South Bay Labor Council's first foray into its new public role. The issue combined concerns of specific unions and community groups. In their opposition to service cuts, local public unions had discovered that tax subsidies that had been provided to corporations were a contributing and important symbolic factor to local government funding shortfalls.[23] At the same time other groups, including the League of Women Voters, had raised concerns that rising "tax expenditures" were undermining local budgets. Normally in the United

States, the main regional-based policy tools for economic development are rooted in city- and town-level government. California, however, had passed legislation that enabled counties to rebate property taxes. As an early campaign, a county subsidy effort offered several attractions. Relative to other municipal subsidy policy changes, the county effort would involve modest amounts of money and thus hopefully less resistance. To secure a county majority required convincing only three board representatives (out of five), compared to six (out of eleven) representatives on the San Jose City Council. Several incidents of the county tax abatements had also directly impacted the SBLC's largest affiliate, the nursing workers in Service Employees International Union (SEIU) Local 715. Finally, since the county government spanned many municipalities, success at this level would provide a regional win that would allow activists to push similar policies at the smaller levels of government.

In 1995, Intel, Cisco Systems, and other successful local corporations asked the Santa Clara County Board of Supervisors to award them substantial property tax breaks to create or retain local jobs. In the past, similar firms had often won tax and regulatory concessions by effectively threatening to leave the region. Following the advice of Greg LeRoy at the Washington, D.C.–based organization Good Jobs First, the SBLC organized a small group of community leaders to request that if the county awarded public funds for a specific purpose, such as the creation of jobs, it should contractually require the firms to live up to their promises. The proposal essentially took the language of business—accountability, measurable outcomes, and performance standards—and applied it to corporate tax breaks.

With Working Partnerships USA then in the making, the SBLC put together a small research team to analyze other communities' controls on corporate tax subsides and organized a coalition with various community groups for a new subsidy policy. An official county task force, in which the labor council participated, proposed that businesses receiving tax rebates be required to provide jobs paying $10 per hour or more, and health insurance, as well as to refund their tax rebates if they failed to generate the promised jobs. In addition, in deciding whether or not to grant rebates, the county would review a firm's labor practices and health and safety policies. Over opposition from employers, the county board unanimously approved the new requirements. The new policy effectively stopped one avenue of property tax giveaways because most companies simply stopped applying for the tax rebates.[24]

The tax subsidies effort demonstrated the strength of integrating research, policy development, and coalition building. It also illustrated how a proactive policy strategy could connect unions and local communities in new alliances.

Living Wages   The 1998 living wage campaign continued the focus on public spending and development policy, but with the three power-building legs now firmly established. The effort proved a key showdown between important elements of the dominant regional power structure and the new capacities of labor and its allies.

The enacted San Jose ordinance required firms with city contracts over $20,000 or direct financial grants over $100,000 to pay what at the time was the highest living-wage standard in the country ($12.27 per hour with health insurance, or $13.52 per hour without it). In addition, the law required companies to provide assurances of good labor relations and to respect the right of workers to organize, and that successor contractors offer jobs to employees of predecessor contractors who performed services to the city.

In addition to opposition led by the Santa Clara County Chamber of Commerce, the powerful local daily, the *San Jose Mercury News,* ran nearly a dozen editorials against the measure, lamenting the "increasing influence" of labor unions on Mayor Susan Hammer, who supported the living wage. "San Jose should not be setting local wage standards for private employers," the paper editorialized. "This is blackmail on behalf of the unions. It has no place in city law."[25]

With 1998 also being a local election year, the living wage issue spilled into city electoral politics. Indeed, it became a central question in the close battle between Cindy Chavez and Tony West for a council seat in District Three. Chavez was Working Partnerships USA's education and outreach director, while West ran a well-funded campaign backed by the chamber of commerce. In its endorsement of West, the *Mercury News* singled out living wages as the key issue in the campaign. It vilified Chavez as a labor leader who "would carry the union agenda and push it as a council member."[26] Chavez won by a few hundred votes because the SBLC led one of the strongest get-out-the-vote operations in the city's recent history. In the end, campaign volunteers could identify by name and address virtually every one of the several hundred new voters who provided Chavez's thin margin of victory. Two weeks later, the San Jose City Council passed the living wage ordinance with the surprise support of one of Mayor Hammer's strongest opponents, David Pandori.

Community Benefits Agreements   The community benefits agreements strategy grew out of the subsidy and living wage work and utilized a similar logic, that promoters of large development projects that needed public approval and/or expenditures should be required to define the specific benefits of their development to the community and be held accountable for delivering these gains. The community benefits efforts not only continued the coalition work of prior campaigns between labor and low-income communities but also promised to change the practice of regional development that typically pitted those sections of the labor movement that hoped to get construction jobs against environmental and community opponents of sprawl or gentrifying development. The pioneering effort also allowed the South Bay Labor Council to work with small businesses and ethnic chambers of commerce often negatively impacted by large-scale development.

The first effort—around a massive 25,000-unit project in the Coyote Valley, a rare 1,700-acre development reserve within the city—focused on affordable housing. On the surface this issue was not a strong "labor" concern. However, with regional housing costs skyrocketing, the issue positioned the SBLC and Working Partnerships USA as advocates for broad community interests. It allowed labor to work in close collaboration with housing advocates, the faith community, and ACORN.[27] And due to the region's high cost of living, efforts to promote affordable housing ultimately benefited many union members. In 2001, the campaign won an agreement from Mayor Ron Gonzales to establish an "inclusionary zoning" provision that required that 5,000 units within the development area be rented or sold to low and/or moderate-income households at below-market prices. The ability of Working Partnerships USA to document both the need for affordable housing and the financial feasibility of the proposal helped secure the victory. The now well-established ability of the SBLC and Working Partnerships to understand the development process and to build coalitions quickly allowed the campaign to intervene in the early stages of the planning process, leaving no time for opposition to come together.[28]

When the CIM Group proposed in 2002 to use public funds to develop three downtown San Jose sites for underground parking, retail, and high-rise residential buildings, the council led a successful coalition to secure a public requirement that CIM negotiate in good faith with the SBLC and its partner community organizations (which included ACORN, the Interfaith Council, and neighborhood associations) to define binding benefits to the community. The final agreement included more than one hundred units of affordable housing, living wage jobs, community amenities (such as space for a child care provider), and space for existing small businesses already in the area. Even the building trades, often skeptical of community benefit agreements as obstacles to construction, embraced the agreements as protection of quality jobs and as a key element of the labor movement's power-building strategy.[29]

Public Transit   Organizing around public transit issues illustrates how the capacity to research and understand public policy allows regional power-building work to connect specific union and community interests. When during the recession of the early part of the new millennium the transit service announced plans to lay off union bus drivers, Working Partnerships USA analyzed the proposed route cuts to find that they were overwhelmingly in the poorer, east side of the county. Transit system analysts had suggested that this was where the cuts should be made because these routes had fewer riders, but the east side residents needed the buses more than anyone else. Working Partnerships USA urged its allies in the local religious community to call policymakers regarding the needs of poor bus riders. The resulting public debate focused mainly on what would be best for the most financially disadvantaged people of the region. In the end, the bus routes and union jobs were saved—the result of good research, pre-established community alliances, and political influence.

Silicon Valley's overcrowded highways have given the business community a strong incentive to get involved with transportation issues. In 2000, the Silicon Valley Manufacturing Group (but not organized labor) backed a half-cent sales tax increase for transit, mainly an extension of metropolitan San Francisco's Bay Area Rapid Transit system to San Jose. But after the economic bust of the turn of the millennium, sales tax revenues plummeted and the system had difficulty maintaining operations. The SBLC took advantage of the situation to work together with businesses on the Valley Transportation Authority commission to use some of the new half-cent sales tax increase to save the threatened bus routes. Both agreed to work for an additional tax to support transit and health care. However, voters in a low-turnout election proved cynical about whether the general tax would actually be used for the stated purposes, and rejected it.

Union Organizing   Helping unions to be successful in organizing was a core strategic goal for the South Bay AFL-CIO upon embarking on its new direction. The SBLC's Strike Support Committee, which mobilized members for rallies and actions, became the Organizing Support Committee. The council focused on providing support and resources for unions that were actively involved in organizing rather than the majority of often smaller locals that were not. This support was often low-profile, but could prove essential for the unions involved. Council support was reciprocated by strong backing of the labor council by these unions.

During organizing campaigns labor council staff often held weekly meetings with lead union organizing staff to map out action plans. It used its ties to elected officials to generate letters to employers urging company neutrality and respect for the right to organize and to remind vendors that labor peace was important in the selection of contractors. Labor-backed officials were expected to use their "bully pulpit" to publicly endorse workers' organizing efforts. The council also drew on its relationships with community groups to, for example, organize delegations of religious leaders to visit employers during a campaign. The Leadership Institute educated participants on the challenges workers confront when they try to organize and brought multiracial teams of workers involved in organizing campaigns to do panel presentations. In other words, the SBLC tried to integrate support for organizing into all of its power building efforts. In doing so it built support not just for a single campaign, but also for ongoing efforts to expand the labor movement's reach.

Specific council-initiated programs also helped particular unions organize. The living wage ordinance, for example, fostered worker organizing. Local unions followed up on the living wage win to organize about two thousand new members and secure raises for five thousand more.[30] It helped the Service Employees International Union (SEIU) with organizing hospital workers and janitors. Growing out of work for labor peace agreements, the labor council helped UNITE HERE—a merging of the former Union of Needletrades, Industrial and Textile Employees (UNITE) and the former Hotel Employees and Restaurant Employees International Union (HERE)—organize all but one of the new hotels built in San Jose by 2007. In 2004, the SBLC joined with the San Jose Convention and Visitors Bureau, the downtown hotels, and the city arts associations as Team San Jose to win a contract to operate the convention center, civic auditorium, and other venues—giving it leverage to protect the workers' right to organize.

Power building work has also shaped public opinion in ways that have helped organizing. For example, Working Partnerships USA's report on temporary workers is credited with helping SEIU Local 715 organize 1,500 workers at Stanford University.[31] Most generally, by establishing organized labor as a visible champion of community well-being, regional power-building work has helped to shift the political and cultural context within which unions organize in Silicon Valley. The SBLC's active role in helping locals organize also had an important side effect: it helped persuade individual unions to support council work that was more experimental and that may have had less immediate payoff to affiliates—but which promised to deliver greater payoff in the long run.

Regional power building offers the ability to support union organizing, but it cannot *create* the actual organizing campaigns because in the United States such decisions are rooted in national union offices. Thus, unionizing in Silicon Valley's largely nonunion high-tech industry depends upon one or more national unions targeting and putting resources into a large-scale organizing attempt. Although some limited organizing efforts were made in the 1980s and '90s such a large-scale effort has yet to emerge.[32] Regional power-building work, however, has begun to change the political and social climate within Silicon Valley in ways that strengthen the possibilities for contemplating future organizing efforts.

Contingent Work   One facet of corporate restructuring that has undermined the ability of unions to organize workers has been the sharp growth in contingent employment. How, for example, can temporary workers organize when the hiring agency and business for whom they do the actual work are two different organizations? Working Partnerships has documented the growth of contingent work and the poor conditions for contingent workers in the region. In doing so it has also acknowledged that some labor market intermediaries providing temporary work are likely to remain an important source of workers for many companies. Yet, most temporary agencies engage in highly exploitative practices that include paying low wages, bestowing few benefits, job discrimination, and various schemes to cheat people.[33] Could a union-oriented temporary agency provide an alternative that would both improve conditions for workers and bring them into greater contact with the labor movement and progressive organizing?

In 1999, Working Partnerships USA created an experimental staffing service that guaranteed workers a living wage and offered health insurance (at $50 per month per person, with the respected Kaiser Permanente health maintenance organization), affordable but custom-tailored training, and career development. Surveys of employers have found pools of managers dissatisfied with the quality and skills of workers provided by many temping agencies.[34] By treating workers better than the temp industry norm, could the Working Partnerships agency offer employers a compelling quality alternative? The new agency consulted with employers to identify needed skills and then worked with a community college to provide workers the necessary classes.

The worker-friendly temp agency appealed to socially conscious clients, including businesses and local governments. The agency plowed its earnings back into the support of higher wages, benefits, and training for workers. It encouraged employers to hire workers full-time rather than charging a fee to convert a temp to a regular worker. In human terms the agency exceeded expectations, placing two thousand employees in jobs within three years, and providing them an unusual combination of living wages, health insurance, training, and career development. Yet as an experiment the agency proved unsustainable. Working Partnerships concluded that weak federal and state regulation allows for irresponsible conduct on the part of for-profit temp agencies. Placed in competition with the abusive commercial firms the more expensive agency could operate only with an ongoing subsidy. When Working Partnerships conducted a multiyear study of labor market intermediaries in two quite different regions—Milwaukee, Wisconsin, and Silicon Valley—it confirmed its conclusion that, without stronger public regulation, competition in the industry will lead to deteriorating conditions for temp workers and obstruct the growth of more responsible, worker-oriented alternatives.

The Community Blueprint Project   Several of the campaigns mentioned herein grew out of the innovative Community Blueprint Project. Through this project, the SBLC and Working Partnerships USA conducted face-to-face conversations with over four hundred current and would-be allies to identify how they would define what community-centered economic development might look like. This process allowed leaders and activists to explain what issues mattered most to their groups.

Using the information from these discussions Working Partnerships identified key indicators for measuring regional patterns. By subsequently conducting research around the indicators, Working Partnerships was able to paint a clear picture of what was happening to working families in the region and identify concrete public policy measures that would address such families' needs. By turning a report on the regional data and policy measures into popular education materials, Blueprint organizers returned to conversations with a wide range of groups about the community's future.

The Community Blueprint Project accomplished several goals: it provided a vehicle with which the SBLC and Working Partnerships USA could introduce themselves to a wide range of community groups and organizations; it further deepened relationships among existing allies; and it identified individuals to invite to participate in the Labor/Community Leadership Institute. In all of these dimensions the project framed Working Partnerships and the South Bay Labor Council as leaders not simply aware of people's issues and concerns but with a positive vision for the regional future.

Power Building in Los Angeles

At the same time that the San Jose movement pursued innovations in northern California, activists in Los Angeles were experimenting in the southern part of the state. This work produced a three-legged model similar in its basic features to that found in Silicon Valley.[35]

Conditions in southern California differed in important ways from those in San Jose. Throughout most of the twentieth century, the San Francisco Bay area boasted the highest union density levels in the state, while metropolitan Los Angeles had a reputation as a "company town" living in the aftermath of the city's famous open shop movement of the century's early decades.[36] However, despite relative weakness, the region's urban scale offered significant potential for building capacity. At roughly ten million residents, Los Angeles County is the most populous in the United States. Reflective of these demographics, as union density in the region has recently grown closer to that of the state average, by 2000 metropolitan Los Angeles was home to 45 percent of California union members. The region's economy has also produced particularly intense conditions of inequality and economic insecurity. Service industry growth and transformation has caused the region to lead the nation in generating poverty-wage jobs.[37] Employers in construction, business services, hospitality, and the retail industries have replaced union members with contracted and contingent workers—especially those who are nonunion and foreign born. Immigrants currently make up an estimated 36.2 percent of the Los Angeles population, and as many as 800,000 of them may be undocumented.[38]

While involving many groups and individuals, regional power building in San Jose was driven by leadership from a single institution, the South Bay AFL-CIO. By contrast, the emergence of regional power building in Los Angeles developed through separate but complementary paths. Key union locals, like HERE Local 11, began developing an innovative grassroots organizing model in the late 1980s. Community-based groups like Action for Grassroots Empowerment and Neighborhood Development Alternatives (AGENDA) and Strategic Actions for a Just Economy (SAJE, an economic justice, community development, and popular education center founded in Los Angeles in 1996) fostered a new type of grassroots organizing based on alliances and movement building. The Los Angeles Alliance for a New Economy (LAANE), founded in 1993, provides crucial capacity for research and policy development and deep coalition building. The Los Angeles County Federation of Labor also leads deep coalition work while building a more unified and aggressive political action program. A variety of educational and leadership development efforts, many based out of the University of California–Los Angeles Labor Center, have also coalesced in the last decade.

Regional work in Los Angeles has established a virtuous cycle of deepening relationships among these core groups that has led to further power building innovation. In his survey of Los Angeles's new progressive infrastructure, Walter Julio Nicholls describes the cycle:

> What makes Los Angeles different is that innovators in this city were able to overcome the constraints imposed upon them by their respective sectors,

find receptive colleagues and friends in other sectors, and embark upon a series of trust-building activities that were later to serve as the relational grounds for the elaboration of more institutionalized forms of coordinated interactions. Once such semi-formalized mechanisms were established, a virtuous cycle of thickening relations and further innovations upon strategic and modes of organizing was initiated. Although this pathway is particular to Los Angeles, many of the processes underlying it are not.[39]

The current makeup of LAANE's board of directors reflects the tight interweaving among these core partners. The chair is María Elena Durazo, executive secretary-treasurer of the County Federation of Labor, while Kent Wong, director of the UCLA Labor Center, serves as secretary. Other board members include Strategic Concepts in Organizing and Policy Education's (SCOPE's) Sabrina Smith, Angelica Salas of the Coalition for Humane Immigrant Rights of Los Angeles, several SEIU and UNITE HERE representatives, and Manuel Pastor, professor of geography at UCLA.

Nicholls's virtuous cycle is reflected in the growing progressive electoral and political clout seen locally and at the state level. It is signaled by the recent gains in union density that have made metropolitan Los Angeles into what one newspaper headline described as "ground zero" in the labor movement's revival. While the mid-1990s movement in Los Angeles was not as formally linked as Silicon Valley's, the two have evolved to share very similar structures—represented by the three legs of regional power building.

1. Research and Policy Development Capacity

In San Jose, the think-and-act tank Working Partnerships USA was founded by South Bay Labor Council leaders. Both organizations are literally under the same roof, and the executive officer of the South Bay AFL-CIO is also Working Partnerships' executive director. Its Los Angeles parallel, the LAANE, was launched by a local and actually preceded the Los Angeles Country Federation of Labor's full transformation. As a central power-building institution LAANE today boasts an accomplished capacity to engage in research, policy development, and coalition building.

In 1993, HERE Local 11, under the leadership of María Elena Durazo, founded what was originally called the Tourism Industry Development

Council (TIDC). As its name suggests, the organization was created to improve the often harsh working conditions found in the area's tourist industry and increase its union density. The TIDC's early work, centered on the 1994 World Cup and airport workers, was only moderately successful, as employers proved adept at using subcontracting to bypass the TIDC's efforts.[40] In 1995, the renamed Los Angeles Alliance for a New Economy turned its attention to securing public policy and building supportive coalitions that would begin to change the climate for organizing. LAANE led a successful campaign to pass the country's second worker-retention ordinance, requiring that existing workers be hired first during a change of contractors. The Los Angeles City ordinance helped save the jobs of hundreds of airport employees, among others.

The election of Miguel Contreras as executive secretary-treasurer of the Los Angeles County Federation of Labor marked a turning point for regional power building and LAANE. A former United Farm Workers (UFW) organizer and HERE leader, Contreras had been part of the core group at Local 11 that started LAANE and now brought the organization into a close relationship with the county federation.

In 1997, LAANE spearheaded a broad coalition to pass Los Angeles's living wage law over a mayoral veto. The ordinance proved a national pioneer in stipulating a higher wage in the absence of health benefits, barring retaliation by employers against workers, and applying living wage requirements to recipients of city financial assistance and leases of city-owned properties. LAANE's living wage work also emerged as a model for aggressive enforcement. The alliance's staff actively monitored the city's contracting and economic development activity in order to intervene in the public process. The living wage coalition successfully pushed the city council to remove responsibility for city enforcement efforts from an unsympathetic and ineffective office to a new staff established for that purpose. LAANE was also the implementation arm of a city-sponsored program to train covered workers on their rights under the living wage ordinance.

With a staff of roughly forty today, LAANE boasts rich capacities. Like Working Partnerships USA, LAANE conducts both broad framing research and targeted investigations that support specific campaigns. As an example of the former, in 2000, the alliance released a report detailing the magnitude of regional social and economic problems produced by the massive growth of low-wage jobs. This report built on earlier studies that exposed the lack of attention to job quality in two of the city's major economic development programs: the Commercial Redevelopment Agency and the mayor's Los Angeles Business Team.[41]

And like Working Partnerships, LAANE plays a direct role in coalition building and policy campaigns. The alliance has been a pioneer in developing the strategy of community benefits agreements (which will be explored in detail in chapter 3). In Los Angeles, these agreements have taken the form of legally binding documents between a developer and a campaign that in turn have been incorporated into the public approval process. The first breakthrough agreement, with the massive Staples Center development, was spearheaded by SAJE and set the framework for future work. LAANE joined with a group formed by SAJE called the Figueroa Corridor Coalition for Economic Justice to secure and implement benefits agreements involving the forty-block strip between the Staples Center basketball arena and the University of Southern California campus. By 2002, the coalition had secured binding agreements with five major entertainment, housing and retail, and industrial development projects. In 2005, it worked with Greg LeRoy and Good Jobs First to produce a detailed guide for securing such agreements used by groups across the country.[42]

2. Fostering More Unified and Aggressive Political Action

Most of the Los Angeles campaigns have depended upon influencing public policy decisions. Such achievements have been possible due to the clear increase in progressive political power in the region over the last decade. While the political work of several key unions and community organizations has contributed to this shift, we have to turn to the transformation of the Los Angles County Federation of Labor to capture the heart of this story.

With roughly 350 affiliated unions representing over 800,000 members, the Los Angles County Federation of Labor has had an extensive membership and resource base from which to draw. Yet for decades the federation practiced a tradition of insider politics focused on union construction work and other benefits for specific affiliates won through close personal relationships with establishment political figures. This tradition often placed the federation in positions hostile to progressive forces among local unions and the broader community. Just before his death in 1996, however, federation leader Jim Wood expressed his desire to have his political director, Miguel Contreras, succeed him. Contreras had learned organizing and movement politics during his years with the UFW and had first come to the city as a trustee for HERE Local 11. Overcoming opposition from the old guard, Contreras became the first person of color to lead the organization. His election came at a time when new leadership emerged in several key affiliate locals and in a context of increasingly aggressive organizing by key unions.

As executive secretary-treasurer, Contreras continued his work to establish the federation as the leader of an energized and broad-based labor-community electoral mobilization. Today, at each election cycle the federation coordinates the fund raising of hundreds of thousands of dollars, internal labor-to-labor mobilizations, and the development of several independent expenditure campaigns, usually constituency-based efforts aimed at immigrants, Latinos, African Americans, or women. Through the federation's leadership, labor has dramatically expanded its technical ability to target voters, the skills of its full-time precinct walkers ("loss-timers" from affiliates on union leave from work), and its pool of weekend volunteers. The federation supplements labor's direct in-person contact with full-time and volunteer phone calls at its forty-station predictive-dialing phone bank and at SEIU Local 99's fixed and mobile predictive-dialing stations.

To pay for these civic mobilization efforts, the Los Angeles County Federation of Labor has secured additional funds (in excess of per-capita payments) from affiliates, often as much as $300,000, to fund the labor-to-labor program and independent expenditure campaigns. In addition, some affiliates are now able to conduct their own independent expenditure campaigns focused, for example, on a separate radio, billboard, or open placement sign as part of labor's overall effort.

The recent electoral record reflects the Los Angeles labor movement's increasingly sophisticated civic mobilization efforts. In 1994, for example, the federation helped progressive union activist Antonio Villaraigosa overcome the old guard Latino leadership to win a state assembly seat in northwest Los Angeles. In 1999, Villaraigosa was elected speaker of the state assembly. Most of the labor movement then worked hard for Villaraigosa when he ran unsuccessfully for mayor against James Hahn in 2001. When Villaraigosa again challenged Hahn in the 2005 election, most of labor officially endorsed Hahn, rewarding him for appointing labor-backed nominees to key boards and cultivating labor support more generally. Sympathies among the labor movements' rank and file, however, backed Villaraigosa. He won election by building on the force of past labor civic campaigns to become the city's first Latino mayor since 1874.

When the Democrats regained control of the state assembly in 1996, Los Angeles labor was a big part of the story through the election of three Democratic challengers. In 2000, the Los Angeles County Federation of Labor broke with a tradition of not opposing incumbent business-oriented Democrats (with moderate prolabor voting records) when it put its now considerable electoral power behind state senator Hilda Solis's successful bid for the congressional house seat held by incumbent Marty Martinez. Solis had led the successful 1986 fight to raise the state's minimum wage, and her 2000 win sent a message that labor wanted, in the words of Contreras, "labor warriors" and "labor champions" in office.

Facing a Los Angeles Area Chamber of Commerce–funded opponent in 2002, the federation's former political director Fabian Núñez won election to the state assembly, despite having never run for office before. In February 2004, he was chosen by his fellow Democrats as the speaker of the assembly. That same year, labor helped progressive community activist Karen Bass become the first African American woman in the state legislature in ten years. In 2008 Bass became speaker of the assembly when Núñez was term-limited out. For some time now, city labor's state and national electoral efforts have complemented the steadily growing progressive influence on the Los Angeles City Council and in surrounding municipalities. Former SEIU organizer and Los Angeles County Federation of Labor political director Martin Ludlow, for example, went from a 13-point deficit in the primary to a commanding runoff victory for a seat on the city council in 2003. The recent election of Mayor Villaraigosa supplemented an already prolabor majority on the city council. By contrast, the Los Angeles County Board of Supervisors has proven far more resistant to labor influence. Part of the difficulty lies with the five huge districts within which supervisors are elected. District Four, for example, stretches at least thirty miles, from parts of Los Angeles, Inglewood, and Culver City in the north to Whittier and La Habra Heights in the south.[43] Nonetheless, progress is being made on this front as well, as a labor-community campaign forced a November 2008 runoff election for a county board seat.

The federation's leadership in building aggressive political action has been intertwined with important alliance work inside and outside of the political system. Federation outreach to the area's immigrant—and especially Latino—communities is particularly notable. Until the mid-1990s, the predominant wisdom within the house of labor saw immigrants as largely unorganizable. Labor and Democratic Party registration work among the city's Latino neighborhoods in the 1980s had produced party membership that was less than 50 percent Democratic and 30 percent Republican. However, newer Latino voters since the Republican anti-immigrant attacks of the 1990s have proven overwhelmingly Democratic. At the same time, organizing campaigns by unions such as the SEIU and UNITE HERE demonstrated the potential militancy of Latinos and other workers from immigrant communities.

Detailed further in chapter 5, the Organization of Los Angeles Workers (OLAW) provided a central vehicle both for building alliances between labor and Latinos and increasing the political clout of both groups. Having previously played a key role in immigrant mobilizations around amnesty, Los Angeles County Federation of Labor, SEIU, and UNITE HERE leaders helped establish OLAW in 2000 to develop a cadre of union members and community activists skilled in getting out the Latino vote. OLAW's first effort focused sixty full-time precinct walkers on two Republican-occupied congressional districts, with the UFW focusing on a third, parallel effort. Two of these three seats became Democratic through work that targeted 40,000 Latinos. For Villaraigosa's first bid for mayor in 2001, OLAW fielded 150 activists for a full six weeks before the election, rising to 450 in the last four days. The organization has since metamorphosed into Strengthening Our Lives (SOL), a statewide voter education organization credited with substantially boosting Latino voter turnout in recent elections.

3. Building Enduring Relationships and Deep Coalitions

The growing relationship between the Los Angeles County Federation of Labor, key unions, and the Latino community in Los Angeles reaches well beyond politics. Indeed, when at least half a million people marched through the city on May 1, 2006, to demand immigrant rights it came as no surprise that newly elected federation executive secretary-treasurer María

Elena Durazo served as master of ceremonies. Through coalition building, political action, legal support, Spanish-language media work, and advocacy for changing the AFL-CIO's policy on immigration, organized labor in Los Angeles has become a central player for Latino advancement.

LAANE has been a particularly active incubator of satellite coalitions and organizations. Like Working Partnerships USA in San Jose, LAANE fostered an interfaith coalition (called Clergy and Laity United for Economic Justice). As part of the long living wage battle in Santa Monica, LAANE formed Santa Monicans for Responsible Tourism (SMART) as a membership-based grassroots organization that went on to support successful worker organizing by HERE in the hotel industry, following the ultimately unsuccessful living wage drive.[44]

Since its founding, LAANE has backed efforts to support the more than 50,000 workers at Los Angeles International Airport. Among other gains, this activism has produced significant growth in union density by UNITE HERE and SEIU.[45] Extending from this work, in 2006 LAANE helped launch the Coalition for a New Century to bring together clergy, labor, community groups, and immigrant rights activists to win better wages, benefits, and working conditions for the 3,500 workers at the thirteen hotels in the Century Corridor near the airport.

LAANE also helped establish the Coalition for Clean and Safe Ports. This alliance of environmental, labor, faith-based, community, and public health organizations works to promote "sustainable trade" at the Ports of Los Angeles and Long Beach. Specifically, poor pay and conditions among the many truck drivers, who are typically and wrongly classified as "independent contractors," spills into high levels of pollution and congestion that greatly impact surrounding communities. The coalition's "Clean Trucks" proposal was adopted by the port and city, and went into effect in October 2008.

Several other key organizations have also proven critical to deep coalition building in addition to the work of the Los Angeles County Federation of Labor and LAANE. After the 1992 civil unrest in Los Angeles, longtime activist Anthony Thigpenn founded Strategic Concepts in Organizing and Policy Education (SCOPE) to help low-income people of color build capacity to influence the policy decisions that shape their lives. SCOPE has more than twenty staff members and organizers, and boasts in-house research and training capacity and a strategic initiatives department.

The group has in turn generated a wide variety of initiatives in the Los Angeles region, in the state, and nationally.

SCOPE's first project was AGENDA (Action for Grassroots Empowerment and Neighborhood Development Alternatives), an organization of residents of South Los Angeles concerned about police accountability, youth education, and economic development. AGENDA's organizers knocked on doors to recruit members, and then cultivated leaders through an educational program that emphasized an analysis of social power and decision making and training about how to wage a public policy campaign. Initially, AGENDA focused on economic prospects for South Los Angeles, trying to influence the post–1992 riots Build L.A. program.

In 1995, it broadened its focus by founding the Los Angeles Metropolitan Alliance with labor, faith-based, and public service provider organizations. The Alliance's regional economic focus promised to help South Los Angeles neighborhoods with access to new jobs in government, health care, and entertainment, and eventually "green jobs" in renewable energy and environmental protection. In the late 1990s, SCOPE initiated the California State Alliance to build on existing community groups to create seven regional organizations covering most of the state. Each group, drawing together community, labor, religious, and environmental allies, did similar economic and political work on three major statewide issue areas—environmental justice, low-wage work, and tax and fiscal policy—in an effort to forge a sense of political unity and not just support for a laundry list of causes.[46]

The electoral field illustrates how SCOPE's work has complemented the regional power-building efforts of the other key institutions. Efforts to build power in the region have had to deal with negotiating the complex terrain of African American and Latino relations. Through unionization, African American workers had made gains in such industries as building services, hotels, home health care, and the public sector. As these industries restructured in the 1980s many black union members lost jobs when employers contracted out work, often using nonunion Latino workers. The political danger of such "black and brown" tensions played itself out in 2001 when the soon-to-be-victorious mayoral candidate James Hahn released a smoking crack-pipe ad with grainy images of opponent Villaraigosa. The ad successfully appealed to Hahn's Anglo voters and an African American base in demographically shifting South Los Angeles.

The following year, SCOPE worked with several SEIU locals and community groups to build the Alliance of Local Leaders for Education (ALLERT) as an OLAW-type labor-community field operation in South Los Angeles. Intentionally developing African American and Latino precinct teams in this mixed community, ALLERT built a capacity to get out the vote over several election cycles that proved key for the victories of Martin Ludlow in 2003 and Karen Bass in 2004 and then Villaraigosa in 2005. In 2008, ALLERT and the Los Angeles County Federation of Labor targeted the county board of supervisors, forcing a runoff election in November.

More recently, SCOPE has pursued a green jobs initiative, the Los Angeles Apollo Alliance, that has worked with building trades unions and the new city administration to retrofit public buildings and to make city construction and maintenance of infrastructure more "green." The overall strategy envisions providing jobs for low-income people of color in work from landscaping to building operation and manufacturing.

University-based educators and researchers have made a range of contributions both in terms of thinking about regional urban questions and in power building leadership development and networking. At UCLA, the Urban Planning Department and the Center for Labor Research and Education worked with SAJE to launch the Community Scholars Program in 1991 in order to allow community activists to use university facilities to develop their research and planning skills. The program brings together groups of ten to fifteen regional leaders with a team of graduate students and faculty to focus on key issues in the regional economy. Past classes have looked at the home health care industry, Wal-Mart, manufacturing, and construction careers.[47] The Center for Labor Research and Education offers the first Spanish-language union leadership program in the country, and also runs programs focused on developing Asian American, African American, and lesbian/gay/bisexual/transgender union leaders. They have also fostered the development of a younger generation, placing about two hundred student interns per year with social justice organizations around the region. While slightly less centralized than San Jose's Civic Leadership Institute, the leadership development programs run by UCLA, SCOPE, and other groups have similarly played a key role in developing a shared vision and connections between labor and community activists.

Local academics have also contributed in terms of research and policy framing. UCLA's Urban Planning Department boasts leading figures in the study of progressive regional thinking, while the Center for Labor Research and Education has been intimately involved in education and strategic planning work integrated into regional power-building efforts. Following Villaraigosa's mayoral win, Larry Frank, the center's staff director and project director for research, became the Los Angeles deputy mayor for neighborhood and community services. The Center for Labor Research and Education also helps facilitate strategic planning for key organizations and the hosting of regular conferences and gatherings that pull together local leaders to discuss organizing and policy goals.

The Payoff for Organizing and Power

As in San Jose, regional power building work in metropolitan Los Angeles has helped unions and community groups organize, build membership, and gain influence. The region's increasing union density offers a good example. The Los Angeles County Federation of Labor has extensively supported worker organizing. Under Contreras, the federation established its Organizing Department to provide a leadership role in initiating organizing. However, the postwar tradition of rooting organizing in national unions, as opposed to cross-union labor bodies, proved too dominant. This initiative—along with similar experiments in other parts of the country—was unable to define a clear role for itself and proved unsustainable. The federation did, however, successfully establish a multimillion-dollar fund that goes to support strategic organizing by area unions. Unlike in the Organizing Department, other federation staff are now assigned directly to the organizing unions.

The political power built by the Los Angeles County Federation of Labor and its allies has created a context and leveraged opportunities to support worker organizing. For example, the federation has recruited labor and community support for many of the public demonstrations during the area's famous Justice for Janitors campaigns. In 1999, the federation's close ally, Antonio Villaraigosa, carried the state legislation that allowed 74,000 area home health care workers to join the SEIU. Drawing on the broad coalition support cultivated by all of the power building institutions, the SEIU has gone from representing 8 percent of workers in hospital-based private-sector health care to over 50 percent.

By the early years of the new millennium, policy and coalition work at Los Angeles International Airport allowed UNITE HERE to go from representing roughly one out of five airport workers in its jurisdiction to four out of five, while the SEIU has moved from representing one in ten workers to more than five in ten. More generally, both unions have drawn on the policy and coalition leverage provided by LAANE's economic development work to support collective bargaining and worker organizing in the building services, hotel, and entertainment industries. UNITE HERE and Teamster organizing has directly drawn on power building coalition work to improve workers' lives at the airport and at the Ports of Los Angeles and Long Beach. In 2007, the Los Angeles City Council passed a "zone based" living wage ordinance that covers the hotels and related establishments surrounding the airport. The measure not only raised wages for thousands of workers at the thirteen hotels but also led to five of them agreeing to let their workers unionize. LAANE and Los Angeles County Federation of Labor efforts to support low-wage workers have also connected to the SEIU's organizing of commercial building security workers. Labor's influence with the new mayor, for example, helped assure employer neutrality during the SEIU campaign to organize security guards in downtown Los Angeles.[48]

Regional power building has also aided union contract campaigns. In the year 2000, for example, the federation coordinated membership mobilization, community outreach, and media work in support of contract battles covering 250,000 workers. In one of these efforts, the federation's then political director, Martin Ludlow, built support among elected officials and church leaders for the United Transportation Union's bargaining, as well as bringing high-profile figures like Jesse Jackson to Los Angeles to broker the dispute.

Finally, the power built by the Los Angeles labor movement has allowed it to assume a more proactive and long-term stance on regional economic development. In 2002, owing to intensive pressure exerted by the movement, LAANE executive director Madeline Janis was appointed to the board of the Los Angeles Community Redevelopment Agency (LACRA), which had a reputation as a "developer's piggy bank." After fighting for several community benefits agreements on individual projects, LAANE leaders wanted to shape policy on a larger scale. LACRA's $750 million annual budget has the potential to make it a significant tool for creating a regional economy that fosters shared prosperity. By identifying and working to reshape key government institutions, the Los Angeles labor movement is taking a step toward assuming a "governing stance" and redefining the playing field.

Regional Power Building Proves Sustainable

While individual initiatives may have had different levels of success, the overall three-legged project of building power in Silicon Valley and Los Angeles has proved sustainable. Several achievements stand out as contributing to the consolidation and growth of this work.

First, regional power building has both grown out of and in turn reinforced and deepened the process of the regional labor movement unifying itself. The work has not only seen greater cooperation among unions but also the growing authority and capacity of the labor council to play a central leadership role within the movement and the community. While most labor councils operate in the clear shadows of the larger unions, the South Bay AFL-CIO and the Los Angeles County Federation of Labor have established themselves as leaders of a broad-based regional labor and progressive movement. Their own leadership reflects this. The two labor councils had visionary political directors in Amy Dean and Miguel Contreras, who each created innovative strategies and then ascended to leadership in the mid-1990s. They were succeeded by allies Phaedra Ellis-Lamkins and María Elena Durazo, who have furthered regional power building.

Second, in founding Working Partnerships USA and LAANE, activists established crucial capacity without which regional power-building work would not have grown strong foundations. These nonprofit organizations combined four key factors: the ability to conduct quality regional research, the capacity to develop concrete public policy proposals, the program skills to handle such complex matters as an alternative staffing agency or the details of establishing a child health care program, and the coalition-building skills and capacity to bring together diverse alliances.

Finally, regional power building has moved beyond specific reforms and organizing initiatives and begun to contest for governing power in both regions. Labor and its allies have engaged the dominant business establishment at the level of ideas by critiquing supposed economic successes and projecting an alternative social vision of a more egalitarian, just, and sustainable society. Both through this broader vision and through many specific coalition campaigns, regional power building has transformed organized labor from an isolated interest group into the leader of a new progressive force representing the hopes and needs of the majority of the population.

Regional Power Building Spreads in California

The early experiments in San Jose and Los Angeles proved significant not simply for changing progressive fortunes in these regions but also in articulating a basic model for building power that other groups could pick up, first in the state and then across the country. The core institutions in both regions have generously aided emerging projects elsewhere.

San Diego

The most striking characteristic of the San Diego experience is its decidedly different political and cultural context. While Bay Area and Los Angeles organizing took place in relatively "liberal" regions, San Diego has been a conservative bastion. Although within the city of San Diego the Democratic registration portion of 39 percent is greater than the 33 percent Republican one, conservatives have long dominated city politics and the county as a whole is decidedly Republican. The area has a strong antiunion culture that dates back to the violent 1912 campaign to suppress the free speech of the Industrial Workers of the World. "This is a place where, most of its history, labor never had any standing," the president of the City Club of San Diego told *San Diego Union-Tribune*. "The leaders of the business community have a deep loathing of labor."[49] Would the power building model established in San Jose and Los Angeles have relevance in such a conservative politicocultural context?

By the mid-1990s, many local union leaders had become frustrated with what they saw as the "sleepy" leadership of the San Diego–Imperial Counties Labor Council (SDICLC). In 1996, they backed Jerry Butkiewicz in a successful insurgent candidacy for labor council secretary-treasurer. Butkiewicz had been an energetic president of the American Postal Workers Union local and labor council liaison to the San Diego United Way. As top SDICLC officer, he opened up the organization to other union leaders, making the council more democratic and increasing union affiliation from 25 percent of the labor movement to nearly 95 percent in 2007. With inspiration and direct support from the Los Angeles and San Jose programs, the SDICLC worked to establish the power-building model.

In 1997, with strong support from local SEIU leader Mary Grillo and Butkiewicz, the SDICLC's political director Donald Cohen created the Center on Policy Initiatives (CPI). The new organization produced framing reports that documented the prosperous region's rising inequality and growing low-wage and temporary work. It documented how public subsidies supported employers, such as Wal-Mart and downtown developers, in the creation of poor-quality jobs. The CPI also analyzed the city's budget problems and criticized the privatization strategy pushed by the city's influential conservative leaders as a solution to the fiscal crisis.

The CPI and the SDICLC used the research to develop a series of policy campaigns around economic development. Their biggest policy victory came in 2005 with the passage of a strong city living wage ordinance. The CPI and the SDICLC have also led efforts to block or change some developments, such as a proposed Wal-Mart Supercenter in the town of San Marcos. The CPI helped rewrite the city's economic development strategy in 2001 to end cash subsidies to tourist businesses unless they meet high-quality job standards, and helped win the 2002 passage of an ordinance requiring housing developers to include affordable units or to pay into a fund to build affordable housing. In 2005, the CPI organized a community coalition that negotiated a community benefits agreement for a downtown development, Ballpark Village, that required living wage jobs, local hiring and job training, affordable rental housing, and cultural and environmental amenities. Since 2000, the SDICLC has sponsored the Employee Rights Center, which recruits law student volunteers to help unorganized workers, many of them immigrants, pursue cases involving unemployment insurance, employment discrimination, workers compensation, labor code violations, back-pay claims and other primarily administrative law violations.

The policy battles have proven viable only because the SDICLC has revamped its political program, starting with a new "labor to neighbor" door-knocking campaign in working class neighborhoods. After the 2006 elections, the council transformed this work into a more formal precinct operation. By early 2007, labor activists had adopted 500 precincts, with the

SDICLC aiming to eventually cover 3,500. In a city where Democrats enjoyed only a fleeting city council majority during the 1990s, labor's new political program established a labor-endorsed Democratic majority through the 2001 and 2002 election cycles. This success was tempered a year later when personal scandal hit several labor-endorsed councilors.[50] The conservative climate also kept the mayor's seat in Republican hands despite several close contests.[51] In 2006, labor failed to defeat two ballot proposals, one requiring voter approval of future municipal worker pension increases and the other authorizing privatization of city jobs. While labor and its allies have enjoyed mixed electoral success, the very fact that local politics has become contested political terrain represents a significant shift.

Because organized labor has become a credible electoral player, it can pursue viable policy campaigns with its allies. In turn, power building has aided in growing union strength through the securing of project labor agreements, "street heat" protests backing striking workers, the pursuit of employer union organizing neutrality agreements, and support for worker organizing.[52] Through policy and electoral campaigns, the SDICLC and the CPI have fostered growing alliances. Key partners have included an environmental health coalition, the Chicano Federation, the Metropolitan Advisory Committee Project (formerly Mexican-American Advisory Committee), the Neighborhood House Association (a primarily African American community social service group), United Way, and Catholic Charities. In addition to serving as an anchor for different issue coalitions, the CPI has also provided support to the Interfaith Committee for Worker Justice of San Diego.

The San Diego experience points to the robust nature of the power building model. Despite the mixed record of success in a conservative political and social context, regional power-building work has been able to take root. Through both success and failure, organizers have been able to establish labor and its community allies as serious regional players that can contest both the political balance of power and the direction of public policy.

The East Bay Area

Power building in the East Bay area illustrates a "convergence of core partners" something like that of Los Angeles, but without the strong labor backbone provided by the Los Angeles County Federation of Labor. The

East Bay area spans the counties of Alameda and Contra Costa, and includes the cities of Oakland, Hayward, Fremont, Richmond, and Berkeley. As with LAANE, a HERE local founded the core power building anchor organization—the East Bay Alliance for a Sustainable Economy (EBASE). HERE Local 2850 president Jim DuPont was motivated by the perceived weaknesses in the local labor movement when compared to success stories elsewhere. "Seeing the success of LAANE and what they were able to do and the ineptness of our own central labor council at the time to do the work we needed done were the motivating factors," DuPont explains. "We needed the living wage work, the building of religious and community coalitions, and creating policies that help working people."[53] LAANE provided crucial guidance to EBASE in its initial years.

EBASE has pursued research, coalition, and policy work similar to LAANE and the other think-and-act tanks that we have described. By 2007, EBASE had led coalitions that won living wage ordinances in six communities, including living wage and worker retention policies at the Port of Oakland and a EBASE/UNITE HERE Local 2850 ballot initiative that established the country's first industry-specific living wage policy that covers wages and workload standards for hotels in the booming Emeryville community. These efforts led to support for worker organizing at the Oakland International Airport and to several hotel campaigns.[54] EBASE has adopted a broad vision of promoting "high road" economic development. Living wage campaigns and support for worker organizing have been accompanied by the promotion of training and hiring of local residents for skilled trades jobs; improving the quality and accessibility of health care; setting community benefit standards for developers; and defending the rights of immigrant workers.

EBASE evolved differently from LAANE, in part because of distinct local conditions. It began work on community benefit agreements for new development later than LAANE because there is less development pressure in many of the areas where EBASE has been active. It also devotes more effort to immigrant rights than LAANE because it did not have a regional body such as the Los Angeles County Federation of Labor taking up some of the work. EBASE played a major role in organizing for the AFL-CIO's 2003 Immigrant Workers Freedom Ride, developed coalitions and campaigns to protect immigrant workers under attack, provided education programs for immigrant worker leaders (through its Freedom

Academy, established in 2005), and produced resource guides for unions and community groups nationwide who were resisting employer retaliation against immigrant workers.

In negotiating agreements concerning development, such as that of a new IKEA store in Emeryville, EBASE has focused especially on the training and hiring of local residents. Its most important development-related work has been with a coalition of groups in Oakland negotiating an agreement for the Oak to Ninth Street Development Project. Partners include the Alameda County AFL-CIO, the Asian-Pacific Environmental Network, the East Bay Asian Youth Center, ACORN, the Oakland Community Organization (part of the PICO National Network of faith-based community organizations), and the Urban Strategies Council, a local low-income advocacy group. EBASE developed a job training and hiring strategy for the project aimed at local Latino and African American residents and an affordable housing requirement tailored for low-income families.

The most significant contrast to LAANE, however, is in the political sphere. Unlike in the Los Angeles experience, EBASE's early development was not accompanied by the transformation of the region's two labor councils. While the Alameda and Contra Costa councils have participated in EBASE work, they do not play leading roles. For one, these councils are smaller than those in Los Angeles and Silicon Valley; even with recent changes, the Alameda Labor Council has only four staff, for example. Even more significantly, until recently neither council had experienced the kind of transformation seen in our other cases. Thus, while building on the electoral work of unions such as UNITE HERE Local 2850, EBASE has not enjoyed a context of overall reinvigorated labor electoral mobilization.

Initially this limitation was offset by the region's relatively liberal political climate. Alameda County votes heavily Democratic in national elections and elects very progressive representatives, such as U.S. Representative Barbara Lee. Contra Costa County is also generally Democratic; its ideological balance extends from solidly left in the western, urban parts to relatively right in the more rural eastern parts. However, as in many "liberal" urban areas, without the counterveiling weight of a full-blown progressive regional power building movement, many local officials prove comparatively conservative around issues of economic development and are heavily influenced by business and developer interests.

What was missing from EBASE's early experience is illustrated by how the recent transformation of the two councils has contributed to power building momentum. For example, although the Alameda Labor Council AFL-CIO had long been on the board of EBASE, the council's involvement increased significantly after Sharon Cornu became executive secretary-treasurer in 2005, following a successful challenge to the incumbent leadership. In 2007, the council worked with EBASE on a living wage campaign for San Leandro, marshaling support for Woodfin Suites hotel workers, and on Oakland Mayor Ron Dellums's development of an economic plan for the city. Cornu views the roles of the council and EBASE as distinct but complementary, with EBASE doing solid policy work and research and the council building political power.[55]

Under Cornu the council has modernized its political operations, with computerized phone banks, new professional staff, and more strategic and long-range planning. It also focused on more aggressive candidate recruitment and endorsements, including support for "long-shot" progressive candidates such as the successful primary bids of Alberto Torrico for state assembly and Ron Dellums for mayor of Oakland. With the help of a local community college, the council has begun to recruit and train labor union members to become qualified nominees for boards and commissions appointed by the candidates that labor helps to elect. With its stepped-up activity, the council has also increased affiliation and participation of unions in its activities.[56]

The central labor council in Contra Costa County began progressive reforms in the late 1990s under former executive secretary-treasurer John Dalrymple, who pulled together a coalition of transit unions to influence county transportation policy, including passage of a half-cent sales tax increase to help the operation of bus lines. Working with a strong United Food and Commercial Workers local, the labor council helped push through local, and eventually countywide, ordinances restricting the size of grocery stores in an effort to block Wal-Mart Supercenters. (In 2004, however, Wal-Mart successfully spent more than half a million dollars on an initiative campaign to override the legislation.) With support from some progressive building trades leaders, the council has also promoted environmental protections in new developments. By 2007, EBASE was participating in a coalition with the council to propose affordable housing, open space, living wage jobs, "green" construction, and other community benefits for redevelopment of a shuttered naval base in Concord.

Regional Power Building Elsewhere in California

Looking back today, the San Jose, Los Angeles, San Diego, and East Bay experiences clearly formed a critical mass for inspiring and aiding the launching of power building programs elsewhere in the state (and the nation)—a process that continues today. Following the election of Governor Grey Davis, LAANE, Working Partnerships USA, EBASE, and the CPI formed a loose network, California Partnerships (which transformed into the national Partnerships for Working Families, described in more detail in chapter 7). This networking of sites fostered concrete support for new projects elsewhere.

The development of a power building program in the North Bay counties of Marin, Sonoma, Mendocino, and Napa is significant in two ways. First, although often seen as an affluent area on the periphery of the labor movement, these counties suffer many of the same problems as the larger Bay Area: the growth of low-wage jobs even during the tech boom, a deficit in affordable housing, and public subsidies for economic development that does not serve community needs. Although the counties often vote for progressive state and national candidates, such as Representative Lynn Wolsey, developers typically overwhelm labor in city and county races. Second, council leaders have been able to put in place a power-building program despite the fact that, like many labor councils not in major urban areas, the Santa Rosa–based North Bay Labor Council operates with no full-time staff. In 2002, council members helped found New Economy Working Solutions (NEWS) as a modest research and action center modeled after the much larger peers elsewhere in the state. Started with funding by SEIU Local 707 (public sector workers), NEWS had two staff members in 2007: an executive director and a living wage coordinator. Despite their modest resources, NEWS and the North Bay Labor Council have led victories on ensuring living wages, facilitating union organizing, creating affordable housing, and promoting responsible development.[57]

NEWS has in turn spun off important regional movements, including the Living Wage Coalition of Sonoma County (with membership comprising more than sixty unions and religious, environmental, political, issue-oriented, and ethnic or civil rights groups), Sonoma County Clergy and Laity United for Economic Justice, and the Sonoma County Accountable Development Coalition. The Living Wage Coalition functions much like a

Jobs with Justice chapter, mobilizing community support for a wide range of labor efforts, while NEWS tilts more toward research and policy advocacy. The Accountable Development Coalition successfully lobbied the Sonoma Marin Area Rail Transit board for a community benefits agreement for a new five-acre development in downtown Santa Rosa near a transit station.[58] More recently, the coalition is campaigning for Sonoma and Petaluma to require community impact reports for any major new development, a tool that strategists think may strengthen the fledgling movements against "big box" retailers. In the face of local developer power, labor and its allies have created an independent political expenditure campaign, the Coalition for a Better Sonoma County. The coalition has succeeded in electing two progressives to the Santa Rosa City Council (one a NEWS board member), but does not yet have a majority on the council.

The city of San Francisco illustrates the importance of labor council transformation. The area has a strong labor tradition reflected in the sophisticated coalition and political work of several key unions—for example, a living-wage coalition developed in the late 1990s with leading roles played by the SEIU, HERE, the San Francisco Labor Council, the Coalition for Immigrant and Refugee Rights, the San Francisco Organizing Project (an affiliate of PICO), the Bay Area Organizing Committee (an affiliate of the Industrial Areas Foundation), and other local groups. The campaign established its own staff and was run as a common effort. A series of enacted living wage policies have covered an increasing number of workers and required such additional dimensions as health insurance, paid vacation, and unpaid family emergency leave. In 2003, a labor-community coalition, involving ACORN, HERE, and Young Workers United (a HERE-sponsored center for young workers in the restaurant and hospitality industry), pushed for a municipal minimum wage. With the active support—but not leadership—of the labor council, the San Francisco Board of Supervisors established the nation's second municipal minimum wage at $8.50 an hour, indexed to inflation. In 2006, a new coalition spurred by Young Workers United campaigned successfully for citywide paid sick leave. Also that year, the board of supervisors passed the labor-community supported Health Access Plan, which established an affordable insurance plan with subsidies for low- to moderate-income individuals and for small- to medium-sized businesses.[59]

All these campaigns reflect a shifting set of alliances among individual unions, the central labor council, community organizations, and progressive local legislators. However, while individual unions and their community allies have been able to achieve much, the lack of a strong leadership role played by the central labor body is reflected in the lack of long-term vision for the city's labor movement as a whole. Coalition work has been undertaken campaign by campaign, while regional power building requires the integration of specific coalition work into a long-term vision. Such a vision requires both a body of leaders who think in terms of the movement as a whole and a research and policy development capacity that builds concrete steps toward that vision.

These needs highlight the significance of efforts to strengthen the San Francisco Labor Council under the leadership of executive director Tim Paulson, brought on in September 2004. Paulson's background spans both the building trades and SEIU, and he has also served as the political director of the San Mateo County Central Labor Council. With a relatively progressive leadership among building trades unions and the expansion of labor council staff capacity, the San Francisco labor movement is moving toward formulation of community-oriented development policies aimed at resolving bruising local conflicts over real estate development and community interests. This effort highlights the need for a research and action center similar to the nonprofits found in other cases.

The way California's pioneering power building efforts were able to cross-fertilize with each other and to foster new work in neighboring areas speaks to the ability of regional power building to impact whole states or even broad sections of the country. Developments in California also suggest that regional power building also lays the groundwork for contesting power at the state level. Indeed, California's regional power-building organizations have begun to tackle more statewide issues. They have started to investigate new communications strategies and policies to break the gridlock on tax and budget issues at the state level that constrain what the labor movement and its allies can accomplish locally. State legislators, with the backing of labor and its allies, have already introduced measures that expand policies and programs nurtured first through regional power-building work. Such initiatives would, for example, extend health care coverage or restrict contracting out when savings are achieved by cutting employee wages or benefits. Such pioneering translation work suggests a long-term potential of assembling regional power building initiatives into a force capable of governing statewide.

Power Building Spreads outside of California

While the chapters to follow will explore many details of power building work elsewhere in the country, we close this chapter by providing an overview of how an experience that began in one state has become a general model used across the country.

Denver provides one of the earliest examples of a labor council–led adoption of regional power building. In 1998, a group of reform-minded labor leaders transformed the rather lackluster Denver Area Labor Federation (DALF) into a base for regional work that self-consciously drew from the California experience. DALF helped establish the Front Range Strategy Center modeled off of the California 501(c)3 nonprofit organizations. DALF and the center in turn established a formal labor-community coalition for influencing regional development projects and, after a grueling three-year battle, secured a community benefits agreement at a major development near the downtown area. At the same time, DALF led a revamping of organized labor's political operations. Because so much of the state's population lives in the Denver region, this growing electoral clout impacted state politics and contributed to stunning Democratic victories in 2004.

More recent labor council–led projects include those in Atlanta and Boston. Atlanta marks the first adoption of the full-blown power building model in the South. A traditionally activist labor council began to revamp its political program in the early years of the new millennium and launched the nonprofit Georgia Stand Up in 2005. The new organization quickly seized an opportunity to intervene in a major regional development project called the Beltline and established a civic leadership institute program modeled after San Jose in 2006. In Boston, around the same time, the Greater Boston Labor Council established Community Labor United (CLU) as a think-and-act tank with a veteran ACORN organizer as its executive director. Community Labor United used the launching of a civic leadership institute as a springboard to generate its first campaign: a labor-community effort that secured prevailing wage and local hiring on a $2.5 million repainting of the Boston schools.

The labor council–led path to regional power building requires a labor council leadership that can successfully move innovation and new programs, making efforts within the AFL-CIO to strengthen its local and state bodies particularly significant. While we will detail this activity in chapter 7, a brief mention of New York State can illustrate the connection to power building. At the turn of the millennium, labor leaders in New York undertook a "New Alliance" process that reformed the state's labor movement by merging many small labor councils into larger area labor federations capable of supporting full-time staff. These new bodies helped lead the revamping of labor's regional political action. And now, as time goes by, they are also providing the base for establishing the other two regional power building legs. For example, the Central New York Labor Federation helped establish the Syracuse Alliance for a New Economy (SANE) in 2007. The following year, SANE launched a civic leadership institute as a vehicle for forming coalitions to intervene in regional economic development projects.

The earliest experience of a convergence-of-core-partners path outside of California took place in Connecticut. The Connecticut Center for a New Economy (CCNE) grew out of several innovative labor-community political and organizing projects within the state that had fallen into decline by the turn of the millennium. Modeled after LAANE, but with a statewide definition, the CCNE's first regional organizing effort was based in New Haven and drew staff, seed funding, and program support from the unions at Yale University. Its first major campaign, a contentious battle for a community benefits agreement at Yale–New Haven Hospital, witnessed deep grassroots neighborhood organizing by CCNE and its labor and community allies. The CCNE has also drawn from the San Jose experience by launching a civic leadership institute in 2007 and a Blueprint Project in 2008. The organization has also established a newer office and regional work in Hartford. Most recently, some of the organizations affiliated with the CCNE are pursing an independent electoral arm (501[c]4).

Power building in Pittsburgh and New Jersey has also emerged along such a convergence model. In 2007, activists from several unions and community groups came together to form Pittsburgh UNITED (Unions and Neighborhoods Invested in Transforming Economic Development). Pittsburgh UNITED was formed with the help of the Partnership for Working Families and modeled after LAANE and other think-and-act tanks. Pittsburgh UNITED jumped right into its first two campaigns, attempting to win community benefits agreements tied to new arena and casino developments. New Jersey's Garden Alliance for a New Economy

(GANE) was also formed recently and based on the support of SEIU and UNITE HERE locals. Like Community Labor United in Boston, GANE hired a former ACORN organizer to begin coalition-building, focused on the northern part of the state. After an initial win on a development in Bayonne, GANE is working to shape projects in Newark and Jersey City.

With a sense that the regional power-building model is not simply a California-specific experience but a strategy of interest to organizers across the country, we now turn to exploring each of the three legs integral to an effective regional program.

The Three Legs of Regional Power Building

3

Developing a Regional
Policy Agenda

While efforts from across the country offer a wealth of particulars, regional power building fully comes into place only when groups are able to develop and integrate the three legs: research and policy development, deep coalitions, and aggressive political action. The next three chapters take up each element in turn. While we draw from the experiences inside and outside of California, we do not restrict ourselves to those regions that have successfully established a fully articulated regional power-building program but also draw on the many regions where leaders have developed separate parts and continue to work to build them into an integrated program. (In chapter 6 we will explore why three of these regions have failed, at least initially, to produce a full-blown power-building strategy.) This chapter explores the first leg by looking at how regional efforts build common policy agendas to put their vision of a social alternative into practice.

Toward Integrated Regional Agendas

Developing a common agenda that unites diverse groups over the long term is not an easy task. This explains why the vast majority of all coalitions in this country form around specific issues and campaigns, and do not last beyond them. The authors have participated in many gatherings that have attempted to produce long-term, integrated agendas. What tends to happen is that each group expresses its specific issues and the coalition as a whole ends up with a laundry-list agenda incorporating each group's separate concerns. The coalition then branches into subgroups where people work on the same issues they did before. Putting a comprehensive reform agenda on paper is relatively easy; building a living program that drives new forms of real cooperation among groups is a far greater challenge.

Soliciting a long list of endorsing organizations in such a "letterhead" coalition is not the solution. Regional power building requires partners who see the new work as a core part of what they do. Such deep commitment can be built only by speaking to each group's fundamental concerns. The trick is to develop an integrative regional agenda that allows groups to address their core issues in more comprehensive and effective ways than when they were simply acting alone. For example, in a region with high real estate and rental prices, a union representing low-wage service workers may strive to raise its members' standard of living through collective bargaining and organizing. Meanwhile, a coalition of religious and community groups struggles to maintain shelters for the homeless that are increasingly being filled with families of working parents. Initially, the union and the homeless coalition might have little reason to work together in any kind of sustained manner.

Enter regional power building and its goal of redefining the regional political economy. Operationally, such an agenda requires creating new possibilities for electing progressive champions as well as developing a shared grassroots capacity to push the kinds of public policy reforms that people could not have hoped for previously. This new context raises the possibility of enacting strong public standards for local development. The standards might include, for example, living wage requirements for employers and affordable housing for developers—two measures that address the income and cost issues faced by both the union and the coalition for the homeless. The two groups can now work together toward addressing their core concerns in a new way connected to a long-term vision.

Over the past several decades many progressive groups have become used to fighting defensive battles. By contrast, the integrative agendas developed through regional power building allow groups to move to the offense—to act rather than react. At the political level, regional power building presents groups a path for moving from separate interest-group access to officeholders to becoming part of a governing coalition—a "New Deal" at a regional level. Over time, such a political transformation can be conducted across many specific issue areas. In our cases, activists have organized coalitions around such diverse arenas as health care for children, funds for community colleges, and immigrant rights.

But such proposals are not simply a laundry list of different groups' demands. Underlying them is a new view of the role of government in shaping the development of society. Policymakers and elected leaders generally assume that business success automatically means community success. This may have held some truth when companies were irrevocably rooted in a particular locale and their growth produced jobs and tax revenues available to local residents. But the new world of globalization has severed corporate success from social well-being. A software company may reinvest its profits in Silicon Valley—or in India or China. It may succeed as a business and yet slash the wages of its Silicon Valley workers.

The new role of government under these conditions is to influence the private sector in ways that restore the link between industry success and community well-being. Rather than simply seeking to maximize profits, corporations must be required to pursue a dual bottom line, to work for both industry success and the well-being of the diverse groups that make up the community.

Why Is Economic Development a Central Focus?

All successful power building strategies have embedded their issue campaigns in a shared general focus on reshaping regional economic development decisions. Why has this arena proven to be the glue that holds together long-term alliances?

In contrast to traditional thinking, regional power building aims to define economic development broadly. The universe of public economic development decisions encompasses much of local government's social and human care spending and policy, as well as regional transportation and other issues. Many of these latter functions take place with county governments or quasi-jurisdictional bodies above the level of the municipality. Regional power building thus operates at a true regional level, using the inherently integrative nature of a broad sense of economic development to build coalitions around the wide range of issues that factor into an area's economic health.

Economic development offers an official arena wherein private employer decisions connect with public authority and resources. It thus encompasses central decision-making authorities that play a role in the currently unsustainable and unjust economy. City and town councils, county boards, economic development bodies, and special public authorities all provide forums within which regional actors debate (or should debate) the community's future. Economic development connects to a wealth of local policy tools potentially responsive to public mobilization. These include tax abatements and public financial assistance, zoning regulations, public acquisition and selling of land, government contracting, local workforce development programs, social service provisions, and leases at airports, port authorities, and other public facilities.

At the same time, as we explored in chapter 1, by thinking regionally power building starts to address the problem of fragmentation in regional governance that undermines effective regional development, whether mainstream or alternative. As power-building campaigns seek to influence specific decision-making bodies, they do so with a broader integrating vision and long-term agenda.

Defining Economic Development Broadly

As mentioned above, regional power building can link so many groups' concerns to "economic development" because it defines this arena in far broader terms than mainstream public policy approaches do. Economic development is not simply about jobs but about healthy communities.

Indeed, the contraction of old welfare-style antipoverty programs over the past few decades means that there is no longer a compartmentalized policy arena within which to confine "social justice" concerns. Today, any effective antipoverty public policy work at the local level has to draw on all the mechanisms available to government. Land use, transportation, housing, contracting, education, and other polices should be evaluated through the lens of social justice. And for regional power building, social justice means focusing on the needs of working families generally, thus linking the needs of the "poor" with the "middle class." In short, most government policy arenas become "economic development."

Questions of affordable housing, transportation, education, and land use apply to both growing and declining regions, although sometimes for different reasons. For example, in growing regions the affordable-housing crisis may link to population growth, while for declining regions it may reflect a decaying older housing stock. In both cases, affordability problems are rooted in a profit-driven housing industry that rewards developers for focusing on upscale housing. Car-dependent commuting presents problems to middle-class and poor workers in both growing and declining communities. Similarly, sprawl-based land use decisions lead to calls for open space and quality of life preservation in growth regions and brownfield redevelopment and neighborhood revitalization in declining areas.

Access to adequate health care is a central regional economic development issue shared by prosperous and depressed regions. The steady decline in the number of families with health insurance and the growing costs foisted onto those with coverage has become a core issue for many would-be regional coalition partners. Exploding health care costs have caused the old economic rules of employer-provided private health insurance to fall apart. These pressures show up at the collective bargaining table, in neighborhood health clinics and poverty programs, and in lost productivity, absenteeism, and greater costs in the workplace. While solving the nation's health care crisis requires federal action, the San Jose Children's Health Initiative, the Yale–New Haven Hospital campaign (both described in chapter 2), and the growing number of state-level policy efforts offer clear examples of taking regional action. And while providing local public sources of health care may seem to aid only nonunion workers, nearly half of those who signed up for the Children's Health Initiative were from union families who, despite being members of the Service Employees International Union (SEIU) or UNITE HERE (a merging of the former Union of Needletrades, Industrial and Textile Employees [UNITE] and the former Hotel Employees and Restaurant Employees International Union [HERE]) could not secure adequate and affordable family health care at the bargaining table.

Affordable housing and renter's rights similarly provide a broad arena that should be part of any progressive vision for regional economic development. During the 1990s and early 2000s, housing costs mushroomed far faster than the general rate of inflation in many parts of the country. The housing construction industry generally prioritizes upscale, high-profit homes. Both the industry and typical public zoning and other incentive mechanisms are generally designed to develop "vacant" land, not redevelop existing urban areas with their more affordable working-class homes. When coupled with stagnating family incomes throughout much of the population, housing market trends have produced broadly felt concerns about affordable, decent housing.

Most mainstream discussions of affordable housing define the issue mainly in terms of median housing prices keyed to what is affordable to white-collar professionals. Regional power-building organizers thus have the opportunity to champion the affordable housing interest of the bottom half of the population. While such inclusive definitions of affordable housing connect to the concerns of antipoverty and low-income neighborhood groups, today's strains connect to other would-be coalition partners as well. For example, as unions organize and bargain among low- and even moderate-income workers, they are representing members for whom affordable housing is a core concern.

The Campaign for Clean and Safe Ports in metropolitan Los Angeles similarly reflects a broad notion of economic development policy. By classifying some 16,000 truckers as "independent contractors," employers have raised profits by shifting costs onto workers. Such drivers are responsible for their own benefits and have to maintain and fuel their trucks. After paying the truck expenses, drivers typically net less than $30,000 annually. The drivers have no control over their work, which is determined by the shipping companies (such as Maersk) and the large merchandise shippers (such as Wal-Mart) through trucking companies that act as brokers or middle agents.

These practices do not simply pull down area living standards but have contributed to the deunionization of the workforce. And they are also responsible for the number one source of pollution in the region. Not able financially to properly maintain their idling trucks, drivers unnecessarily pollute the air in ways that harm themselves and surrounding areas. The Campaign for Clean and Safe Ports brings together labor unions, community groups, faith-based groups, and environmentalists to improve the working conditions for truckers who service the Ports of Los Angeles and Long Beach. The coalition passed its Clean Trucks proposal in 2008, inspiring similar coalitions to form elsewhere.

Immigrant rights are also an economic development issue faced in both declining and growing regions. In September 2004, Working Partnerships USA released a report, *The Economic Effects of Immigration in Santa Clara County and California,*[1] documenting the economic benefits of immigration to the San Jose area and to California in general. The report argues that regional economic success and robust public resources depend upon immigration. Regional power-building efforts in several parts of the country have organized around immigrant rights not simply because it is the right thing to do but because fostering prosperous immigrant communities is a fundamental engine for generating regional prosperity more broadly. The efforts of the Los Angeles AFL-CIO around community college funding similarly reflect a broad understanding of what constitutes economic development.

Quite often, official economic development agencies and policies operate disconnected from other arenas of public spending. Many public bodies simultaneously attempt to lure employer investment for "good jobs" while destroying well-paid jobs through contracting out public work.

Regional power building can open up fiscal debates to broad questions about the region's future. The Boston school refurbishing campaign offers a good example of how regional power building can use a broad frame to intervene in public spending decisions. On the one hand, the effort brought together the International Union of Painters and Allied Trades Union and minority community groups to win prevailing wage and apprenticeship programs that benefited two immediate constituencies. Given the history of tensions between the region's building trades unions and people of color, this marked a significantly new dynamic. On the other hand, the specific policy victory and labor-minority alliance developed within a broader frame that viewed issues of public spending not simply as a fiscal concern but as a question of what kind of communities public policy was attempting to build.

Protecting the right of workers to organize should be a central aspect of any progressive economic development agenda. In growing regions, unionization provides a mechanism for sustaining economic growth by sharing prosperity broadly. In depressed regions, unionization provides an economic stimulus to broaden purchasing power and growing the region's middle class. Regional power building ultimately aims to create union cities. By contrast, for many, unions are either an obstacle or something not even considered as part of economic development. Yet the only way to achieve a regional economy that is prosperous, socially just, and equitable is through the ability of workers to have some say in the workplace. Through unions, workers are able to secure a greater share of the economic pie, stabilize employment, and raise productivity and firm performance. A more unionized community is a community that has greater aggregate wealth and healthier consumer markets.

Regional power building supports a worker's right to organize at many levels. Concrete immediate policy reforms and community benefits agreements provide direct leverage to deactivate employer antiunion efforts. The coalition relationships developed throughout regional power-building work provide allies to support worker struggles. And over the long term, regional power building allows organized labor to be seen by increasing parts of the community as a central institution dedicated to the long-term welfare of the community and the region.

Building Policy Capacity: The Role of "Think-and-Act Tanks"

The development of regional policy proposals that integrate the needs of multiple constituencies is demanding work. It can rarely be done simply on volunteer energy. Because public economic development programs, public spending, and other policies are typically cloaked in secrecy, finding out what public money goes to who or discovering development negotiations before key decisions have been made requires a significant amount of time and technical expertise. The opposition often has a pool of paid staff whose work must be effectively countered. While allied academics can help with this and broader framing, research into regional power building works best when there is some in-house capacity to manage the research agenda.

Similarly, the energy required to build and grow a coalition relationship among a wide range of groups over the long term requires more ongoing attention than volunteers alone can provide. While using staff time from unions and allied groups can work for specific campaigns, at some point the coalition work of regional power building will grow to require ongoing staffing.

It comes as no surprise, therefore, that our discussions throughout this book reference time and again some form of local nonprofit organization with dedicated staff. Here we complete this picture by identifying the key elements that make these organizations distinct. They can be referred to by a range of general labels. The national resource center Partnership for Working Families calls them "policy action centers"; we refer to them here as "think-and-act tanks." Regardless of their name, size, or origin, all of these organizations combine research with policy advocacy and direct organizing.

The Los Angeles Alliance for a New Economy (LAANE) and Working Partnerships USA in San Jose represent two of the largest and oldest examples of the regional power building think-and-act tank. Both operate with three to four dozen staff. Elsewhere in California, the Center for Policy Initiatives in San Diego boasts a dozen staff, the East Bay Alliance for a Sustainable Economy (EBASE) fifteen, the Coastal Alliance United for a Sustainable Economy (Ventura County) six, and New Economy Working Solutions (Sonoma County) two. Outside of California, the Front Range Economic Strategy Center (FRESC) in Denver grew to eight paid staff by 2006 from its founding by one person in 2002. The more recent Georgia Stand Up in Atlanta and Community Labor United in Boston have started up with just a couple of full-time people. Many of these nonprofits were founded directly by their areas' central labor council leadership. Others formed independently from a partnership of one or more unions, but work closely with their local labor councils.

Although many regional power-building projects have built nonprofits from scratch using the models first developed in California, others have tried to establish similar capacities using differing paths. For example, the "think" and "act" capacities in Cleveland are housed in separate organizations. Labor council leader John Ryan redefined labor's traditional community service arm, the United Labor Agency (ULA), to move into power-building-related coalition work. He also used the ULA to seed Policy Matters Ohio as a more traditional think tank that combines regional power-related research with state research and contracts with specific area unions and state level policy work. The Connecticut Center for a New Economy (CCNE) presents yet another path; it began with a statewide focus, but then invested heavily in regional think-and-act staffing, first in New Haven and more recently in Hartford.

Thinking

The research can begin quite modestly. For example, researchers can construct an early framing report using readily available government data assembled to make the case for a growing crisis of working families in the region. As research capacity develops, reports delve more deeply into specific areas. Researchers may focus on specific aspects of the strains on working families, such as the lack of affordable housing, poverty wages in specific industries, poor conditions in growing temporary and contingent work arrangements, or the increasing number of families without health insurance.

A second major research focus pieces together and then critiques public policy. LAANE, for example, produced a series of reports exposing the lack of standards and poor results found in the city's specific economic development programs. In 2005, FRESC issued a series of reports under the umbrella title of *Are We Getting Our Money's Worth? Tax-Increment Financing and Urban Redevelopment in Denver.*

In addition to in-house research, think-and-act tanks also build capacity through alliances with progressive academics. While helping directly with research, these figures and their institutional affiliations also lend credibility that it is not "just labor" arguing, for example, that success for industry requires success for workers. Academic connections are not restricted to simply regional institutions. For example, Working Partnerships USA has collaborated with regional partners (such as academics at the University of California–Santa Cruz) while also working with institutions elsewhere (such as the Center on Wisconsin Strategy at the University of Wisconsin–Madison). Nonacademic support groups such as Good Jobs First, The Partnership for Working Families, and Building Partnerships have also provided research support.

Research in and of itself does not distinguish these power-building institutions from more traditional think tanks. All across the country, and in many different arenas of concern, progressive think tanks are engaged in research and conduct media campaigns to get information out into the public debate. Think tank staff may also engage in lobbying and expert testimony. While such institutions were once concentrated inside the Washington, D.C., Beltway, an increasing number of them have emerged at state and regional levels as well.

Acting

What most distinguishes power-building research institutions from their more traditional think tank counterparts, however, is their *acting* role. Research such as "state of working people" reports and critiques of economic development programs are not the end but the starting point for their work. These power building nonprofits integrate their research directly into coalition campaigns. Evaluations of the economic and social impact of a proposed Wal-Mart, for example, have been central tools in local battles against this corporation.

Research also develops technical expertise needed directly in policy advocacy and organizing. LAANE, for example, did not simply provide background research for regional living wage campaigns; it also established extensive monitoring of city contracts and subsidies, and developed sophisticated expertise in living wage enforcement by dedicating extensive staff time to these projects.[2] This capacity not only supported one of the more aggressive and effective living wage enforcement efforts in the country but also provided concrete support for worker organizing, such as among the over 50,000 employees at Los Angeles International Airport.[3]

The *act* part of think-and-act tanks also includes a central role in direct organizing. This often takes the form of coalition building. Their staff often do much of the legwork to pull together and support coalitions that have worked for specific community benefits agreements, for example. In several cases where a local interfaith worker support network did not exist, the tank helped to incubate one—providing both staff and office space. In San Diego, the Center for Policy Initiatives similarly supports a student organizing project.

The CCNE's work on medical debt illustrates the integration of policy work, research, and coalition building. As part of their campaign for a community benefits agreement at Yale–New Haven Hospital, CCNE staff and allies systematically knocked on doors in the neighborhood surrounding the hospital. These conversations not only built grassroots support for the benefits campaign but also revealed story after story of residents who faced garnished wages and home foreclosures from the hospital's aggressive debt collection. The CCNE then produced three reports: *Yale Don't Lien on Me: The Attack on Homeownership by the Yale–New Haven Health System and Yale School of Medicine; Uncharitable Care: Yale–New Haven Hospital's Charity Care and Collection Practices;* and *Coming to a Town Near You? Charity and Collections at Bridgeport Hospital, Member of Yale–New Haven Health.*[4] These reports systematically exposed aggressive debt collection and weak use of charitable funds available to offset residents' debt. The research in turn fed back into organizing both for the community benefit demands and what became an independent medical debt campaign.

Think-and-act tanks aim to construct a long-term cross-institutional community leadership team. They provide the organizational home for all of the civic leadership institutes further explored in chapter 4. Their staff facilitate class discussions, recruit guest instructors, and organize logistics, and their research becomes a central and necessary part of the institute curriculum. They also maintain relationships among participants and active ongoing coalition work after the institute has finished its work.

Finding resources to establish and maintain these nonprofit organizations presents a central challenge to all power building leaders. Indeed, as we saw in chapter 2, how funding and subsequent capacity comes together can shape a particular organization's balance between thinking and acting.

Unions and other groups have often provided seed money to bring on a new organization's first staff person. Fund-raising events have also brought in some money. However, the budgets of all these nonprofits have been grown and maintained over time, mainly through foundation grants. Getting start-up resources—the first $50,000 to $150,000 to hire one or two staff—has proven relatively doable. The greatest challenge comes with expanding the scale of the work to go beyond this initial nucleus. The numbers of and levels of commitments from regional funders may hit limits, while national foundations have to set priorities. Furthermore, foundations that are focused on supporting certain strategies at one point in time may change their focus.

Part of the solution lies in ongoing work within the foundation world to cultivate and maintain greater involvement by both regional and national foundations. The New World Foundation, for example, has attempted to raise greater awareness of power building work within the foundation world. Drawing parallels to the investments of the New Right in civic education and mobilization, the foundation argues for greater funding to what it calls "new majority structures." The authors of the foundation's "Building the New Majority" pamphlet identify many of the nonprofits that we have covered here as examples of these structures.[5] The foundation has established its own $3 million annual fund to help support these structures and called on other funders similarly to expand their support for such work.

In chapter 7 we will return to issues of funding by raising questions about how to diversify the funding base to go outside of the foundation world. Specifically, we will consider the potential for greater funding coming from the labor movement—including the significant sums of money that the labor movement currently places into electoral work that builds only ad hoc structures during campaign seasons.

What's Wrong with Current Regional Development Strategies?

To establish a progressive voice in defining who is at the table and what the framework is for regional economic development requires an understanding of the limitations of current mainstream approaches to the subject.

While mainstream thinking on economic development ranges along a spectrum from more free-market fundamentalist to more free-market liberal approaches, they all represent variations of a basic growth coalition as described in chapter 1.[6] In general, the free-market orientation dominant in growth coalitions presumes business as the lead active agent, with public policy supporting business initiative. It defines unions and community groups as special interests that need to be either accommodated or confined depending upon whether the outlook is more liberal or fundamentalist. Growth coalitions generally have no room for labor and its allies to play leadership roles as experts for defining holistic economic health.

The free-market framework presumes that what is good for private employers is naturally good for the general community. By contrast, progressive approaches assert that this connection is problematic. Business success can come either at the benefit or the expense of community well-being. More positive outcomes require deliberate efforts to build institutions and economic rules that will produce mutual benefit. When applied to public policy, free-market approaches suffer many limitations both at the level of conception and in how concrete policy tools are used.

Flawed Assumptions of Conventional Economic Development Policy

Free-market approaches are embedded in a worldview of isolated individualism. They assume that both business leaders and workers freely enter a pluralistic, unstructured society of individuals who succeed and fail based primarily on their own efforts. Isolated individualism is reflected in concrete public policy in several ways. At the level of individual workers, it shows up in the tremendous weight mainstream economic development discussions give to education (the development of "human capital"). If only workers can get the appropriate training, they can secure a job or a better job based on their increased skills.

Governor Jennifer Granholm of Michigan, for example, tried to officially set a statewide goal to double the number of college graduates and provide for all workers to gain some kind of post–high school education. While this approach is certainly better than the cut-taxes, deregulate approach of her Republican predecessor, it failed to ask what kind of jobs employers are actually creating. Who is going to do all the jobs for which employers do not require much education? Which jobs that require greater education actually provide family-supporting employment, and which do not?

At best, education without a broader restructuring of labor markets represents an individual solution in which workers move up and down the scales of the existing economy—one displacing another. At worst, education alone simply creates more highly credentialed workers stuck in the same poor-quality jobs. Indeed, among today's best educated workers are adjunct faculty—Ph.D. educated workers piecing together a "full-time" job by teaching a class or two at several schools, usually with no benefits and making far less than a family-supporting wage.

At the firm level, isolated individualism translates into business models that revolve around individual entrepreneurship. While separate firms do enter into partnership agreements with each other, many opportunities for industrywide cooperation at the regional level typically go underutilized. Even worse, customer-supplier relationships among American companies can be downright predatory—as in the infamous case of the pressures Wal-Mart puts on its suppliers, not only demanding deeper-than-usual discounts but also reneging on contracts and finding excuses to return goods that are not selling well.[7] As a result, many collective problems that might include regional solutions around such areas as developing and adopting new technology, researching and developing new products, marketing, and workforce development often remain unresolved due to a lack of regional cooperative effort. Public policy all too often focuses on attracting the high profile corporate investor at the expense of more holistic economic planning.

Because of its free-market framework, mainstream economic development measures success and failure in quite narrow business terms. Mainstream debates tend to focus on quantity, such as job numbers and investment figures. Public and business officials like to talk about "X hundred new jobs created" or "Y amount of dollars invested." Progressives, by contrast, should also ask about quality: What are the wages and benefits of the "new" jobs? Are these new jobs in fact new, or is the firm simply moving jobs from one location to another?

How poverty is addressed illustrates the difference between mainstream and progressive approaches. Mainstream approaches typically focus on simple aggregate figures, such as the federal poverty guidelines that set a yearly income level per household size. In isolation, such measures become consistent with a deficit conception of poverty. The poor represent a lack of income. The solution lies in attracting outside private investors to provide jobs to fill the emptiness.

Because it does not delve deeply into quality measures, mainstream economic development thinking typically cannot even conceive that business investment decisions might be the cause of poverty. When think-and-act tanks research the details of wages and benefits, they draw attention to the reality that most poor in America do in fact work; the problem is not simply access to jobs, but access to *decent* jobs. Levels of poverty are signs of the balance or imbalance of power between workers and employers.

In part because large-scale deals can bring fanfare-filled public announcements of "new" jobs, mainstream economic development practice tends to focus on attracting new investment at the expense of efforts to retain existing jobs. Such priorities are consistent with a bias that sees solutions in expertise and resources outside the community rather than within it.

Finally, because it places business leaders in the driver's seat, the free-market framework typically relegates government policy roles to a passive and reactive role. Rather than actively seeking out collective problems and solutions to the operations of regional industries, most economic development officials largely stay out of industry decision making. They typically limit their energies to providing infrastructure, subsidies, and supporting narrow and isolated workforce development—hoping that the market will then respond with investments.

Such a narrow focus often does not even serve the interests of employers. Workforce development offers a case in point. It is woefully underfunded and generally does not connect to employer needs. Unlike most other developed nations, the United States has no national public framework for developing effective worker training. Thus, such training crystallizes at the regional level as ad hoc and uncoordinated efforts. As a result, employers experience ongoing skill shortages among occupations that do not require a college degree. And many professional fields have no system for developing and certifying worker skills once those workers leave college.

Flawed Use of Policy Tools

Inadequate measures, individualistic worldviews, and passivity combine to undermine the way in which public policy tools are used to promote community success. Typically, specific mainstream economic development actions suffer from lax or nonexistent standards, a secretive process, and narrowness in what government policy tools are actually used for "economic development."

When LAANE researched two of Los Angeles's major economic development programs, it found millions of dollars in public subsidies spent with little effective criteria for community well-being. Job quality, for example, was not a criterion used in either program! Public efforts were not targeted specifically toward underserved communities. Indeed, the city had no coherent strategy for targeting key industry sectors but focused its energy on attracting individual firms. LAANE's reports recommended far less emphasis on retail development and much more attention to smaller projects. The research fed successful campaigns around living wage policies, labor peace compacts, and community benefits agreements.[8]

The lax standards revealed in Los Angeles are all too typical. Due to the business-driven nature of the current public process, such community-destroying employers as Wal-Mart enjoy lucrative economic development assistance from communities across the country.

In their work on regional economic development policy, researchers Manuel Pastor, Peter Dreier, J. Eugene Grigsby, and Marta López-Garza note that questions of equity and distributions of wealth are typically the weakest concerns in official economic development thinking. Yet their research data suggest that levels of equity and community empowerment are actually key to a region's overall economic well-being.[9]

The nonprofit Good Jobs First operates as a national clearinghouse and support service for progressive subsidy reform campaigns. According to their data, state and local government subsidies to attract business investment have grown markedly over the past few decades. In 1977, for example, only twenty-eight states had programs to grant businesses property tax abatements for machinery and equipment; by 1993, forty-one states had such programs. In 1977, only thirteen states provided subsidized loans for machinery and equipment; by 1993, forty-two did. And over this sixteen-year period, state governments with laws empowering local governments to provide businesses loans increased from eight to forty-five.

In theory, packages of tax abatements, tax increment financing, subsidized loans, free land, and the like help a state or municipality either attract new jobs or retain existing ones. However, as the deals get ever more lucrative, and as subsidies become something that firms take for granted, critics question what the public really gets in return for its generosity. Indeed, a growing body of research suggests that most subsidies deliver very little. Typically, company commitments to jobs are vague. Often subsidized firms merely pledge not to eliminate jobs. Promised new jobs often do not materialize and existing jobs are lost anyway.

Even worse, as data from Good Jobs First research in Minnesota and Maine have showed, companies may simply use state and local subsidies to relocate from one part of the state to another. The research also reveals that subsidized employers all too often pay wages below the state average for their industry![10] Subsidies also go to firms with clear track records in violating labor, social, and environmental laws.

Indeed, research suggests that firm location and investment decisions are based upon a variety of factors not related to subsidies. Firms apparently make their basic investment decisions first and then go to states and local governments demanding a public gift. They all too often encounter public development officials convinced that if the public does not offer some kind of subsidy, the firm will go elsewhere. As Larry Ledebur and

Douglas Woodward argue: "Most studies show that incentives have little influence on location decisions.... It is not surprising... Governments have little or no control over the fundamental determinants of a firm's demand and costs.... Recent evidence... suggests that incentive bidding tends to feed on itself, with more expensive items often added at the last minute in an attempt to keep ahead of the competition. These hastily-assembled packages act like economic steroids."[11]

In return for generous public gifts, public officials typically ask little in return. Only nine of thirty-four states responding to a 1993 National Governors Association inquiry could identify any sort of reporting requirements for companies receiving public incentives. Only eight states told the association that job quality (and not just quantity) was even one of several criteria used to determine which companies get aid. Two-thirds of the thirty-six states responding to a National Association of State Development Agencies study could not even say what percentage of their incentive dollars was going to various types of businesses.[12]

These lax standards naturally grow out of the typically secretive process within which so much economic development policy occurs. The more firms negotiate with public officials privately, the more likely they are to be in the driver's seat without having to face broader responsibilities. Often a public consultation process either does not happen at all or comes after the main decisions have been made. Furthermore, information on subsidy, zoning, and other public policy practices is rarely accessible via a single governmental agency or readily available for public viewing. In Detroit, for example, the official body charged with overseeing the city's empowerment zone during the administration of President Bill Clinton did not even collect information on which companies had applied for or received the zone's many tax credits. These data were simply a private matter between the Internal Revenue Service and each firm!

Subsidy deals typically are done with minimal public record keeping—when approved, the tax break or subsidy is simply recorded in the minutes of a city council meeting. Progressive researchers then must comb through these records to piece together the big picture. The overall secrecy and lack of transparency commonly found in economic development policy helps explain why regional power-building efforts need the capacity of a LAANE, FRESC, or similar institution to effectively understand and critique mainstream economic development policy.

On the flip side, bringing public-private decisions into public view offers a rich arena in which regional power building may begin to redefine regional economic development. Our discussion points to why the insertion of a public benefit process into the Beltline Project in Atlanta (detailed in chapter 6) represented a significant first step in efforts to build regional power there.

The secretive nature of economic development work also reflects a final limitation: the fragmentation among public policy tools. Focused on attracting investors to bring in "new" jobs, mainstream approaches confine "economic development policy" to the official "economic development" authorities that are unconnected to other areas of government. Most of the human services or social service functions of government—such as housing, transportation, and (ironically) education—typically are not defined as "economic development." Certainly the various arms of government policy do not commonly add up to a greater vision of integrated progress. One of the tasks in developing a regional power-building agenda is asserting that most areas of governmental policy represent "economic development" policy that should be subject to integrated social justice criteria.

Building an Alternative Vision and Practice

Building regional power cannot simply involve identifying the limitations of mainstream economic development. The critique must also pave the way for the main work of developing an alternative. Activists must build a progressive regional economic development regime by working simultaneously at two levels: redefining the nature of the "big picture" problem and solutions and making on-the-ground changes by redirecting concrete policy levers.

Reframing the Big Picture

In issuing its first two research reports in San Jose—*Shock Absorbers in the Flexible Economy: The Rise of Contingent Employment in Silicon Valley* and *Growing Together or Drifting Apart? Working Families and Business in the New Economy*—Working Partnerships USA and the South Bay Labor Council aimed not simply to expose the underside of Silicon Valley's new economy for working families but also to begin to change the frame within which regional economic development was discussed.[13]

Since its early reports, Working Partnerships USA has documented the steady loss of health care coverage among working families and the decreasing availability of affordable housing, as well as the continued creation of low-quality jobs in the region. In 2007, it returned to a broad framing report with a new version of *Growing Together* titled *Life in the Valley Economy: Silicon Valley Progress Report 2007*.[14] The findings were compelling. With incomes stagnating or falling and the cost of living continuing to climb, the vast majority of working- and middle-class families in Santa Clara County remained worse off than they were in 2000. Although official unemployment numbers remained low, all too many workers had been forced to accept substandard, insecure jobs. Racial disparities in jobs, housing, and education continued to plague the region.

The combination of framing reports that document broad patterns in the economic quality of life for working families with research on specific industries, employment situations, or issue concerns can be found in other power building cases. The Center for Policy Initiatives, for example, issued its first report, *Prosperity and Poverty in the New Economy: A Report on the Social and Economic Status of Working People in San Diego County,* in 1998 to paint a broad picture of San Diego's regional economy from the viewpoint of working families.[15] Its next report then focused on leading industry sectors; *Planning for Shared Prosperity or Growing Inequality? An In-Depth Look at San Diego's Leading Industry Clusters* revealed that mainstream economic development discussions were half right in that targeted sectors did in fact provide overall higher wages and higher levels of education attainment.[16] However, the fact that 22 percent of these sectors' jobs paid below $18,000 per year meant that they were also contributing to the substantial increase of the working poor within the region.

Between 2001 and 2006, the Center for Policy Initiatives issued a series of focused reports on such areas as contingent and temporary employment, the regional cost of living, and examinations of downtown development using social justice criteria.

In Denver, the research agenda developed in a different order. To support the community benefits campaign at the redevelopment of a city landmark, the former Gates Rubber Factory, FRESC issued a series of issue briefs specific to that development pointing to the opportunities for affordable housing, quality jobs, and high-road construction. Before and after, FRESC published critiques of specific development deals and programs. Then in 2006, it unveiled *The Denver Atlas: A Region in Living Color* that visually documented the broad regional trends impacting working families.[17]

The combination of broad picture and more targeted research aims to articulate a new framework for discussing the region's economic health and planning. At a general level, the stories being told in different regions are similar, reflecting broad national trends. Conventional regional discussions do not examine the real indicators for how working families are doing. Looking at a wider set of measures reveals that prosperity in a region is not being broadly shared. The region's current path is producing a complex mixture of strains experienced by a wide range of working families. Public policy is currently contributing to rather than attempting to redirect these negative patterns. A new path is needed.

At a concrete level this framing work translates into several practical applications. It forms the starting point for establishing a core of diverse leaders with a shared understanding of regional power building. Indeed, the Civic Leadership Institute curriculum, explored in chapter 4, is built around such research. Framing research also translates into on-the-ground media work both to secure specific news coverage and to shift the way regional economic development questions are framed. For example, Working Partnerships drew national media attention when its early research revealed that the much-hyped opportunities of Silicon Valley's "new economy" were producing a large poverty-wage and contingent economy. Fully half the population of the region did not have jobs that could adequately meet the area's cost of living! Framing research is also used to educate supported candidates—helping to frame both their election campaigns and approach to public policy. Finally, broader research leads into more targeted areas that, in one way or another, connect into concrete policy development and organizing.

Embodying the Vision in Concrete Policy Campaigns

To continuously inject its new frame into public debates, regional power building has to connect broad framing work with tangible policy and other campaigns. Our regional power building cases reveal a range of specific tools that all share a key common characteristic: they connect specific winnable reforms and policy levers to the general concerns raised by progressive reframing.

Living Wage Campaigns   Living wage campaigns illustrate this connection of a general critique to specific reforms. The actual reform of requiring companies that receive public funds to pay a living wage is a fairly simple measure that local governments generally have the power to enact. Because battles over local living wage ordinances usually do not draw in large corporate players, many campaigns can prevail over the opposition of regional chambers of commerce and their local business allies.

But while the portion of an area's working poor that is covered is quite modest, the living wage concept speaks to big questions about poverty wages, public spending, and the role of local government in private economic decisions. Indeed, the tendency of the business opposition to speak of living wage ordinances as if they were across-the-board minimum wage laws or some even greater attempt at government control over the economy reflects the broad issues embedded in this very specific reform.

It is precisely this ability to connect the specific with the general that accounts for the rapid spread of living wage organizing in the late 1990s and the first decade of the new millennium. By the middle of 2006, a diverse collection of 140 municipalities across the nation had passed some form of living wage measure. Living wage campaigns served as an early coalition-building effort in nearly all of our regional power-building cases.[18]

Subsidy Accountability Campaigns   Living wage campaigns provide one way for grassroots coalitions to enter the broader subsidy reform arena, but progressive campaigns can also reform subsidy policy in other ways. Governments can require subsidized firms to commit to job numbers and require them to pay back subsidies in proportion to which the promised jobs do not materialize. They can include provisions that allow local governments to impose harsh penalties when subsidy recipients break local, state, and federal labor, environmental, and other laws. Public bodies can conduct environmental, economic, and social impact studies before granting subsidies. Most important, public subsidies should be part of a coherent public plan for regional economic development that guides when such outlays are appropriate and when they are not. Clearly, the question of public subsidies allows progressive alliances to work on very specific policy reforms while also raising very large unifying questions. The Washington, D.C.–based Good Jobs First offers a clearinghouse for information on subsidy reform.[19]

Community Benefits Agreements   Having achieved success around living wage and subsidy organizing, power building efforts in California began to experiment with a new strategy for intervening in economic development that has now become part of the basic tool kit for many regional efforts: the community benefits agreement (CBA). CBAs can take the form of legally binding documents signed between a grassroots coalition and the developer of a specific large-scale project. The developer commits to such measures as building a certain percentage of affordable housing, living wage requirements for leasing businesses space and funds for child care or youth centers, resources for community development projects, local hiring, prevailing wage construction, and neutrality and "card check" union recognition (recognition of the union by the employer when a majority of workers sign membership cards) for worker organizing drives. The CBA is then incorporated into official public approval documents. A CBA can also take the form of direct requirements that are passed by regional government independent of any agreements with developers to place public requirements on specific private development activity.

Because many different issues can be covered by a CBA, a broad coalition of union and community partners can pursue their core goals through such agreements. In return, the developer receives the support of the coalition in moving through the public approval process. Community benefits campaigns take advantage of the reality that, for developers, time is money. The support or opposition of a grassroots coalition can potentially have a major impact on both the speed and final outcome of the public process.

LAANE's pioneering Accountable Development Project won its first three CBAs in 2001. The breakthrough agreement with the massive Staples Center development was won in coalition with Strategic Actions for a Just Economy and set the pattern for future work. For their third CBA, the developer—seeking to show community support during the public approval process—actually approached the campaign. This work in Los Angeles and other California cities aims to establish a track record of enough CBAs that coalitions begin to transform the regional development process.

CBAs set a precedent for public bodies to undertake formal evaluations of the social and economic impact of proposed development and to seek binding developer commitments around tangible benefits to the community. Ultimately, as cities demonstrate the value of requiring clear community benefits, they lay the groundwork for power building coalitions to push for state legislation that will transform local and state economic development work generally.

The growing breadth of CBA work in Los Angeles can be seen in subsequent campaigns. In 2002, when Los Angeles designated the impoverished Adams–La Brea neighborhood as a redevelopment area, LAANE helped form the Adams–La Brea Neighborhood Committee. Over a period of several years, the committee persuaded the Los Angeles City Council to terminate negotiations with the original developer and to open up a new request for proposals with the community's base demands incorporated in the requirements. That same year, labor and community pressure led to the appointment of LAANE executive director Madeline Janis to the Los Angeles Community Redevelopment Agency, from where she has been able to help tie community benefits to more than one hundred projects in recent years.

In 2004, Los Angeles activists won the largest CBA in the country at the $500 million expansion of the massive Los Angeles International Airport. The new measure grew out of years of worker organizing and legislative action around a facility that employs over 50,000 workers. That same year, the LAANE-incubated Coalition for a Better Inglewood defeated a ballot proposal that would have allowed Wal-Mart to enter that community. Organizers followed up on this victory with an effort to compel the company to enter into a CBA for its renewed attempts to build a store. In 2006, the coalition won Inglewood City Council approval for the nation's fourth superstore ordinance requiring companies to pay for an economic impact study of their proposed store site before permits can be approved. The law also mandates a public hearing to review the findings.

Getting the first pathbreaking community benefits agreement is not easy. In Denver, it took three long years to win a CBA at Cherokee Denver LLC's high-profile redevelopment of the fifty-acre Gates Rubber Factory. Cherokee planned to create a mixed business and residential use neighborhood that modeled attractive urban density and transit-oriented development. During this time leaders of the effort risked the criticism—from skeptics within their own ranks—that they were wasting scarce time and resources. The Campaign for Responsible Development first raised its public demands at a May 2003 Denver Planning Board meeting. Coalition members objected to the Gates redevelopment plan's lack of clear commitment around affordable housing, high-paying jobs, and neighborhood and park investments. In the end, the planning board voted to send the plans for a special "urban renewal district" to the Denver City Council in order to allow the developer to apply for tax subsidies. However, the board did criticize the city's economic development officials for their slowness in sharing information on the project with the public. In June, the campaign called on the city council not to approve the renewal district until the development plan included a CBA. Although the council approved the district, the fact that there had even been a public debate during what was normally a quiet rubber-stamp process did demonstrate that something new was afoot.

While Steve Moyski, president of the development company Cherokee Denver LLC, was officially willing to negotiate with the campaign, he was not willing to discuss the whole package of demands until the city made a clear commitment on the amount of public subsidy the development would receive. The coalition scored an initial victory when Moyski agreed to limit commercial space to buildings less than 80,000 square feet, essentially meeting a demand by the food and commercial workers union to close out "big box" retailers. Moyski also initially agreed to attend a January 2004 meeting of three hundred campaign supporters, but pulled out when he heard of potential media coverage. A few days later, he resigned his position with Cherokee Denver.

It was not until January 2006—after three years of coalition building and growing political action by organized labor and its allies—that the campaign secured a community benefits agreement with the developer. The next month the Denver City Council approved $126 million in direct public subsidies for the project, whose plan now included the CBA's framework. Under the agreement, Denver's living-wage ordinance will be extended to include the site's parking lot attendants and security personnel. The plan secured prevailing wages on the publicly funded construction and the choice for a union construction manager and general contractor. Cherokee agreed to include 20 percent of rental units for lower-income working families. The CBA also enhanced a "first source" local hiring system that recruits local residents to fill new positions and, for the first time, prioritizes immediately adjacent low-income neighborhoods. Most important, the hard-fought campaign's victory set a precedent for negotiating tangible and binding community benefits on future public-supported development in Denver. Indeed, Denver's Office of Economic Development officially praised the agreement as a model for future large subsidized projects in Colorado.

In Milwaukee, the Good Jobs and Livable Neighborhoods Coalition faced a similarly difficult three-year battle to secure a CBA for development of a sixty-four-acre parcel of land in downtown Milwaukee. The project encompassed parcels owned by the city, county, and private land holders and involved nearly $20 million of direct city spending and subsidies. Although local officials hailed the Park East corridor project as a catalyst for downtown redevelopment, the public review process focused mainly on aesthetics, planning codes, and physical infrastructure. Job creation and job quality was not a consideration.

In December 2002, a small group of organizations stopped the city's Park East Redevelopment Plan from being passed through the Milwaukee Common Council and County Board of Supervisors, after which it could not have been amended. That bought time to grow a coalition and raise public visibility through prayer vigils, rallies at the site, phone banking, and the turning out of crowds for public meetings. Unwilling to either approve the project or a CBA during an election year, the city council at first took no action, then drafted several watered-down CBAs, and finally in June 2004 approved the development plan with no CBA attached. The Milwaukee County Board of Supervisors, however, proved far more receptive to the campaign. In February 2005 they overrode the county supervisor's veto to enact a CBA on their sixteen-acre Park East parcel that included many, although not all, of the campaign's demands.

Milwaukee's Good Jobs and Livable Neighborhoods Coalition became the first in the nation to win a CBA through legislation rather than by direct negotiations with the developer. The fact that coalition meetings continued to draw healthy attendance despite the drawn-out battle testifies to the compelling nature of these fights. As of 2007, the coalition—with its core partners in the International Union of Painters and Allied Trades, the SEIU, the Housing Alliance, and the interfaith Milwaukee Innercity Congregations Allied for Hope (associated with the Gamaliel

Foundation)—continues mobilizing coalition members around new developments in the Park East parcel.[20]

Sectoral Development Strategies   Broad notions of what "economic development" entails provide a correction to the common myopic focus on jobs by highlighting the many dimensions that contribute to true community well-being and social equity. However, regional power building must ultimately still grapple with questions of how a region creates family-supporting jobs. Supporting worker union organizing and requiring living wages from employers provide part of the solution, yet since in a capitalist society most job creation is controlled by the private sector, power-building leaders—especially those in depressed areas—must come to terms with the issue of how to foster business investments in decent jobs.

The concept of sectoral development planning provides a powerful tool. In recent years some currents within mainstream economic development circles have realized the virtues of thinking and planning around whole regional industries or groups of industries. Indeed, industrial "cluster" approaches have become a major concept. In part, this reflects the reality that globalization has increased the importance of regional economies as sites for decision making.

Although welcome as compared with traditional ad hoc firm-by-firm practices, such cluster strategies typically suffer from many of the same limitations that mainstream economic development work shares generally. They tend to focus on business-oriented and aggregate measures of success that fail to connect to the specific needs and realities of moderate- and low-income families. Cluster innovators often share the "better business climate" ideology that tends to favor "free market" initiatives over government regulation.

Rarely do these initiatives include proper representation by groups and individuals from the working-class and low-income communities in which the clusters will be located. As a result, such strategies may not only fail to help those most in need but also "cluster people out" of their neighborhoods in much the same way that poor families were "urban renewed" out of their homes in the 1960s and '70s.[21]

Our cases, however, include examples of progressive sectoral thinking that address these limitations and take that concept in the direction of power building. Similar to mainstream thinking, these progressive approaches seek to build a collective "industry table" that allows employers to address common problems that prove difficult to solve at the individual firm level. Unlike mainstream practice, progressive sectoral work includes labor and community groups as central players; in doing so it builds the work around the goal of creating and retaining family supporting jobs to which local residents have access.

The Wisconsin Regional Training Partnership (WRTP) in metropolitan Milwaukee provides a well-established example of a labor-driven progressive sectoral strategy.[22] Formed in 1992, the partnership brings together unions and community partners with over one hundred firms in the metalworking, machinery, plastics, and equipment industries that employ over 65,000 workers—roughly one third of the area's industrial workforce. In joining the WRTP, employers agree to follow a basic code of conduct supporting broad worker skill development, worker involvement in the firm, collective problem solving, and a vision of high-performance workplaces that support high standards of living.

The WRTP allows employers to pool resources into common worker training programs administered by staff with strong union backgrounds. The training draws expertise from the Milwaukee Area Technical College. It also establishes ongoing peer-to-peer learning networks. Because the WRTP programs are developed through extensive worker input, they prove far more effective than management-centered training both in terms of providing effective workplace skills and allowing workers to improve themselves more generally. Because they fear losing workers to other firms, management-developed programs tend to focus narrowly on very job-specific skill sets. Because it is focused on developing a regional workforce that all member firms can draw upon, the WRTP can pursue a much more holistic notion of worker development.

The WRTP provides a regular forum through which employers and unions share knowledge and jointly work at problem solving in the areas of technology, marketing, and workplace organization. Once again, the ability of unions and workers to participate as equal partners has proven a key factor of success. New technology or various schemes to reorganize work can benefit workers enormously, yet workers may be reluctant to share knowledge about their jobs if they fear a management-driven process will cut jobs or degrade their work. By building a forum for joint labor-management collaboration, the WRTP has helped all sides develop a level of trust necessary for effective workplace change.

Although the city lost 40,000 (one-third) of its manufacturing jobs in the 1980s, in the 1990s employment not only stabilized but employers added six thousand new jobs after the WRTP's creation. Success has also been shown through the model's expansion. With a grant from the U.S. Department of Labor, new partnerships were pursued in construction, data networking, health care, hospitality, and transportation. In nearby Madison, the related Jobs with a Future initiative grew out of a blue-ribbon commission of local business, labor, nonprofit organization, and public leaders constituted in 1995 by the Dane County Board of Supervisors.

The work by the Center on Wisconsin Strategy (COWS) to support the Milwaukee and Madison efforts demonstrates how systematic research can pave the way for concrete strategies. COWS research identified those industries that both enjoyed a regional specialization or significant concentration and offered or had the potential to provide family-supporting jobs. Interviews and focus groups with specific employers helped isolate those industries for which collective problem solving offered the greatest potential rewards. Along the way, conversations with employers also helped build relationships.

In a way generally similar to that of the WRTP, the labor-driven Economic Development Group in Buffalo, New York, was able to build progressive sectoral work with area businesses because it provides a means for effectively addressing basic collective problems that firms cannot solve on their own, including affordable and sustainable electricity and a downtown building heating system. In the same way, the group was able to take leadership around worker training precisely because the most effective programs need to have the worker and community buy-in that unions and independent community partners are uniquely positioned to provide.

Progressive sectoral strategies are not a magic wand. They do not change the basic profit-seeking, competitive logic inherent in capitalism. Firms can pursue antiworker, community-destroying "low-road" profit strategies as much as they can the kinds of "high-road" approaches supported by progressive sectoral partnerships. The context within which firms operate is important. In both Wisconsin and Buffalo, the sectoral work was supported in various ways by public institutions. Even more important, relatively high union density in the target industries had fostered firms more open to partnerships by making low-road strategies more difficult and high-road approaches a logical extension of the investments made in a unionized workforce. Progressive sectoral work attempts to further build high-road commitments by meshing firms in new institutional relationships.[23]

Such sectoral work establishes a new institutional table that moves crucial aspects of firm success into collective discussions at which labor and its community allies become equal partners. Sectoral partnerships thus assert what regional power building work attempts to establish generally—that labor and grassroots community leaders are just as much "experts" and stewards of the economy as business managers.

Developing a Sophisticated Approach to Business

Regional power building's policy work as described above naturally leads to a sophisticated approach toward employers. While individual campaigns may target and pressure specific employers, regional power building aims to change the regional economic and policy rules, not to declare a frontal assault on the very system of corporate America. Indeed, depending upon the issues, regional power building policy work can involve coalitions with specific employer groups.

Private employers in a region do not constitute a monolithic entity. Effective power-building organizers must develop a sophisticated approach that distinguishes among different parts of the business establishment whole. Most regional chamber of commerce bodies, for example, might focus on lower business taxes, deregulation, and tax subsidies while opposing such labor and community efforts as minimum wage and living wage laws.

However, these regional chambers do not reflect the opinion or interests of all employers. In San Jose, for example, the South Bay Labor Council (SBLC) realized that the big Silicon Valley technology companies had interests very different from those of the contractors, developers, landowners, and big-box retailers that it confronted in its economic development work. These technology companies do not compete primarily on low labor costs but by attracting skilled knowledge workers and keeping this workforce in the area even when individuals change companies. The Silicon Valley Manufacturing Group (a regional industry association) and the Joint Venture–Silicon Valley Network (a public-private consortium) have both focused on managing the urban system in ways that maintain a high quality of life and enhance the region's long-term economic competitiveness.

Thus, on the question of public transit the SBLC was able to work with the Silicon Valley Manufacturing Group, or SVMG (known since 2006 as the Silicon Valley Leadership Group), an alliance of the major corporations in the region heavily drawn from the electronics industry. Though the SBLC had to overcome the protests of the CEO of the SVMG in passing subsidy accountability legislation, it was careful not to paint employers with a broad brush or to demonize the business power structure. Instead, the SBLC realized that because of their direct interest in attracting and retaining knowledge workers, manufacturing firms were naturally led to support decent public transit options and affordable housing for these workers.

The dot-com bust of 2000 and the resulting plunge in sales tax revenue left the Santa Clara Valley Transportation Authority not only with no money for a Bay Area Rapid Transit extension but also insufficient funds for basic operating expenses. Finding a common interest, labor and the SVMG worked together to develop a financing, service, and revenue strategy. In 2000, voters approved a half-cent sales tax increase for transit, primarily for BART. When the Transportation Authority threatened 20 percent bus service cuts, the business group joined labor in persuading it to use some of its new half-cent tax revenue increase for basic services, despite legal questions raised by opponents.

In 2006, the Silicon Valley Leadership Group and labor worked hard to pass another half-cent sales tax increase for general revenue with an implied promise that it would be split between health and transportation services. Despite a well-funded, vigorous campaign with widespread endorsements, the referendum failed amid voter skepticism that the money would be used as promised.

Such tactical alliances with regional business players work because labor and its community allies, having pursued the strategies explored in this chapter, can approach cooperation from a position of independence. Without their own understanding of how the regional political economy works and a strong sense of what they want to achieve, progressive leaders risk getting co-opted into a nice-sounding corporate agenda that fails to deliver on social justice concerns. Even when they worked with manufacturers on transit funding, for example, the South Bay Labor Council leaders realized that their understanding of the issue differed from their employer counterparts. Both sides addressed different constituencies. While the manufacturers focused on better-paid "knowledge economy" (based on high-tech information industries) workers, the council tried to represent the interests of the vast majority of working people generally, and the large section of working families squeezed by a knowledge economy of very high paid and very low paid workers in particular. Thus, the SBLC and its allies supported employers on the general goal of increasing public transit funding but simultaneously tried to shape the agenda in a more progressive direction that spoke to the needs of lower-income working families.

A similar dynamic was at play during the council's work with the manufacturing interests around affordable housing. While the two sides could cooperate around the general issue of affordable housing, the council realized that the definition of what was "affordable" differed widely between the technology firms' knowledge economy professionals as well as middle-income union members and the broad population of low-income service workers that were the labor movement's constituency.

In addition to having an independent analysis of how interests did and did not overlap, power building organizers sat down with business leaders within the context of their own new efforts to build their movement's political and organizing capacity. A mobilized constituency allowed labor and its allies to interact with business figures from positions of mutual respect and strength. Such respect can be built at the individual as well as institutional levels. Power building leaders can get to know key business leaders as individuals while still keeping in mind that these people are both empowered and constrained by the institutional interests of which they are a part.

In San Jose, for example, Working Partnerships USA's community services director Steve Preminger had gotten to know Eric Benhamou, chairman and CEO of 3Com Corporation, in 1996. Both had participated in a seminar sponsored by the American Leadership Forum, which brings together top leaders of large and small companies, nonprofit groups, clergy, the judicial system, and the labor movement to develop leadership as well as friendship among these people of varied backgrounds. In 2000 the SEIU was running a contract campaign to pressure the large corporations who contracted for building services to support the union's demand for living wage contracts. Drawing on his relationship with Benhamou, Preminger set up a meeting with Benhamou, Amy Dean, Justice for Janitors leader Chava Bustamante, and other labor representatives to explain poor working conditions for janitors. The labor leaders asked Benhamou to help contact other employers and accept a code of conduct—a concept that Working Partnerships is still promoting. Benhamou did contact other executives, and wrote a letter that was published in the *San Jose Mercury News* arguing that Silicon Valley's technology firms had a social and business responsibility to support the janitors' wage demands. He wrote,

> We also expect the least skilled of our jobs to command decent wages, and to enable all these workers to live and function within our society. Failure to acknowledge that such a threshold exists borders on irresponsibility.
>
> For some, it is a plain moral question of social equity. For others, it is a pragmatic need to address a business risk before it develops into a crisis. For others yet, it is a matter of dealing with the guilty feeling one experiences at the thought that yesterday's business lunch leftovers were magically cleaned up at night by someone who lives in a storage shed.
>
> The current situation with our janitors is a symptom of a broader problem. We are pricing basic living standards beyond the reach of an untolerably high percentage of the population. This problem is of our own making. Not unlike our well-chronicled educational system debacle, it can be solved with a little money spent now, or allowed to fester over time at a much greater cost to us all. As leaders of the high-tech industry, we are being put to the test. While some may ignore a serious problem in the making for a while longer, I trust many will join me and San Jose Mayor Ron Gonzales and see in the janitors' case an opportunity to make our ideas known about which kind of a Silicon Valley we stand for.[24]

The SEIU was able to secure living wage contracts without a strike.

Looking at the cases we researched for this book highlights overall the importance of making sophisticated distinctions. In building regional power, progressive leaders are not launching a frontal assault on corporate America. As new and fragile projects, local power building efforts can get started in part because organizers do not have to confront a united business power structure led by the most powerful corporate players. In the core arena around which power building organizes—regional economic development policy—area business players have a wide range of interests, ranging from seeing such concerns as a central focus, with mild interest, or with a general lack of concern.

The sharpest confrontations typically come with those components of the business community that have the greatest direct financial or ideological commitments to the local status quo. Thus, in pushing a living wage or responsible development policy before a local public board, activists will likely confront figures from low-road contractors, retailers, hotel and restaurant owners, developers, and/or the local chamber of commerce. By contrast, executives from Microsoft, Lockheed-Martin, or Exxon-Mobile are not likely to make an appearance.

In many regions, ethnic chambers of commerce may not share the same interests as the official regional chamber of commerce, despite sharing the same root name. Many ethnic chambers of commerce represent genuinely small family-run businesses. Thus, in San Jose, for example, organizers could bring several ethnic chambers into the labor-community coalition that passed an anti–big-box store ordinance, despite the opposition of San Jose Silicon Valley Chamber of Commerce. The anti–big-box campaign spoke to the direct survival interests of many ethnic-owned small businesses.

The campaign allowed the South Bay Labor Council to develop relationships with leaders of Hispanic, Vietnamese, Filipino, and other ethnic chambers of commerce. When the SBLC and Working Partnerships USA led a subsequent living wage campaign, the Vietnamese chamber of commerce supported the measure, while the Hispanic counterpart remained neutral—rather than following the strong opposition of the regional chamber.

Reflecting its relationships with these ethnic chambers, the SBLC pushed for a final ordinance that included provisions to review all public contract bids. The goal was to identify those bids that could be broken up and thus made more accessible for smaller businesses—consciously countering the general tendency in government to lump public contract work together and in turn favor large contractors.

The council and several ethnic chambers worked together against Proposition 209, which ended affirmative action for California government and higher education. More recently, labor and the ethnic chambers of commerce—especially the African American, Hispanic, and Vietnamese chambers—and a small business group called Downtown Retail Advocates worked together to promote a community benefits agreement for a downtown housing and retail development by the CIM Group. The ethnic and small-business groups were interested in requiring that the developers promote existing businesses as well as any new businesses, since their own ethnic-owned and small businesses would suffer during development and they believed the whole region should benefit from the new development and the ensuing influx of new residents. The existing San Jose Chamber of Commerce (now called the San Jose Silicon Valley Chamber of Commerce) was strongly opposed to any community benefits agreement and even opposed the specific development, since it was associated with labor as a major promoter.

Business and the High Road

The concept of high-road and low-road business strategies has proven an effective tool for labor and community groups around the country to approach business from a position of both independence and possible collaboration.[25] Not all firms, even within the same industry, compete in the same way. Management can take the high road, focusing upon the quality of the company's goods or services and its internal ability to rapidly and effectively adjust to changing markets over time. To pursue such a high road, firms must invest in and listen to their workers, offer family-supporting wages and benefits that keep experienced workers around, and look for opportunities to partner with community institutions and active governments.

By contrast, companies can take the low road, simply focusing on cutting short-term costs. Since labor is the cost that management most directly controls, low-road firms typically undermine wages and benefits, outsource work, downsize and overwork laborers, and reinforce a top-down management style.

The choice between high- and low-road strategies is faced by firms in every industry. The retail sector, for example, may seem custom-made for the low road; yet bulk discounter Costco boasts a higher rate of profit per employee than arch–low road competitor Sam's Club (a division of Wal-Mart) precisely by paying significantly higher wages, reducing employee turnover, and investing in a workforce that can sell a higher profit mix of items.

The choices that firms make between the high and low roads is of great concern to the community. High-road strategies tend to internalize more costs, raise community standards, and favor environmentally and socially sustainable business practices, and high-road firms tend to look for partnerships that can help them address the many challenges that prove difficult for individual firms to solve on their own. For these firms, unions can become proven partners in raising productivity, and community organizations and active local governments are something to be embraced, not feared. By contrast, because low-road strategies push costs onto the community, the workforce, and the environment, such firms fight unionization, community organizing, and "government interference in the market" at all costs.

The high road–low road distinction has direct application for regional power building since it poses the key question of which road regional economic development policy is promoting. The passive, market-oriented models that predominate in the United States tacitly favor the low road since they rely on individual firms making decisions in isolation. The high road, by contrast, requires active cooperation, collective resources, and, ultimately, sharing power. The progressive economic development strategies that we describe in this book are essentially efforts to use public authority and resources to promote the high road.

In seeking to block the low road and pave the high road, regional power-building coalitions have a framework for both confronting and cooperating with employers. They can also approach the political structure from a standpoint not by being probusiness or antibusiness but by asking, What kind of businesses are we trying to promote?

This chapter's example of Buffalo's Economic Development Group illustrates a sophisticated approach informed by high road–low road distinctions.[26] Power building in Buffalo clearly involves deliberate high-road cooperation with employers. Through the Champions Network, the union, the community, and business leaders promote the Buffalo-Niagara region as a high-performance place for doing business. Three committees of the Network have focused on voter registration and civic involvement, the retooling of public development incentives around high-road criteria, and, through the Believe in Buffalo-Niagara campaign, collected 100,000 signatures on a letter touting the region's virtues and dynamism.

In 2007, the Champions Network planned an economic development trade show focusing on sustainable energy, high-tech manufacturing, the health and bioscience industries, transportation and trade, arts and culture, and education. More informally, the network helps to educate employers on the value of organized labor in the community and to promote a better understanding of common concerns. At the same time, the projects promoted by the Economic Development Group—electrical power, heating, and workforce training—all combine community and leader concerns with core interests of the business community.

Three factors support high-road cooperation in Buffalo. First, Buffalo is a union town; despite erosion in union density, in 2003 more than one-fourth of the city's workforce was unionized, placing it in thirteenth place for unionization among the 260 U.S. metropolitan areas.[27] As a result, the region offers a core of employers with high employment standards positioned to understand the benefits of working with unions.

Second, unions and their community allies have been able to approach management from a position of independence. The Economic Development Group was founded as a gathering of labor leaders that grew into a fully staffed agency. The Champions Network grew out of research and a conference sponsored by the local branch of Cornell University's School of Industrial and Labor Relations. Key Cornell faculty combined a prounion, progressive perspective with the credibility of a program that serves both labor and management. In both cases labor and its community allies were able to draw on prior experience and progressive-oriented local research to develop a clear sense of what they wanted in a high-road relationship. Unlike many management-driven civic partnerships, labor unions and the community in Buffalo entered into cooperation with management as equal partners and, in many ways, as the key drivers of the agenda.

Third, in addition to promoting the high road, power building in Buffalo also involves organizing to block the low road through the Coalition for Economic Justice. Governed by a board of union and religious leaders, the coalition not only organizes community support for local strikes but also confronts such low-road companies as Wal-Mart, Cintas, and other local employers who try to prosper at the expense of workers and the community. Power building in Buffalo thus builds a complex labor-community capacity to cooperate with good companies, confront bad companies, and to both cooperate or conflict with companies whose actions may be good or bad on different issues and at different times.

Winning the Battle of Ideas: The Role of Values and Vision

Building an agenda for regional power is more than simply a sum of its parts. While we have explored many particular policy reforms and research arenas, these components represent maneuvers in a general battle for ideas.

The New Right did not simply organize around its constituent parts. Its "values" organizing linked to a distinct social vision in which social ills reflect questions of individualized responsibility, the belief that America's problems come from moral decay fostered by an immoral liberal elite, and a commitment that government can and should be a force for enacting individual morality. The New Right's vision of the good society also intertwines with a powerful corporate ideology that equates personal freedom with unregulated capitalism.

To the extent to which they have enjoyed success in the battle of ideas, conservatives have done so because they face weak countervisions. Ever since the decline of the New Deal coalition, liberals and progressives have remained fragmented over the "big picture." In one reflection of this impasse, in election after election poll data reveal that the public does not view Democratic election campaigns, at least until recently, as offering any clear social or economic vision.

An effective social vision that has life and breath on the ground is not born from the heads of intellectuals but grows out of the values and ideas articulated in grassroots battles. While the full social vision that will come out of regional power building remains a work in progress, we can identify within that policy work the emerging values and ideas that point toward a future vision of the good society.

Regional power-building efforts offer values that clearly contrast with those of the New Right. Grassroots campaigns place personal responsibility in the context of institutional accountability. What kind of society are our centers of wealth and power promoting? What is the moral behavior of society's main economic and political institutions? Social, moral, and economic decay come not from a liberal elite but from corporate profit seeking and amoral markets not governed by public authority. Individual success comes not from "being left alone" but by gaining access to shared resources and opportunities.

Regional power building works to reestablish the basic idea that government has a role to play in building an economy and society that works for everyone. It points toward a vision that "another world is possible." Much of establishment thinking offers the rather fatalistic message that individuals should hold on to what they have in an inherently unjust world. By contrast, regional power building offers the promise that through democratic action the economic and political rules of our regions, states, and ultimately our country can be changed to foster shared prosperity and a brighter future for coming generations.

4

Deep Coalitions

"Teamsters and Turtles Together at Last"—so ran a famous headline on the 1999 World Trade Organization protests in Seattle. It reflected the co-operation among unions, environmentalists (some of whom in fact were dressed as sea turtles in Seattle), faith-based communities, women's groups, and a wide range of community organizations that has grown steadily over the past two decades.[1] The coalition work that is central to regional power building both reflects this general trend and represents its deepening.

Regional power building is founded upon the growing opportunity to build broad alliances. Without coalitions, power building is simply not pos-sible. The list of supporting organizations in Connecticut and a sample co-alition from Los Angeles (see tables 4.1 and 4.2) offer two typical examples of the kinds of broad coalitions that regional power building fosters.

Power building, however, goes beyond the general sense of coalition building. For example, since the mid-1990s, labor-community coalitions have enacted living wage ordinances in over 140 communities. While all point to positive trends in growing progressive activism, the formal coali-

TABLE 4.1. Community Organized for Responsible Development, Connecticut

---

Amistad Catholic Worker
Asociación Ministerial Evangelistica Hispana de New Haven
Bridge of Life Ministries
Bristol Street Blockwatch
Brookside Tenant Council
Brookside Youth Alternative
Cathedral of Higher Praise, Church of God of Prophecy
Cedar Hill Block Watch
Centro Cristiano Restauración
Coalition of Black Trade Unionists
Common Ground for Good Government
District 1199 New England Health Care Employees Union, Service Employees
    International Union
Essex TRC
Grandparents on the Move
Hospital Debt Justice Project
Iglesia Cristiana Fe
Iglesia Unida al Calvario
Knowing God Ministries
Liberty Square Cooperative One
Mt. Zion Missionary Baptist Church
New Growth Outreach Ministries
New Haven Green Party
New Haven People's Center
New Haven Student Fair Share Coalition
People Against Injustice
Radio Amor
Regalo de Dios
Sacred Heart RC Church
Second Star of Jacob
Sisters with a New Attitude
St. Andrews Episcopal Church
St. Martin DePorres Church
Trade Union Plaza
Trowbridge Renaissance
Undergraduate Organizing Committee
Unidad Latina en Acción
UNITE HERE Locals 34, 35, 217 and Graduate Employees and
    Students Organization
Urban Design League
Varick A.M.E. Zion Church
Vecinos en Acción/Neighbors in Action
West Village Resident Council
Westville Progressive Action

---

tion partnerships behind the vast majority of these efforts did not continue after the living-wage campaign ended. Even fewer produced ongoing alliances that integrated the three elements of regional power building: policy work, strategic relationship building, and aggressive political action.

TABLE 4.2. The Coalition for Clean and Safe Ports, Los Angeles

Change to Win
Clergy and Laity United for Economic Justice
Coalition for a Safe Environment
Coalition for Clean Air
Coalition for Humane Immigrant Rights of Los Angeles
Harbor–Watts Economic Development Corporation
Hermandad Mexicana Latinoamericana
International Association of Machinists Lodge 1484
Los Angeles Alliance for a New Economy
Long Beach Alliance for Children with Asthma
Los Angeles County Federation of Labor
Mexican American Political Association
Natural Resources Defense Council
Physicians for Social Responsibility
Service Employees International Union Local 1877
Southern California Council of Laborers
Teamsters Joint Council 42 and Teamsters Locals 63, 848, and 952
UNITE HERE Local 681

This is not to denigrate the living wage movement. As we will see, issue campaigns produce lasting and deepening relationships only when they are part of a broader effort to do so. Without planning and investment in a larger program, formal coalitions around issue campaigns will naturally rise and fade around the unifying issue. Deep coalitions are a leg of the model that must be deliberately built.

Strategic Coalition Building

Leaders of regional power building work select issue campaigns based upon how such work will support their strategic relationship-building goals. In San Jose, California, the South Bay Labor Council's Housing for All campaign illustrates a careful choice chosen to develop strategic relationships among partners key to building power over the long term.

A study by Working Partnerships USA found that regional median home prices had increased from $311,146 in 1997 to $513,950 in 2000. The same report offered public policy solutions that would result in 8,600 new units of affordable housing.[2] It would have been possible to develop a strategy based on building new affordable housing units to address the housing crunch that was hitting relatively well-paid union members; however, the South Bay Labor Council's first Housing for All policy push focused on the interests of lower-income renters. With a rental vacancy rate falling to 1.1 percent by 2000, average rental costs had climbed 61 percent in three years. In this environment, some landlords were evicting lower-income tenants to clear the way for wealthier renters. To stop that, the council fought for and won an eviction protection ordinance.

The campaign to protect renters accomplished several goals for the SBLC. It forged a strong alliance with the local tenants' rights movement, producing a great deal of goodwill and credibility that labor was not simply seeking community alliances for its own narrow benefit. It also allowed organized labor to distinguish itself from Silicon Valley's big employers, for whom "affordable housing" meant homes for the higher-paid knowledge economy workers that these firms hoped to attract to the region. By contrast, labor spoke as a representative of the interests of the working majority—uniting middle-income earners with those trapped in the region's mushrooming low-wage "new economy" jobs.

Over the long term, such strategic campaigns help redefine labor's image in the community. Building labor's political influence and organizing more workers shifts from being a "special interest" to a mechanism for growing power that benefits a range of community organizations and the community at large. The research around the eviction protection campaign showed that the high cost of housing and rent in Silicon Valley made tenants' rights organizing directly relevant to union members in lower-wage jobs who either struggled with rent or made long commutes from lower-rent areas. For tenants' rights groups, labor's participation brought to bear significant political clout well beyond what they could have achieved on their own. For both labor and community, the campaign helped to build greater trust and sense of shared values.

Australian scholar Amanda Tattersall, an activist who has helped build many labor-community coalitions, provides a helpful framework for thinking about the distinct kinds of coalitions fostered by regional power building work. Tattersall distinguishes among four types of coalitions. Table 4.3 summarizes a modified version of her model.[3]

The vast majority of all labor-community cooperation happens in ad hoc or support coalitions. These are relatively easy to build, and require the least commitment of resources and strategic energy. Even coalitions that involve mutual support or deep relations among core partners will often have other groups involved only in a support or ad hoc role. Long

TABLE 4.3. A Framework of Union-Community Coalitions

	Ad hoc coalition	Support coalition	Mutual-support coalition	Deep coalition
Nature of common interest	- Specific group's agenda/issue/event - Can be initiated by union or community organization	- Specific group's agenda/issue/event - Issue indiscriminate, no necessary connection to organization members	- Mutual direct interest of participating organizations	- Issue framed as social vision for working people
Structure and strategy	- Episodic engagement - Tactical, not strategic, engagement	- Short-term coalition - Some formal shared decision making - Informal union dominance or limited union engagement - Hasty, reactive engagement - Between organizations with different or similar political practices	- Coalition includes leadership and officials - Joint decision-making structure, trust - Midterm focus and planning - Participating organizations have trust, similar culture/political practices	- Layered decision-making structures, connections between union and community groups at membership level - Long-term strategic plan to build power
Organization/union participation	- Instrumental engagement - Campaign distant from members	- Union officials, campaign distant from union members	- Union vision framed as "community" issues - Some mobilizations of members through union - Greater buy-in	- Union actively engaging rank and file - Significant buy-in, financial resources
Scale	- Any place	- Coalition operating at same scale as decision makers	- Effective longer-term scale at same site of decision maker	- Mobilizing capacity at several levels, including local
Shared capacities	None	Temporary ————————————————————————→ Lasting Specific areas ————————————————————→ Many complementary areas Possible areas include: research, leadership and staff development, campaign methodologies, media and communications, fundraising.		

lists of endorsing organizations, for example, do not necessarily reflect who is doing the core organizing work of the coalition. Leaders who pursue regional power-building strategies self-consciously seek opportunities to foster mutual support and deep relations among a core group of partners. The ultimate goal is to move interaction between key labor and community groups from transactional relationships ("I'll scratch your back if you scratch mine") to relationships based on intertwined interests and strongly shared values. Building power in the region becomes a way of not only supporting the interests of each group's constituency but also making the values that are ultimately shared by core partners (such as social justice, fairness, and sustainability) a force that steers the region's political economy.

Such an approach to coalition building has three important implications. First, groups are not simply supporting each other's organizational agendas. Coalition activity can include, for example, community support for union organizing and contract campaigns. However, the overall basis for alliance building lies in a process by which labor and community groups develop new mutual agendas that transcend their traditional activities. This transcendent character can be seen in such efforts as living wage campaigns, community benefits agreements, the San Jose Children's Health Initiative, and labor protections for immigrant workers. In each case, the direct organizational interests of key partners became embedded in a larger community cause and set of shared values around which the campaigns were organized.

Ultimately, such mutual interest and common values transcend individual campaigns to become a shared commitment to building progressive power within the region systematically over time. Cooperation becomes not only a way of accomplishing the immediate tasks at hand, but also a vehicle for growing the capacity of each core partner to exercise power individually—and collectively as part of a coherent regional progressive movement. Leaders of the core power building partners see their work self-consciously in terms of growing a movement of working people that can transform their region, state, and ultimately the nation.

Second, such a commitment to building a broad movement does not mean a loss of the self-interest of the organizations involved. Labor and community leaders do not build power for its own sake or become active in coalitions because it is the "right thing to do." They do so because establishing alliances, passing specific government policies, and growing political influence over the long term help them address the central goals of their constituencies. Through power building, however, organizational interest becomes defined in more than narrow or simply immediate terms. Indeed, power building participation can reflect a significant broadening by an organization in its conception of how it can accomplish its core interests. Thus, growing a constituency for power building efforts involves a twin process of defining the work to speak to different partners' core goals while at the some time encouraging them to view the building of a shared capacity for regional power as a necessary step for fully pursuing those core interests.

Third, while coalition work often involves a broad range of groups that vary from campaign to campaign, power building requires deliberate efforts to establish deeper relationships among a set of core partners. In San Jose, for example, cooperation between the SBLC and the Association of Community Organizations for Reform Now (ACORN) around renters' rights and affordable housing produced a more formal partnership. In the summer and fall of 2003, a joint grassroots organizing team combining labor and ACORN organizers conducted door-to-door neighborhood visits in poor, predominantly immigrant neighborhoods in support of a new community benefits initiative campaign. This partnership added new ACORN members, greater community support for the community benefits initiative, and a stronger electoral base for labor.

ACORN became a key partner for the SBLC because both organizations focus on establishing long-term grassroots institutional power. In an article on labor-ACORN partnerships across the nation, ACORN executive director Steve Kest emphasizes this point, arguing that unlike "advocacy" or "policy" groups, ACORN builds membership organizations in low- and moderate-income communities in ways that parallel organized labor's workplace membership. He quotes the opening of the memorandum of understanding signed in March 2003 between San Jose ACORN and the SBLC:

The underlying philosophy of the partnership between the SBLC and ACORN is one that is founded upon the belief that institutional power must be built in order to advance the political, economic, and social interest of working families. The SBLC and ACORN have unique capacities that together allow working families to advocate for their interests in the community, workplace, and halls of government. Those actions not only achieve immediate outcomes but also strategically position these organizations to advocate for working families on an on-going basis, building lasting, meaningful power.[4]

From the SBLC's perspective, labor could build neither strong workplace organizations nor lasting political power unless it had robust community partners. Recognizing that long-term labor-community alliances must be built around real grassroots community capacity, Nathan Cummings Foundation program officer Andrea Kydd made the foundation's first grant to Working Partnerships USA to build the capacity of labor's community partners.

The labor-Latino political alliance in Los Angeles similarly reflects deep coalition building. Neither set of groups can attain long-term power in the region without such an alliance. Just as organized labor seeks to rebuild its membership base (including that among immigrant workers), many organizations in immigrant communities struggle with institutional stability and capacity. Furthermore, immigrant communities need to grow lasting political participation among community members in order to gain long-term political influence. Thus, in a way similar to the labor-ACORN partnership in San Jose, union organizing and political action in Los Angeles (and elsewhere) becomes a path for Latino empowerment. In turn, Latino political and institutional development strengthens labor.

Because of this broad strategic perspective, power building coalition work looks different from labor-community alliances around single campaigns. For example, in Boston, Community Labor United's first public action was not an issue campaign but the launching of its Building Partnerships' Civic Network Leadership Institute. The program brought together specifically targeted union, community, and political leaders to discuss building power to shape the region's political economy. CLU staff had spent six months having one-on-one conversations with a wide range of labor and community groups to assess their interests, capacity, and potential as core partners. These preparations also led to the formation of a strategy committee of seven labor and nine community core partners. The committee selects major campaigns for CLU to work on based upon each issue's potential to contribute to the larger regional power building goals.

CLU's first campaign, around repainting Boston's public schools, should be seen in light of the broader power building process. The effort secured a commitment to union jobs and local hiring on this multimillion-dollar project and was attractive as a first effort for several reasons. It brought together two sets of organizations (the building trades unions and low-income community groups) that were needed for long-term power building but had a history of tension between them. Furthermore, because of labor's political clout (including the Greater Boston Labor Council and the International Union of Painters and Allied Trades) the effort promised a relatively quick and achievable win that would help establish CLU's credibility and set the stage for more elaborate and potentially much longer economic development campaigns.

Because it looks toward establishing long-term power at a regional level, power building coalition work must look beyond the "usual suspects" of groups that share a general progressive outlook. The Connecticut Center for a New Economy (CCNE) uses a three-layer model to guide its strategic thinking consisting of three circles labeled one, two, and three (figure 4.1).

The "ones" represent the groups and individuals that share the same general progressive vision and are actively working to make it happen; power building begins among these groups. The "twos" share the same basic values and would likely support power building if they were organized or exposed to progressive regional thinking. The "threes" currently support the corporate regional agenda. Regional strategizing looks to building alliances among the first layer in order to move into the second layer and to eventually win over or neutralize parts of the third layer. The CCNE's community organizing work in New Haven (described later in this chapter) represents a systematic effort to reach out to the "twos."

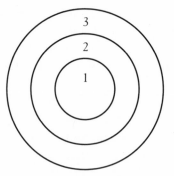

Figure 4.1 Three layers of group outreach

The targeting of the Organization of Los Angeles Workers (OLAW) reflects a similar sort of strategic thinking. Rather than simply concentrating voter mobilization efforts on traditionally Latino neighborhoods, OLAW targeted specific Republican districts that could become contested terrain due to recent influxes of Latino residents (those in the districts who are natural "twos").

The CCNE's three-layer framework also helps unpack coalition categories that are often quite general. For example, to build regional power, leaders must involve "the faith community." But what does this mean in practice? The three-layer framework helps distinguish between the contributions of potential faith-based allies. For example, the fifty faith-based groups associated nationally with Interfaith Worker Justice bring together liberal and progressive clergy and laity—the faith-based "ones"—into an organizational structure that allows them to be more systematically active in worker struggles. By contrast, the roughly sixty faith-based organizing efforts associated with the Gamaliel Foundation aim first to organize the faith community in low-income and heavily minority neighborhoods in their regions. This work is among more of the "twos" of faith institutions that might not start as self-consciously progressive or particularly involved in "political" issues. Both approaches help move toward power building, but by reaching out to slightly different constituencies.

In short, regional power building involves a sophisticated, multilayered approach to coalition work. Specific issue campaigns may encompass a broad set of supporting groups while a core of institutional partners drive the campaign. Similarly, long-term relationship building simultaneously seeks to broaden the array of supportive groups while deepening relationships among the most integrated partners.

Deep coalition building may also require regional power-building planners to think beyond the universe of groups that are currently organized. Power building in Boston and New Haven provides an instructive contrast between strategic environments. The Boston area enjoys a dense fabric of nonprofit community-oriented organizations. Thus, CLU and the Greater Boston Labor Council naturally focused on bringing together targeted groups. By contrast, the CCNE and the Yale University unions faced a reality that grassroots organization among residents in the low-income neighborhoods surrounding the university was relatively sparse. Thus, the CCNE chose to devote significant staff time to direct community organizing.

During the summer and fall of 2004, the CCNE conducted a systematic door-knocking effort to learn about the community, listen to those who would be affected by the Yale–New Haven Hospital expansion, and build a grassroots network among residents. Staff from the CCNE and the Yale unions, plus approximately seventy volunteers, went door-to-door five days a week, visiting over eight hundred homes. In addition to talking to residents about the hospital, the organizers also tried to get people to register to vote. Reflecting its long-term strategic orientation, the CCNE secured a grant to purchase hand-held personal digital assistants. The technology was used to track houses visited, record survey data, and build a systematic database on area residents that would be useful in future campaigns.[5]

Similarly, when beginning a series of campaigns focused on the service industry in the beachfront city of Santa Monica, California, the Los Angeles Alliance for a New Economy (LAANE) established Santa Monicans for Responsible Tourism (SMART). As a grassroots organization of several hundred members, SMART developed and fought a long battle with the tourist industry over a zone-based living wage law that would have required all employers within the city's lucrative coastal zone to pay a living wage. Although the battle was lost in 2002, when a successful industry-backed referendum canceled the ordinance, the years of activism did help workers in four out of ten luxury hotels (representing half of the hotel workforce) successfully organize with UNITE HERE—a merging of the former Union of Needletrades, Industrial and Textile Employees (UNITE) and the former Hotel Employees and Restaurant Employees International Union (HERE)—and achieve gains. In addition, the coalition was able to pass a citywide living wage ordinance and persuade the school board to adopt a labor peace ordinance for a hotel on property it owned.

In this chapter, we explore three main aspects of deep coalition building: strengthening relationships within the labor movement, connecting unions with communities of color and immigrant communities, and links between labor and faith-based organizations.

Making Labor a Strong Regional Partner

People outside the labor movement often assume that organized labor is a monolithic entity. Yet even in regions with the most dynamic power building efforts, unions differ widely in terms of their perceived interests and their level of participation and support. Even without differing evaluations of regional power-building work, unions can find themselves in conflict over issues of who gets to organize and represent specific groups of workers, who did or did not make bargaining concessions that impacted other unions, and which unions endorsed which candidates. Thus, unifying the "house of labor" at a regional level is an objective of power building that must be continuously pursued.

San Diego provides one example of the disunity that has afflicted many local labor movements at one time or another. Despite the city's intense antiunion climate, "unions used to spend all their time fighting with each other," according to San Diego and Imperial Counties Labor Council leader Jerry Butkiewicz. But, "We've united all the unions together into one union called the labor council, and now we spend all the time fighting the enemy, the antiunion establishment."[6] The council's coalition efforts have not always worked perfectly. At times, one or more of the four municipal unions (including an independent union not eligible for membership in the labor council) have taken positions in elections that are at odds with the rest of organized labor. But Butkiewicz works toward unity by arranging interviews with every candidate seeking endorsement by top officers, political committee members, and other activists in local unions. While in theory such a process should be the labor council norm, as we will explore in the next chapter actually achieving it is not always easy or straightforward.

In San Jose, the ability of the South Bay Labor Council to pursue innovative power building work under Amy Dean benefited enormously from the success of Dean's predecessor, Rick Sawyer, in forging a sense of common purpose among the council's affiliates through intensive one-on-one work with union leaders. Sawyer's legacy highlights the importance of bringing together the Left and Right within the labor movement. How can power building forge a regional electoral majority if it cannot speak to both wings within the house of labor?

The challenges facing labor today compel unions of all types to rethink their basic strategies. The results do not always fit with labor's familiar past divisions. For example, while it may seem that alliances with immigrant groups are the innovations of such "sympathetic" unions as the Service Employees International Union (SEIU) and UNITE HERE, recent years have also seen "unsympathetic" building trades leaders pursue work with both immigrants and minority communities. In San Jose, for example, Loyd Williams of the United Association of Plumbers and Pipefitters proved instrumental within the SBLC and the Santa Clara and San Benito Building Trades Council by helping connect the trades into the immigrant worker activism begun by the organizing of those in the janitor trade. Indeed, Williams helped get all the building trades unions into the battle against Proposition 187. The proposition, which denied public services to undocumented immigrants, was passed by voters but overturned by federal courts. Similarly, while some power building labor councils are led by individuals whose background comes out of such "left" bodies as the United Farm Workers of America, the SEIU, and Jobs with Justice, in at least three cases—those of Atlanta, Seattle, and Houston—key initiative has come from labor council leaders whose homes are in the construction trades.

As with regional coalition work generally, some unions must become key driving players while others provide varying levels of support. Which unions have tended to become core players who contribute the most resources, leadership, and integration of power building work into their internal operations? Providing the pioneer cases, the California experience reveals the strong link between worker organizing and power building work. Los Angeles saw the consolidation of the SEIU's national Justice for Janitors campaign—an organizing and bargaining effort built around mass mobilization and community support. Similarly, the state has been home to other community-based union campaigns. It also saw the largest organizing victory in decades when 75,000 home health care workers joined the SEIU thanks to political action granting them a legal context for bargaining. Unions that pursue aggressive organizing on a regional scale are naturally drawn to coalition work, political action, and other elements of regional power building. In California (and elsewhere) the aggressively organizing unions have proven core players in developing a regional power-building program.

Active organizing can, however, come from very different parts of the labor movement. While the service economy in the United States is growing, the construction industry also provides major job growth. Thus, the "old" craft-organizing strategies of the building trades continue to have relevance to the twenty-first century and help explain why construction trade leaders have proven key innovators. Indeed, the craft union model for organizing highly skilled workers who migrate from job to job and employer to employer has direct application in such "new economy" businesses as software and other technology industries.

Unions organizing on a geographical basis typically provide core leadership for regional power-building work. By contrast, manufacturing unions have often been marginal players in current regional power building. This is especially noticeable in cities like Cleveland and Seattle that have traditionally strong unionized manufacturing industries. Taking manufacturing unions as a general category (and recognizing that there are exceptions) these unions are relatively behind in mounting the type of industry organizing efforts that have emerged among key service industry unions. Furthermore, when they do organizing these unions can face employers far less rooted in regional markets. Manufacturers can integrate production systems across different regions, and their customer base may be more national and international than that of more regionally rooted industries like health care, building services, construction, and entertainment. Leverage to aid worker organizing in manufacturing thus can come less from an ability to influence regional economic development decisions and more from such sources as leveraging supplier-customer relations between union and nonunion firms and potential disruptions of "just in time delivery" systems between firms.[7]

We should note, however, that regional work in Buffalo, New York, and Milwaukee, Wisconsin, demonstrates that there are potential paths for manufacturing unions to reach power building strategies. As we argued in chapter 1, even big manufacturers are not disconnected from what happens at the regional level. They rely upon attracting and retaining appropriate workers, having strong relationships with regional supplier firms, and benefiting from effective regional transportation systems. Reflecting these regional connections, manufacturing unions can have interests in regional power building, although the specific type of regional work may take a different form (sectoral initiatives rather than community benefits campaigns, for example).

Having discussed general categories of unions we should note that the stance of locals from even the same national union can vary region by region. The United Food and Commercial Workers International Union (UFCW) in Seattle, for example, has expressed keen interest in power building work, while in Colorado the UFCW left the state AFL-CIO and

the Denver Area Labor Federation after Change to Win split from the
AFL-CIO in 2005.[8]

One implication of the above discussion is that when a labor council or
similar leader embarks on the path of power building, he or she is taking
risks to manage a complex set of relationships. Regional power building
bolsters the growth strategies of a council's most active affiliates. Yet, leadership in a local labor council or area labor federation is ultimately a political position won by election. Council leaders need to maintain a majority
base. Traditionally, such political environments have encouraged council
policies around the lowest common denominator. By contrast, regional
power building work may prompt varied opinions by the less active affiliates on the wisdom of allocating scarce movement resources to work that
often feels experimental. Efforts among immigrant and minority communities, in particular, can generate differing opinions among affiliates, since
the full virtues of such connections are hardly universally accepted within
the American labor movement.

The same is true of economic development work. Our cases include
examples in which economic development coalitions helped forge new alliances between building trades unions and minority and immigrant communities and examples of how ongoing tensions between the two groups
undermined such work. Economic development campaigns can offer new
opportunities for building trades unions to connect to such communities
while exerting greater leverage over public construction. However, such
campaigns can also seem to threaten traditional trades strategies that have
sought project labor agreements on their own. Indeed, developers may actively try to break off the building trades unions from broader coalitions
through separate deals.

This conflicted political environment helps explain the general pattern,
found over the second half of the twentieth century, in which labor councils attracted cautious leaders not known for particularly bold experimentation. As a result, local councils did not figure into the strategies of many
of the more innovative unions. Yet, our cases reveal that over the past decade this situation has begun to change. Labor movement revival requires
dynamic cross-union regional labor bodies that can forge powerful coalitions inside and outside the house of labor. A new generation of local labor
council and area labor federation leaders continues to develop within this
climate of crisis.

These innovators have to negotiate difficult tensions between asserting a bold path and building consensus. For example, in choosing to support MaryBe McMillan for North Carolina AFL-CIO secretary-treasurer, federation president James Andrews had to decide between having a particularly skilled labor-community leader, activist, and researcher in one of the organization's three full-time positions and accommodating the expectations of his largest affiliate that one of their members would occupy the post. (We will discuss state-based power building in North Carolina in chapter 7.) John Ryan's election to head Cleveland's North Shore Federation AFL-CIO of Labor with 54 percent of the vote marked both the overturning of an old guard and a significant split among affiliates, especially between the public sector and the building trades locals. Following his victory, Ryan methodically worked to win over affiliates that had voted for his opponent. Researchers Stephanie Luce and Mark Nelson found that "many interviewees commented positively on Ryan's leadership skills—particularly his ability to mend fences with the Building Trades without alienating his initial base."[9]

In reviewing the leadership experiences found among our cases, we see both success and failure in negotiating the tension between innovation and consensus. Indeed, in some of the cases where the mantle of power building leadership has changed hands we find affiliate support breaking down or coming together over similar programming due to different leadership styles that either attract or alienate affiliates that are not yet on board with the core program.

Efforts to win consent within a regional house of labor for a new path are made easier today by the examples and direct support offered by the pioneering initiatives described in this book. For example, in founding Community Labor United Building Partnerships, leaders of the Greater Boston Labor Council did not have to spend a half-decade cultivating interest with the building trades; they could instead call on the help of building trades leaders in San Jose who could explain from a trades perspective and by pointing to concrete outcomes why power-building work was crucial for union revival in the construction industry.

When the initiative for power building first comes out of individual unions and allied groups, such as Jobs with Justice, tensions can develop with a more traditional or less capable labor council. In one case, the prior leaders of a local labor council literally attempted to shut down a Jobs with Justice chapter that they saw as a direct threat to their leadership position.

In other cases developing regional strategies may so redefine council staff roles that leaders confront the challenging choice between laying off dedicated individuals or attempting to build new strategies with staff whose skills and perspectives do not fit current needs.

An opposite dynamic is also a danger when groups such as Jobs with Justice have traditionally filled mobilizing roles not provided by a central labor body. As a previously moribund council becomes more effective, it may draw in many of the roles and resources previously held by an active Jobs with Justice chapter. In several of our cases the new leadership of the council came directly from Jobs with Justice. Ironically, subsequent power building by the council led to a crisis of purpose for the Jobs with Justice chapter.

Labor-Community Alliances

While unions and community groups work together in regions across the country, power building requires deep alliances between labor and community partners committed to organizing and a shared vision of social justice. The landscape of community groups in most regions is even more complex and fragmented than that of labor, making it essential to differentiate between organizations while seeking core partners.

Community-based organizations are often divided into three types based on their primary mission and method of intervention. Some provide *services* to meet direct needs of disadvantaged communities (e.g., food banks or homeless shelters); others *advocate* for change on behalf of some population (e.g., the Children's Defense Fund), while others *organize* the affected constituency to take action on their own behalf (e.g., Association of Community Organizations for Reform Now). While all three types of community groups can be valuable members of campaign coalitions, those focused on organizing and mobilizing a mass membership tend to make the most effective core partners for power building.

The field of community organizing can be further divided into two main wings: those that recruit individuals directly as members and those that bring together institutions like churches. Membership-based organizations are often centered around neighborhood boundaries and ideally function like community labor union locals. The most prominent national membership organization is probably the Association of Community Organizations for Reform Now (ACORN), and most cities also have neighborhood associations (of widely varying strength and effectiveness).

Institutional organizing is inherently coalition-based. Paralleling central labor councils, such efforts strive to bring together all the significant membership-based organizations within a certain area to work toward a common agenda. Primarily faith-based networks like the Gamaliel Foundation, the Industrial Areas Foundation, and the Pacific Institute for Community Organization are the most prominent practitioners of this approach in U.S. cities. When at their best, these organizations work through their member congregations to educate and mobilize a broad cross-section of the local community around shared values.

Both types of organization are central players in regional power building, and labor leaders should be aware of the differences between them. Since institutional organizing involves managing diverse coalitions (like leading a labor council), they are sometimes unable to move as fast on issues as more centralized unions. Membership-based organizations tend to be more geographically concentrated, which can narrow their interests and impact, but also make them more likely to be able to exert significant leverage over politicians in certain districts. Most centrally, both the unions and community groups within the core leadership group should have the capacity to move their memberships and an interest in expanding their capacity to do so. Whatever the organizational type, two constituencies are particularly key components of the power building alliance with labor: communities of color and communities of faith.

Labor–Minority–Immigrant Alliances

Every case of regional power building includes some significant outreach by labor to minority communities—most often African Americans, Latinos, and immigrants. Several logics appear to be at work. The low-income organizing of specific unions has enmeshed them in minority communities. Alliances around broader community issues reflect these unions' organizing campaigns that have involved significant community outreach. In the process of organizing, unionization has been framed within the community as a key dimension for its development. As Kate Bronfenbrenner has documented, in general minority workers are particularly receptive to unionization.[10]

New coalition work has had to address past tensions between organized labor and minority communities. For example, the preapprenticeship training and minority hiring programs found in several cases responded to a history of conflict over job access between the building trades unions and African American and Latino communities. Part of the problem lies in the fact that the labor movement has not been impervious to the racism endemic to the broader U.S. society. Racism in America, however, is not simply a question of individual attitudes—although these certainly play a role—but in the design and function of society's major institutions. In the nineteenth century, the institutional racism in the construction trades and other craft unions was often blatant—the organizations simply had bylaws banning African Americans (as well as the foreign-born and women) from membership. By the mid-twentieth century, when these provisions were dropped, the issue for the unionized construction trades involved a tradition of recruiting new members through the family and friends of existing members. Even without overtly racist prejudice this tradition ensured that unions that had originally allowed whites-only membership would continue to comprise largely white members.

How to overcome this pattern, however, is not straightforward, especially in light of the decline in union construction jobs. Unlike the situation with most unions, where the employer does the hiring, the building trades unions have maintained a "closed shop" arrangement in which they provide the workforce for union contractors. Because work assignments end when the construction project is completed, the building trades unions are continuously responsible to the membership for finding them new work, leading to particularly intense conflict with community groups. The community justifiably looks at the largely white composition of the trades and demands more hiring of minority workers. Every newly trained apprentice, however, is another worker for whom the union needs to find a job. When union construction work grows, this need is less of a tension than when the available union work shrinks, as it has in most places over the last several decades.

However, the very shrinking of union work provides a potential for bringing together the building trades with minority communities, since construction is a growing industry overall. Over the past twenty years, nonunion contractors have used their base in residential construction to move into the core areas of unionized industrial construction jobs. They have used African American, Latino, and immigrant workers as a source of both skilled and unskilled labor.[11] Indeed, Robert Hunter of the right-wing Mackinaw Center in Michigan made the case quite clearly in a 1997 article. On the surface he expressed great concern over the apparent racism found in the building trades. His solution, however, was not to increase African American union membership, but "to end the unions' monopoly power in public construction by getting rid of 'project labor agreements,' which mandate that all contractors must employ members of a designated union for all labor performed on the site"—in other words, train blacks as a nonunion construction work force in order to bust the trade unions.[12] As Hunter's proposition indicates, either the building trades unions will find ways to build alliances with minority communities or minority workers will provide a weapon for employers to use against them.

Power building in Boston illustrates the possibility of building trades-minority cooperation. Boston Public Schools planned a multimillion-dollar repainting project that could easily have become nonunion and used largely white suburban workers; neither the building trades nor groups in minority communities were in a position alone to change this picture. By furthering an alliance between the International Union of Painters and Allied Trades and minority groups, Community Labor United led a successful campaign that secured the work as union jobs that would allocate substantial slots for minority apprenticeships. Similar union-minority partnerships have emerged in other power building cases. The glue in such cases is provided by the fact that, by cooperating, both the building trades and minority groups can expand the amount of union construction work, thus helping the trades increase union density while also pulling in more minority workers. We should also note that because of the aging of the union construction workforce in many parts of the country, retirement within the trades also provides a possible avenue for mitigating the minority-apprenticeship/jobs-for-existing-members tension.

The new connections between labor and minority communities can also reflect a common dilemma of local political marginalization or declining influence. For minority communities the local political power structure has either locked them out altogether or their representation is dominated by business-oriented, middle-class elites. Basic math on potential voter numbers naturally suggests political alliances—neither labor nor specific minority communities alone have the strength to achieve regional electoral power in most parts of the country, making crossing racial lines a key dimension of the political programs that we will detail in chapter 6. The community benefits agreement model explored in chapter 3 similarly has an inherent logic for crossing racial boundaries in general, and bringing the building trades into coalitions with minority groups in particular.

In the spring of 2006, several hundred thousand immigrants marched in the streets of Chicago, starting off a national wave of such marches. Activists and media within immigrant communities organized the protests to counter efforts in the U.S. Congress to criminalize undocumented workers and to fight for a secure status in this country. While not the core initiator of the marches, organized labor in many communities played an important role. This is particularly true of many of our power building cases. As mentioned previously, in Los Angeles, María Elena Durazo, president of UNITE HERE Local 11, served as master of ceremonies for the May 1, 2006, march. She was elected leader of the Los Angeles County Federation of Labor two weeks later. Much of the march organizing took place in labor-related meeting spaces. The spring 2006 civic leadership institute in Denver focused entirely on immigrant rights issues—providing an opportunity for immigrant leaders to connect with labor and other community groups. In most of our cases, power building leaders spent an active spring involved in the protest wave.

Regional power-building activists could connect to the immigrant marches because relationships with local immigrant communities had already become part of their organizing. Many of the core union partners in regional power building are organizing in industries that have large proportions of immigrant workers. This applies not simply to occupations like janitorial, laundry, grounds keeping, grocery, and hotel workers, but also to less obvious industries, such as construction, where immigrant workers are increasingly employed. Indeed, as a wide range of employers shift to contingent and outsourced employment arrangements, immigrant workers come to fill a significant proportion of such positions.[13]

As immigrant communities grow around the country they have the potential to change many regional political dynamics. While only one of many immigrant groups, Latinos have become the most rapidly expanding group in the U.S. electorate. While some Latinos are highly concentrated in urban centers, over half live in metropolitan area suburbs. Latinos are already over 12 percent of the population in California, Texas, Florida, New Mexico, Colorado, New York, and New Jersey. Seven of the ten states with the fastest growing Latino populations are in the conservative bastion of the Old South.[14]

Realization of this political power potential is not automatic. In Los Angeles, mobilization for a new political alignment of labor and Latinos in Los Angeles was sparked in early 2000, when labor led a coalition of immigrants' rights organizations in an amnesty campaign that filled the Los Angeles Sports Arena with 16,000 supporters, and with over 4,000 more cheering outside. The County Federation of Labor and key unions then helped set up the Organization of Los Angeles Workers (OLAW) to develop a cadre of skilled union members who would work on political campaigns.[15]

In addition to HERE Local 11, SEIU Local 1877 (Justice for Janitors), and UNITE members, full-time walkers came from the Coalition for Humane Immigrant Rights of Los Angeles, Hermandad Mexicana Nacional, Clinica Romero (a Salvadoran immigrant solidarity organization), and a number of Mexican and Guatemalan hometown associations.[16] The power of OLAW came from its ability to operate outside traditionally progressive Latino communities to target those growing Latino populations in traditionally Republican districts. By registering people to vote and getting them to the polls, OLAW helped make Los Angeles a Democratic and labor stronghold. SEIU international vice president Eliseo Medina explains OLAW's work:

> Sometimes the details are important.... We made up *compromisos,* commitment sheets, on NCR paper. The person at the door signed and kept one copy, and the other copy went into our data bank. That built in a lot of accountability with our lost-timers because they had to show a signature, not just circle a code.... And the commitment was focused on making voting a social act. The commitment forms said, '*Por Los Angeles amnistia, por derechos, mi familia vota 100 percento.*' [For amnesty, for rights, my family is voting 100 percent.] ... We tried to make everything a family act to magnify the work and make it resonate.[17]

OLAW and the County Federation also worked with Spanish-language Univision (channel 34) to conduct citizenship fairs. As Larry Frank and Kent Wong describe,

> At the Lincoln Park event, every consulate in Los Angeles set up a booth and over 3,000 people attended to inquire about the citizenship process as

it relates to their country of origin. Channel 34 set up call-in shows with a toll-free number into the SEIU Local 99 phone bank. Univision started conducting other call-in shows with labor, marketing them *"Treinta Cuatro en Su Lado"* [Channel 34 on Your Side]. They advertised and televised a question and answer session with immigration attorneys, and the union recruited fifty immigration attorneys to staff SEIU Local 99's call center. That session led to over 200,000 phone requests. For a question and answer session on L.A. schools, the union recruited school district and union representatives to field another barrage of questions, and a session on community-police relations filled the phone bank with LAPD community affairs representatives. In this way, Eliseo Medina explains:

> With the phone bank at Local 99, the TV has the SEIU logo behind all of the experts and people start to understand that labor has a role on all these key issues.... As a result of these and other efforts, the new voters in L.A. are now almost as progressive as the San Francisco voter base. With nine to ten million non-citizen permanent residents, many of them in key states such as Florida, New Mexico and Arizona, whoever is figuring out how to do this work can make all the difference.[18]

While Los Angeles may be an obvious location for labor-immigrant alliances, Houston is not. Yet, during the past ten years immigrants have made up 70 percent of the city's growth, and the Latino population overtook the Anglo population by the 2000 census, representing 38 percent as compared to 30 percent of residents.

When elected to the leadership of Houston's Harris County AFL-CIO Council in 1995, Dale Wortham and Richard Shaw saw an opportunity to reach out to the Latino community around several initiatives. The council helped build the Justice and Equality in the Workplace Partnership for immigrants whose employers violate labor and other laws. Officially billed as an Equal Employment Opportunity Commission initiative, the partnership includes the consulates of Mexico, Guatemala, El Salvador, and Colombia; U.S. agencies including the Department of Labor Wage and Hour Division, the Department of Justice, and the Occupational Safety and Health Administration (OSHA); the Houston Mayor's Office of Immigrant and Refugee Affairs; the Galveston-Houston Catholic Diocese, the Mexican American Legal Defense and Educational Fund, and the Interfaith Committee for Worker Justice; and, of course, the Harris County AFL-CIO Council. By posting a single phone number on billboards throughout the city the partnership helped an estimated 1,900 individuals recover over $1.3 million in back wages between July 2001 and June 2003.[19]

The Harris County Council also supported the new Mayor's Office of Immigrant and Refugee Affairs (MOIRA), staffed by Benito Juarez, an immigrant rights activist. The creation of MOIRA was originally part of a political platform in 2001, supported by the Harris County AFL-CIO Council, which helped reelect Mayor Lee Brown, an African American, over a serious challenge by city council member Orlando Sanchez, a Cuban American Republican. With Sanchez winning the Anglo and Latino vote, Brown won a narrow reelection thanks to huge African American turn-out and the labor council's get-out-the-vote drive. Like the Workplace Partnership, MOIRA provides referrals to help immigrants and refugees. Nonpayment of wages is the most frequent complaint, with workplace safety also high on the list.

City funds currently support three organized day-labor sites in Houston, including the Oscar Romero Day Labor Center, where the Harris County Council is helping to promote worker education programs covering OSHA safety rights, discrimination, and wage and hour laws. Currently the council is working with immigrant and faith-based groups to try to expand its Community Services Program into a more comprehensive workers center that would provide employment services, training and education programs, and emergency health, clothing, and legal assistance.

Connecting immigrant empowerment to the broader struggle for progressive power is not easy. Except for SEIU Local 105, organizers of the Denver civic leadership institute on immigration had a hard time attracting labor leaders. Immigrant rights work is controversial in many parts of the labor movement. Just as the movement has not been immune to racism, so too it is not resistant to anti-immigrant sentiment. This can be true even among African American union members who understand the oppression of racism. In many parts of the country unionized industries—ranging from manufacturing to the public sector—that have traditionally provided "middle class" job opportunities for African Americans have contracted out work to nonunion firms. In order to cut costs these contractors may often draw heavily upon immigrant workers as the most vulnerable and seemingly controllable part of the workforce. Thus, unionized African Americans can literally be replaced with nonunion Latinos and immigrants.

In South Los Angeles, this tension was augmented by demographic shifts as historically black neighborhoods with black elected representatives have become more "brown" as African Americans move out and Latinos move in. In his 2001 mayoral campaign, James Hahn won office though gaining black support in South Los Angeles against Latino- and labor-backed candidate Antonio Villaraigosa by directly drawing on anti-immigrant sentiment. Power building leaders responded by developing a united African American–Latino political mobilization program in South Los Angeles and by running progressive candidates with strong credentials in both African American and Latino communities. The result: Villaraigosa beat Hahn in the next election for mayor. We will examine the Alliance of Local Leaders for Education, Registration, and Turnout program more fully in the next chapter; here we note simply that the key ingredients for success were core partner organizations on both the union and community sides with strong roots in the African American and Latino communities. These partners could thus directly confront interracial tensions by, for example, deliberately organizing door-knocking teams that partnered African American and Latino activists.

With leadership coming from California, pro–immigrant rights leaders within the labor movement succeeded in changing the AFL-CIO's policy on immigration in 2000. Having long promoted anti-immigrant policies of aggressive law enforcement, border policing, and employer sanctions for hiring undocumented workers, the national federation switched to supporting workers regardless of their immigration status and focusing enforcement efforts on employers of the nation's labor laws that protect all workers and for whom employer violations (such as not paying wages at all or paying below the minimum wage) are especially egregious against immigrant workers.

The AFL-CIO followed up the new policy by developing the 2003 Immigrant Worker Freedom Rides. Modeled after the historic civil rights rides of the 1960s, the program sent eighteen buses with nine hundred riders traveling from the West Coast across the country to New York City and Washington, D.C., to highlight the need to strengthen immigrant rights. Most of our power building cases come from among the 103 cities where the freedom riders stopped.

Just as those outside the labor movement cannot assume a unified labor monolith, labor leaders and others seeking to build minority and immigrant alliances should not presume that such communities speak with one voice. Indeed, such communities may not even enjoy clear organizational structures with which to partner. The existing constituency organizations built in such communities may not work as part of clear national networks, and they often struggle to find funding.[20] Thus, building regional power requires both finding the existing organizations that are active and helping to build and strengthen the civic infrastructure within minority and immigrant communities.

The immigrant–minority–labor electoral work described herein reflects this imperative. Unlike traditional single-election get-out-the-vote operations, these projects seek to expand the electorate by registering and mobilizing new voters—and by connecting them to structures that remain in the community and press for progressive reform on an ongoing basis year after year. This need to grow organizational capacity is another reason why partnerships between central labor councils and a group such as ACORN are so central to power building work.

Labor-Interfaith Alliances

Deeply rooted interfaith involvement is a key alliance necessary for long-term regional power building. Many unions that are doing aggressive organizing work realize the importance of interfaith connections. However, they often seek such alliances only when they need help on their organizing drives. As Kim Bobo, founder and executive director of the national group Interfaith Worker Justice, explains in an article on labor-interfaith collaboration, "Even though there is much more strategic involvement of religious leaders early in a campaign than there was a few years ago, the biggest complaint from the religious community is that they get called at the last minute to show up at a rally and say a prayer.... The last-minute calls are so common that they have names: 'Rent a Priest,' 'Call a Collar,' and 'Dial a Minister.'"[21]

The most effective labor-interfaith alliances are partnerships built over the long term around a shared agenda of economic justice—one that reflects the core interests of both partners. Religious groups thus turn out to help organizing drives because labor has been there for faith communities and both sets of partners have worked together to shift the political power dynamics in their region. Such strategic and long-term labor-community cooperation typically requires growing the institutional capacity of the faith community. As Bobo argues, "the most effective interfaith religion-labor groups have staff devoted exclusively to building the coalition and reaching out to the religious community on a systematic basis."[22]

Sometimes outreach to the faith community involves fostering and deepening cooperation with existing faith-based networks—such as those fostered by the Gamaliel Foundation or Interfaith Worker Justice. Other times a vehicle for cooperation has to be established. With no explicit worker-oriented interfaith group in Los Angeles, for example, LAANE used its living wage organizing to foster Clergy and Laity United for Economic Justice (CLUE), for which LAANE provided office space and staffing support. Today CLUE works as an association of six hundred faith leaders focused on responding to the crisis of poverty.

Since the successful living wage campaign, CLUE has been deeply involved in supporting Justice for Janitors, the grocery workers, and other labor struggles. For example, when the Westside Hotels balked at a first contract with the hotel workers union to gradually raise housekeepers' wages from $8.15 to $11.05 per hour, CLUE dispatched small teams in full ministerial garb to deliver brief sermons on workplace fairness while ordering coffee at several hotel dining rooms. On April 8, 1998, a procession of sixty ministers, priests, and rabbis marched through Beverly Hills to deposit bitter herbs outside the Rodeo Summit Hotel, which still had not signed the HERE agreement, and offer milk and honey to the two hotels that had. Two months later the Rodeo Summit signed as well. CLUE has organized similar religious support for a campaign against a union-busting hotel in Santa Monica, an organizing drive at St. Francis Hospital, and protests over the University of Southern California's decisions to contract out work to low-wage employers.

In addition to CLUE, the Los Angeles County Federation of Labor has developed a strong working relationship with the city's Catholic archdiocese, holding an annual workers' mass on Labor Day at Cardinal Roger Mahoney's new Cathedral of Our Lady of the Angels. And on the Sunday before Labor Day, the County Federation continues to build its Labor in the Pulpit program, primarily in South Los Angeles.

Incubating new organizational structures to establish deep relationships can present challenges. For example, in San Jose the Interfaith

Council (TIC) on Race, Religion, Economic and Social Justice was jump-started and nurtured by the South Bay Labor Council in 1997. Researchers Barbara Byrd and Nari Rhee observe that the TIC

> has grown more independent over time, though it still receives staff and a small amount of financial support from the Labor Council. Current TIC chair Rabbi Melanie Aron explains that the organization struggled to find its own voice while still working closely with the Council on the living wage campaign, the Children's Healthcare Initiative and immigrant issues. The move toward more independence was driven, she says, by faith leaders' need to find a religious framework for their activities and to educate their own congregations on the connection between faith and social justice, not simply to respond to Labor Council requests for assistance. In fact, the TIC was independently involved in affordable housing advocacy prior to labor's involvement. But Rabbi Aron also commends the Labor Council on their understanding of the need to have a real collaboration, not simply to approach the Interfaith Council when they need a religious presence on a picket line. San Jose Newspaper Guild Executive Officer Luther Jackson who serves on the TIC by virtue of his leadership in the Unitarian church asserts, "Our work is based on justice theology, not just responding to 'dial a collar' requests from unions. We're working to build an authentic organization of our own."[23]

Fostering Bridge Builders: Civic Leadership Institutes

Since labor and community leaders seek to build progressive power over the span of decades, their efforts must both expand the ranks of current power building leadership and ensure replacements for the current core. Over the years, employer interests have invested heavily in regional leadership development and networking through such programs as the American Leadership Forum. These efforts reflect an understanding that developing relationships among individuals is the first step toward building strong relationships among institutions. In order to build lasting governing majorities over the long term, progressives must do the same.

The San Jose Labor/Community Leadership Institute described in chapter 2 has been a pioneer for similar programs across the country. While these are now generally called civic leadership institutes, the basic model remains the same: bringing together primary and secondary leadership from labor, religious, community, and political groups in a four- to eight-session program to develop their understanding of the regional political economy and a common vision of progressive change. Participation is through invitation, and leaders typically pay to participate.

In his book on coalitions between unions and the environmental and peace movements, *Coalitions across the Class Divide: Lessons from the Labor, Peace, and Environmental Movements,* Fred Rose identifies the key role played by bridge builders.[24] Because their background spans more than one movement, bridge builders can help bring together organizations that might not normally work together. Bridge builders understand where different groups are coming from, can speak their language, and can draw upon the personal relationships and credibility that they have with different groups.

Civic leadership institutes essentially work to establish cadres of bridge builders with a distinct twist. Ideally, institute graduates not only gain an understanding of the issues and reality confronting various groups but also emerge with a shared analysis of the regional political economy and a common vision for building real power.

The bridge building outcomes arise not only at the level of overall strategic thinking, but also through many individualized relationships. For example, during an early San Jose civic leadership institute, Loyd Williams, president of the large Plumbers, Steamfitters and Refrigeration Fitters Local 393, met immigrant rights activist Maria Ferrer from the campaign against Proposition 227 (an anti–bilingual education measure). Because of the relationship they forged, Local 393 turned over its entire phone bank apparatus to help defeat this measure.[25]

Institute bridge building can also directly connect to the power building political program. Cindy Chavez, for example, who as education and outreach director for the South Bay Labor Council helped develop the Labor/Community Leadership Institute, notes that a majority of the current San Jose City Council members have attended programs at the institute.[26]

Through the nonprofit Building Partnerships USA, Amy Dean and David Reynolds have worked with others to spread the leadership institute model around the country. Building Partnerships has developed a starting curriculum adaptable to local situations. From 2005 to 2007, pilot institutes ran in Denver, Boston, Atlanta, New Haven, and Milwaukee, with other regions in the planning pipeline. Table 4.4 outlines the

TABLE 4.4. Civic Leadership Institute Core Curriculum

Part One: Understanding Our Region
Module One: Understanding the Regional Economy
Module Two: Voices of the Past, Paths for the Future
Module Three: Rebuilding America's Social Contract Region by Region

Part Two: Rebuilding Democratic Institutions
Module Four: Activist Government in a New Economy
Module Five: Using Power Analysis
Module Six: Strengthening Our Democratic Grassroots Institutions
Module Seven: Confirming Our Vision, Planning Next Steps

seven modules that run roughly three hours each. Actual programs vary considerably based on local needs and audience.

The institute's first half encourages participants to see how their neighborhood or industry links to a shared regional experience and structure. The region represents a distinct level at which key economic and political decisions are made. By understanding how the region works and by collectively organizing, participants can have an impact on the future for working families in the general area, and for their constituency in particular.

The first module taps participants' experiences to examine the economic patterns that strain the lives of working families, but with a distinct twist: the module emphasizes regional decisions. Material from local business-oriented employer and civic groups illustrates that in an age of "globalization" regional economies become more, not less, significant. Even those employers whose markets are national or international nevertheless often take regional public policy very seriously.

In the second module, participants examine key past decisions and struggles that have shaped the current course of their region. This scan of history helps participants lay out the basic power structure of their region. With an eye toward building future coalitions, they also examine which grassroots groups have had access to the power structure, which have been closed out, and how such patterns may have weakened potential desired outcomes.

The third module then looks toward forging a new regional calculus by having participants explore the regional power-building strategies profiled in this book. How might such strategies be developed and adapted to a specific region?

Having developed a common "big picture" regional analysis, the curriculum moves in the second half to exploring specific nuts and bolts details.

The fourth and sixth modules focus, in turn, on the two institutions found within our current society most capable of impacting private economic decisions. The fourth module examines the role of regional public policy. Participants examine the powers and limitations of local and regional government, the role of public boards and planning bodies, and the various strategies of grassroots coalitions to get regional public authorities to shape private business decisions.

The sixth module examines the decisive role that unions play in shaping private and public decisions. Through collective bargaining, unions help shape firm decisions, and as membership organizations engaged in political action they offer the single greatest political capacity on the left side of the political spectrum. In both their workplace and political roles unions serve as key champions of community wellbeing. Hearing the stories of local workers who have attempted to organize highlights the importance of working to protect organizing as a basic civil right that is key to the future well-being of the community. In addition to unions, the sixth module also allows participants from other types of groups to talk about their grassroots efforts, challenges, and common cause.

In between, during the fifth module, participants learn how to use the power analysis tool developed by Strategic Concepts in Organizing and Policy Education/Action for Grassroots Empowerment and Neighborhood Development Alternatives in Los Angeles. Using a current or potentially future issue or campaign, participants chart out key decision-making bodies, possible opposition groups, potential allies, and the relative power of each. The tool allows participants to isolate specific strategic needs—whether they be to target specific public bodies, minimize the opposition from certain groups, gain support from others, or develop capacities of key allies.

In the seventh module, participants and institute organizers discuss various plans for the future, depending upon the particular regional situation.

This curriculum provides for an institute program that runs one or two sessions per year. In addition to the subject matter, the institute curriculum offers several other important characteristics. Because the lesson materials are rooted in concrete regional reality, the curriculum includes a clear research agenda. The original San Jose institute was able to foster a new regional understanding because it drew upon groundbreaking research on the regional economy and the public and private power structures done by Working Partnerships USA. The new institutes that are being fostered around the country are similarly rooted in some form of organization with a similar think-and-act capacity.

In addition to providing detailed research, these organizations are critical for maintaining relationships and work among participants both before and after their participation at the institute. People go through the institute not simply to gain knowledge and perspective as an intellectual exercise but to be able to better work together in ways that build collective power over the long term. As with Working Partnerships USA, the convening organizations need the capacity to translate the organizing ideas fostered in the institute into concrete coalition work. Similarly, preparation for the institute does not simply focus on the mechanics of pulling together an education program. Designing an effective institute requires organizers to think about their long-term plan—how the institute fits into a larger picture of regional activism. At the same time, the one-on-one recruiting of participants should prove an involved and prolonged process as the goal is not simply to get people in to a room together but to build a relationship with them by discussing their constituencies' issues and organizational needs, links to regional decisions, and so forth.

The importance of relationship building is reflected in the use of participatory adult-education methods. Initial pilots revealed that the emphasis on detailed information in parts of the original curriculum resulted in institute sessions organized around presentations by academic specialists. Unfortunately, higher education in the United States is a bastion of an obsolete "banking" model of education in which instructors simply transfer knowledge into the blank heads of students, mainly through lectures. For an institute designed to build personal relationships among leaders, the limitations of the banking model are obvious.

Modern progressive teaching methods view learning as a more collaborative process between students and teacher, with emphasis on using students' prior experiences and knowledge. To maximize broad class participation, the institute curriculum was revised to train facilitators to use a wide range of teaching methods (small group discussion, role plays, simulations, videos, partnering, etc.). Carefully chosen short supplemental presentations by guest speakers serve as tools for enhancing class interaction rather than dominating the agenda.

The actual curriculum and timing for launching new institute programs depends upon the potential for ongoing work by the groups being brought together. The Boston institute took one step in fostering a new self-conscious program for building long-term power out of the promising seeds laid by past single-issue coalition experiences. One outcome of the first Boston institute was a new type of coalition between the International Union of Painters and Allied Trades and low-income neighborhood groups. The alliance successfully secured prevailing wages, union apprenticeships, and community first-source hiring for multimillion-dollar local school renovation work. Atlanta's institute program focused on helping leaders, especially at the neighborhood level, increase their capacity by understanding how regional public policy decisions were made, the agenda of the current governing regime, and ways to impact these decisions by mobilizing at the grassroots.

5

From Access to Governance

Building Aggressive Political Action

The political work of regional power building stands out for two distinct characteristics, which are explored in this chapter. First, it aims to build a rich and ongoing capacity to mobilize at the grassroots level both during and between elections. Second, electoral activity closely integrates with regional power building's other two legs to form a larger process aimed at building capacity to govern.

These two characteristics stand in contrast to many of the reforms seen on the liberal-to-left side of the political spectrum over the last two decades. These efforts have taken diverse forms, from organized labor's retooling of its political action since the election of AFL-CIO president John Sweeney, to campaigns such as Barack Obama's 2008 presidential bid, to new organizations such as MoveOn.org, to a wide range of grassroots civic engagement programs. While this general wave of innovation is certainly welcome, we believe that the two distinct characteristics found in regional power building's political work provide key ingredients necessary to move from simply electing and having access to sympathetic officeholders to actually forming part of a governing regime.

The Limits of Actually Existing Electoral "Democracy"

While we will return to the issue of governing later in this chapter, to fully appreciate the significance of regional power building's political work we must start with the limitations of the current electoral process.[1] American electoral democracy operates with a large gap between the formal mechanisms of electoral representation and the actual substance found in the current electoral process. On the one hand, the United States enjoys a broad franchise and a formally open electoral system that permits most adults to run for office. (We should note that the franchise took two centuries of grassroots struggle to broaden from white, male, property-owning voting restrictions common during the nation's founding to the official universal adult suffrage of today.[2]) On the other hand, the actual conduct of elections filters the popular will so as to marginalize the interests of the majority from the actual process of governing. These limits can be summarized as follows:

- *The domination of elections by corporate money.* As elections move from local to national, the levels of funds needed to realistically run for office increase dramatically to the millions required to run for the U.S. Senate or the presidency. Among industrialized democracies, the costs of running American election campaigns are already quite expensive, and they continue to rise far faster than the rate of inflation.[3] The United States stands out for its weak system of public election campaign financing.[4] At the same time, the high costs also reflect our nation's abnormally long election seasons—with the starkest contract being between U.S. presidential campaigns of well over a year and the one- or two-month campaign seasons common in Canada, Europe, and elsewhere. Absent significant grassroots mobilization that can raise significant funds in small amounts, high-cost elections mean candidate reliance on corporate money. According to the Center for Responsive Politics, in 2004 and 2006 business accounted for 74 and 72 percent, respectively, of all campaign contributions. The next strongest group, organized labor, contributed 3 and 4.2 percent.[5]
- *The domination of elections by corporate media.* Media consolidation has meant that most of what Americans can readily see on television, listen to on radio, and read in print is primarily controlled by a handful of large corporations.[6] The dominant treatment of elections by this corporate media is characterized by "horse race" coverage—who is where in the polls, what is this or that campaign's current strategy, and so forth. Media electoral coverage provides very

little actual analysis of what candidates are pledging to do and rarely offers any detail on what experienced candidates may have actually done or how they have voted while in office.

- *The domination of elections by advertising strategies.* Historians have well documented how the rise of modern advertising methods in the late nineteenth century quickly became the dominant tool for elite-funded electoral efforts. Today, the standard campaign model offered by the political consultant industry focuses on image appeal, name recognition, and mudslinging. To put the matter rather crassly, our nation chooses its political representatives much in the same way that it chooses between competing brands of soft drinks or soaps.

- *The dominance of two elite parties.* The American electoral system is distinctly biased toward maintaining dominance by only two political parties—both of which have elite and corporate origins. The mechanisms include the "winner take all in a single district" representation system (as opposed to the proportion representation systems dominant in most of the world), two-party-oriented ballot-access rules, and a corporate media that marginalizes and ignores any serious third party effort.[7]

- *Weak party structures and the dominance of individualized candidacies.* Political parties do not exist in the United States in terms of the classic definition of a party as a coherent and structured grassroots organization. Legally, both the Democratic and Republican Parties exist as fifty state–based entities (both parties' national committees are not executive bodies that organizationally control the state and local parties). The introduction of the primary and caucus system and other reforms at the turn of the twentieth century broke down party organizational authority. Today candidates run for office primarily as individuals with separate campaign organizations. An individual that enjoys substantial private funding and/or grassroots mobilization can become a party's official nominee regardless of the preference of official party leaders or official members. Certainly party structures in the United States do not provide ordinary citizens meaningful channels through which to participate in politics in any organizational way similar to that provided by the grassroots parties developed by the European labor movement (and the U.S. populist and socialist movements) in the late nineteenth and early twentieth centuries.[8]

These five characteristics reflect a form of "filtered democracy" that formally allows democratic participation but substantially limits popular influence in actual practice. The openness of the system is reflected in the ability of grassroots campaigns to elect progressive champions—including sending such figures as Bernie Sanders, Paul Wellstone, and Dennis Ku-cinich to Congress. Yet absent a sustained, long-term, and well-developed organizing strategy that unites America's progressive social movements, the current system guarantees that officeholders mainly reflect strong links to corporate America.

The contradiction between form and practice is reflected in a final characteristic of American politics: the nation's infamously low voter turnout. The United States ranks at the bottom of lists of voter participation among industrial democracies. Despite the upsurge in national turnout from 54 percent in 2000 to 60 percent in 2004, two out of five eligible voters did not participate in this 2004 presidential election year. For off-year elections voter turnout drops to below 40 percent, and for local races the proportions get even lower.[9]

Even among those who vote, enthusiasm for the electoral process is hardly vigorous. As a 1999 Keystone Research Center report on Pennsylvania notes, "'Over half of middle- and low-income Americans believe, "People like me don't have any say about what the government does." Only 30 percent of Americans held this view in the 1960s.'"[10] The typical voting base today has a pronounced white and upper-middle class bias, as shown in table 5.1.[11]

Census data from 1996 have showed that while 73 percent of those in managerial and professional jobs voted, only 43 percent of those employed as operators, fabricators, and laborers did so.[12]

Low voter participation is the natural outcome of a political system dominated by the characteristics explored above. It allows elite rule to hide behind a veil of formal democracy. In a demobilized and cynical electorate, the major parties can compete narrowly on images that do not challenge corporate power or raise questions about the nature of class or race in America. Hearing a debate that seems to have little to do with their reality, many working people simply stay home on Election Day. Those who do vote often do so around motivations other than their core concerns. For example, a 2006 survey of Republican union members identified health care costs, education, jobs, the economy, and taxes as respondents' top concerns. Yet, when asked which party was better on these specific issues, the respondents gave the Democrats only a slight advantage on standing up to big corporations and none on health care or pensions.[13]

Focus group research conducted by David Reynolds of Republican- and independent-registered public employee union members in Michigan

TABLE 5.1. Voter Turnout in 2004, by Selected Criteria

	Voted (%)	Did not vote (%)
Overall	58	42
Family income		
Under $15,000	38	62
$15,000–$29,999	48	52
$30,000–$49,999	58	42
$50,000–$99,999	70	30
$100,000 or more	78	22
Race		
White	66	34
Black	56	44
Hispanic	28	72
Unemployed	46	54
High school education	52	41
Bachelor's degree	72	27

Source: U.S. Census Bureau, *Current Population Survey,* November 2004.
Note: Proportion among those reported voted and did not vote in 2004 November election.

found that these people had the same top concerns as their Democratic-registered counterparts: health care, job security, and pensions. Yet they saw politicians in general as not offering any believable program or message around such concerns. Thus, on Election Day they made their choices based on an assessment of either each candidate's personal character or on what they consciously identified as secondary issues, such as abortion rights or gun control. How many Democratic voters similarly go to the polls not convinced that electoral success will deliver substantive change on their day-to-day concerns? With such distrust found among those who actually do vote, it comes as no surprise that so many Americans simply do not bother. Yet, rather than blaming a small corporate elite for dominating the country, people simply come to see "politics" as inherently distasteful and not worthy of great attention.

The above critique offers important implications for what a successful progressive electoral response must entail. On the one hand, the reality of popular demobilization and alienation from politics, coupled with the formal mechanisms of electoral democracy, means that a movement that finds ways to successfully reengage ordinary citizens in active politics can turn formality into actual governance. In his classic work *The*

Semisovereign People: A Realist's View of Democracy in America, political scientist E. E. Schattschneider wrote, over three decades ago, "Anyone who finds out how to involve the forty million [nonvoters] in American politics will run the country for a generation."[14]

On the other hand, the challenge is much deeper than simply getting out the vote. Indeed, the current political process ensures that most newly mobilized voters will likely lapse back into apathy once the get-out-the-vote campaigns are no longer active. Get-out-the-vote work has to be part of a broader strategy to transform the very nature of the political process so that ordinary people experience something quite different than distrustful "politics." In other words, to mobilize decisive political majorities, organized labor and its allies have to redefine the political process by engaging Americans in a new politics of substance. To do so requires building capacities that organized political parties should offer but in America do not: agenda and policy creation, grassroots alliance building, candidate development, and grassroots voter mobilization structures—in other words, the very elements core to regional power building. None of these capacities can grow from Washington-based political strategies focused solely on national elections that "drop everything" for the next "critical election." Such strategies maintain the image-driven, status quo political process that has already turned off most Americans.

Organized Labor Rethinks Politics

The strengths and limitations of how the labor movement has tried to revamp its political action since the mid-1990s illustrate the gaps in strategy that regional power building can fill. Coming to office in the wake of labor's narrow defeat over the North American Free Trade Agreement and the subsequent Republican takeover of Congress, the new Sweeney administration at the AFL-CIO officially challenged organized labor to rethink labor's electoral politics.

Labor's traditional methods focused on donating money to candidates, informing members of union endorsements (primarily through the mail), and some get-out-the-vote work, mainly through modest volunteer phone banks. The limitation of these traditional methods became clear in the 1980s. Epitomizing the phenomenon of the "Reagan Democrats," union members in heavily working-class Macomb County, Michigan, for example, helped send Ronald Reagan to the presidency either by voting Republican or by not voting at all. Organized labor had politically become increasingly disconnected from the sentiments of a fair number of its members.

The Sweeney administration led a call to shift organized labor's emphasis to place greater weight on issues rather than on individual candidates. Rather than simply telling members who to vote for, labor's election efforts would educate members on working families' issues that made political action important. Organized labor's political action also moved beyond contests for elected office; the labor movement in a growing number of states began going to the ballot box to pass progressive initiatives such as raising the minimum wage. Between elections, the AFL-CIO also led labor mobilizations on substantive fights around raising the minimum wage, blocking free trade agreements, and protecting Social Security.

To varying degrees, many unions and the AFL-CIO also invested in workplace "worker-to-worker" programs and community "labor-neighbor" initiatives. Both represented attempts to revive person-to-person political contacts. Labor also shifted greater resources into election field operations—offering candidates more on-the-ground activism rather than simply donations. The overall resources raised by organized labor for political action also increased substantially.

In California, labor's new political approach was tested in 1998 when a corporate-funded counterattack threatened to disable union political capacity altogether. The Republican creators of Proposition 226 claimed that the measure would give union members greater control over how their unions engaged in politics. In reality, the measure would have required unions to get renewed written permission every year from each member before they could use union dues for any purpose outside of narrow collective bargaining. Proposition 226 would have essentially cut off funds not simply for educating members during elections and for getting out the vote but for union lobbying activity as well.[15]

Backers of Proposition 226 hoped that a win in California would prove a stepping-stone to other states. With millions of corporate dollars flowing into its coffers, the "Yes on 226" committee seemed headed to victory. Just four months before the election, polls showed that 71 percent of union members supported the proposition, with only 26 percent prepared to vote against it. The numbers were far worse among the general public.

The campaign against Proposition 226 witnessed an unprecedented level of labor unity inside California as well as model integration of national labor support with a state-based effort. Labor leaders realized that if they followed conventional political wisdom and focused on the traditional tools of direct mail and advertising, they would be playing on the opposition's ground and likely lose. Instead, they geared up for old-fashioned people-to-people politics. The No on 226 campaign prepared to recruit and train 28,000 union member volunteers. Each union developed its own distinct approach for educating its own membership. Programs varied from twenty to forty minutes in length at work sites to several hours at union halls. For example:

- The Teamsters had member volunteers talk one-on-one with fellow members about why union political action was important, how it worked, and why Proposition 226 was a major threat to them.
- In one county, the American Federation of State, County and Municipal Employees (AFSCME) ran several half-hour sessions at work to discuss the proposition.
- The United Brotherhood of Carpenters and Joiners of America and the International Union of Painters and Allied Trades unions used their apprentice classes to teach about the relation between unions and politics.
- The Sheet Metal Workers International Association used its retirees' council to organize retired workers.
- Most important, throughout the state, individual workers talked to other workers—either at work or by going door-to-door.

While these specific methods may not seem particularly innovative or unique, much of organized labor had not used such extensive member-to-member political contacts in decades. This contact was also supported with mailings and information in union newsletters and other publications. Union activists met with newspaper editorial boards, persuading several major papers to come out against Proposition 226. Volunteers turned out members for rallies at events in which Governor Pete Wilson campaigned in favor of the proposition; reaching out to the community, activists got over one hundred organizations—from the Sierra Club to the Heart and Lung Association to the League of Women Voters—to publicly oppose it. More than forty employers and thirty-two local governments formally expressed their opposition as well.

The election on June 2, 1998, delivered a "political miracle." The returns showed that 71 percent of union members and 53.5 percent of all voters cast their ballot against Proposition 226. Support for the measure dropped 17 points and opposition to it had increased by 28 points in just four months.

The work of David Reynolds with Michigan unions over the past several election cycles is reflective of the California experience as applied to candidate-oriented elections.[16] New political programs have been based upon building workplace volunteer networks of individuals who hand out information and have ongoing conversations with five to fifteen coworkers throughout a campaign season. Rather than "telling members who to vote for" these worker-to-worker programs begin by surveying members about their issue priorities, experiences, and policy preferences on specific issues, as well as preferences on receiving political information. The campaign volunteers then distribute factual and policy information about the top concerns identified through such surveying. Although this material may refer to specific legislative and executive actions, it largely avoids mentioning candidates. As election day nears, these campaigns then distribute candidate comparisons and voting records focused on the issues highlighted by the flyers. In the final weeks, union volunteers ask members to sign pledges to vote. During and after the election campaign members are also asked to register and to donate to union political action funds.

This program goes further in emphasizing issues rather than candidates than most worker-to-worker or labor-to-neighbor efforts. Many union and AFL-CIO "issue flyers" profile an endorsed candidate or give candidate comparisons—although they do so around the substantive concerns expressed by members. All of these programs, however, attempt to mobilize members using an "old style," grassroots, person-to-person politics. In recent election cycles both the AFL-CIO and many unions have put greater staff and other resources into building up such a grassroots capacity.

Labor's grassroots mobilization efforts have delivered measurable results. During the second half of the 1990s, union electoral efforts succeeded in getting an increasing portion of union members to the polls. Despite declining union density in the workplace, union households went from providing 19 percent of all voters in 1992 to 26 percent in 2000. For the 2006 midterm elections, the AFL-CIO claimed that 205,000 union members had knocked on more than 8.25 million doors, made 30 million phone calls, and passed out more than 14 million leaflets at workplaces and in neighborhoods. That year one quarter of the electorate came from union households. Union members voted for labor-endorsed candidates by a margin of 74 percent to 26 percent, compared to a narrow 2-point Democratic margin among nonunion voters.[17]

Labor's increasingly effective electoral operations allowed labor leaders to lay claim to helping stall the "Republican Revolution" and build a Democratic congressional majority. The 2004 presidential election, however, illustrated quite well the limits of labor's electoral program. Despite continued high union member turnout, the 2004 voting pattern did not differ substantially from that of 2000's close race.

Despite notable gains, labor's new electoral politics continues to suffer significant limitations. It remains essentially an election-by-election strategy. Issue mobilizations (such as those around the minimum wage) remain isolated and separated from election efforts. Labor's concerted electoral work also remains focused mainly on national elections, and secondarily on state elections. Local elections—often out of sync with national election cycles—receive little coordinated attention. National labor leaders tend to view grassroots political mobilization primarily as a vehicle for pushing national priorities, not as a central mechanism for growing a progressive future through regional work to build coalitions, policy agendas, and governing capacity.

This election-by-election and national focus makes labor's political efforts highly episodic. Much of the mobilization structure created during an election season—with substantial amounts of labor movement money—does not continue after an election. This is especially true of political operations that "parachute" staff from other regions into battleground areas. Within unions, worker-to-worker volunteer structures are typically thought about and organized separately from other union activity. Rare is the union that translates its electoral volunteer networks into either active local elections or contract campaigns or similar workplace actions. Despite continued talk of the need "to keep things going after the election," labor's political capacity tends to disappear until the next national or major state election. These limitations are exacerbated by the "drop everything" approach in which the next election is always seen as the critical election and resources that could go to patient long-term capacity building get consumed in a flurry of short-term activity.

Finally, despite concerted efforts to focus on issues, labor's political strategy remains candidate-centered and candidate-dependent. While issue information can help union members and the broader community to distinguish between greater and lesser evils, there is no guarantee that labor-endorsed candidates actually champion labor's agenda. For example, when campaigning in Florida in 2004, John Kerry said little about the minimum wage proposal on the ballot in that state—even though it was so popular that it passed with a 70 percent vote. Labor's work to develop an autonomous election mobilization capacity has thus far not been accompanied with a corresponding ability to place an independent agenda into the public debate or develop a full cadre of candidates to champion such an agenda.

The 2005 split within the AFL-CIO did little to change these limitations. The "change to win" unions argued for organized labor to exercise greater political independence. However, as long as union political action remains geared toward individual elections and primarily focused on national contests, this call means very little in terms of actual practice. Without an ongoing program to develop a concrete operational agenda, and candidates who will run on that agenda, organized labor will continue to have to support lesser evils. Organized labor and progressives more generally are not simply "one election away" from changing the country—regardless of the Democratic gains of 2008. Building real national power requires a significant long-term investment in ongoing capacity at the grassroots level.

Establishing Aggressive Regional Political Action

The tools used for aggressive political action are not unique to regional power building but have provided a repertoire available to grassroots groups for decades. Some, such as building regional endorsement unity among union affiliates, have served as ideals that nevertheless prove difficult to sustain in practice. Within the regional power-building model, leaders who pursue aggressive political action aim to establish such ingredients in a manner that accomplishes two goals. First, the tools represent a systematic and lasting regional capacity for political work. Second, electoral action becomes fully integrated into the larger agenda for building regional power. In this section we examine the first goal before turning to the question of integration at the end of the chapter.

Building Political Unity among Unions

Simply examining national general elections may leave the impression of great political unity among organized labor—after all, how often do unions endorse Republicans for national office? Yet a look into the primary season reveals a far more complicated picture and much less unity. Labor fragmentation can be even more visible in local politics. Most local contests are nonpartisan, and thus do not involve clear party divisions. In other cases, one party so predominates within a municipality that the primary is the most significant election.

Traditional insider access–oriented politics also encourages fragmentation, as individual unions are concerned less with overall policy direction or ideology than with specific concessions from elected officials. Public sector unions, for example, seek bargaining rights and contract bargaining help. Building trades seek prevailing wage requirements on public-funded construction.

Individual unions build relationships with specific officeholders who may not prove particularly good for broader progressive or labor politics but may deliver on specific actions. When faced with a progressive challenger, these unions may resist cutting ties with someone known to deliver on their immediate concerns, even to elect someone who might be a better choice overall. Unions may also make different endorsements based on varying assessments of each candidate's chances for winning.

Political divisions among organized labor have often led to electoral loss. Colorado's story of Democrats taking control of one house in the state legislature in 2000, only to lose control in 2002, and to then take both houses in 2004 reflects a story of political unity, then division, then unity in the state's labor movement.

Electoral unity goes beyond simply endorsing the same candidates, however. Endorsing an individual is one matter; mobilizing serious resources in support of their campaign is another. Because of limited resources, labor and its allies' electoral efforts need to target specific races and specific communities. However, unions in a region may disagree on electoral priorities.

Our nation's candidate-centered politics encourages fragmentation of electoral work as unions plug into separate candidate campaigns.

Even when the labor movement achieves relative internal unity, divisive forces may put it at odds with allied progressive groups. For example, having helped build Antonio Villaraigosa's political career and having campaigned strenuously for his candidacy for mayor in 2001, most of labor in Los Angeles backed incumbent mayor James Hahn in 2005. Unlike Villaraigosa, Hahn did not champion a progressive shift in city policies. However, Hahn had reached out to connect with unions on a series of specific labor concerns and had the electoral advantages of an incumbent. Ironically, Villaraigosa beat Hahn by building on the political grassroots foundations labor had established over the preceding years, including the voter mobilization of the Alliance of Local Leaders for Education, Registration and Turnout in South Los Angeles (detailed later in this chapter).

Seeking a clear mechanism for building political unity among unions and for connecting labor's politics to community allies involves first strengthening an existing institution. In theory, central labor councils provide the cross-union vehicle through which local unions come together, endorse candidates, and decide on which races and communities to target. In reality, individual unions often jealously guard their resources for political operations almost as much as their organizing programs. Thus, establishing a central labor council or area federation as the true leader of a politically coherent regional labor movement typically represents a major accomplishment.

The Cleveland AFL-CIO's revamping of its political program under John Ryan illustrates how a central labor council can nurture labor unity in the political arena. Through many one-on-one discussions with affiliate leaders, the federation persuaded affiliate locals to assign a political coordinator to work with the group. The political coordinators work together to make endorsement and targeting decisions, and then go back to "sell" those decisions to their members in each local.

The coordinators have worked to get rank-and-file union members involved in various ways. For example, the Cleveland AFL-CIO has helped set up meetings between elected representatives and rank-and-file union members in their home districts. These gatherings have given the members confidence to speak up about their issues, and let them see that public officials are not so different from themselves, perhaps even helping the members consider running for office themselves someday. It also helps show the representatives the "real face" of labor: They hear directly from union members rather than a paid political lobbyist.

The South Bay Labor Council (SBLC) in San Jose, California, has also succeeded over time in establishing a unified candidate-endorsement process. While individual unions may enter the process with disagreements, rarely do locals break ranks with the final decision. This basic endorsement unity provides the foundation for building an overall unity in grassroots civic engagement operations. Today, the labor council can, for several weeks, coordinate up to forty affiliate staff members whose union work would traditionally have been done independently. Affiliates have bought into the council-led program, in part because the electoral work is integrated into a broader plan to build labor and community power in the region—and thus offers compelling potential long-term gains in the fortunes of the area's labor movement.

Building Unified Field Operations

Getting unions to fully coordinate around candidate endorsements and electoral targeting represents an important first step. Regional power building, however, requires that organized labor go beyond common endorsements to develop a capacity for coordinated grassroots field operations for electoral mobilization. This requires union locals to share lost-timers—members who are put on union leave for union work—with the coordinating central labor body.

Traditionally, each union places this central resource of union political action—as well as member volunteers—under the direction of the union's local or regional political staff. To maximize labor's political strength, however, power-building central labor councils must seek a more involved role in directing this resource. The Denver Area Labor Federation's work provides a good illustration of how greater shared control by the labor council helped build labor's overall political strength. Starting in 1998, DALF asked its affiliates to participate in a "lost-time program" in which participating affiliates have members work on election campaigns under the direction and leadership of DALF. This program put DALF at the center of the campaigns, with staff and rank-and-file activists taking direction from and reporting to the labor movement as a whole rather than the political candidate for each campaign.

The new political program has developed through a mix of local and state elections. At the local level, in 1999, DALF led a successful effort that resulted in two new school board members. These individuals helped convince other board members to recognize the right of district service employees to form a union and, in the spring of 2000, 125 part-time custodians joined the Communication Workers of America. In early 2003, the federation held a strategic planning session that included community allies with affiliate leaders to plan for the May primaries and June city elections. In the end, five of six DALF-supported candidates won city council office seats. However, the DALF-endorsed mayoral candidate, Don Mares, lost in a landslide to rival John Hickenlooper amid a split within the ranks of labor. While the building trades and other unions came out as strong Mares supporters, Hickenlooper had won endorsements from the police, sheriff, and firefighters unions.

The Denver case illustrates in a particularly clear way the implications of regional work for state governing power. Indeed, local political work in Denver is intertwined with battles over the state's balance of power. Of Colorado's 4.7 million residents, over 2 million live in the greater Denver area. One-half of Denver's voters are registered as Democratic, compared to one-third statewide. The first test of DALF's new political program came in a state, not local contest—the narrow loss of the DALF-supported candidate for governor in 1998. Denver area political mobilization made the difference, however, in 2000 when the Democrats took control of the state senate for the first time in twenty-four years. Six of the seven seats targeted by the labor movement statewide were in the metropolitan Denver area. In all of these districts, Republican and independent voters outnumbered Democrats. Using lost-timers, DALF ran a major voter registration, education, and get-out-the-vote program targeting union households. More than seven thousand voters were registered, and exit polling revealed that 80 percent of union Republicans swung their vote on the state senate candidate. Labor disunity two years later contributed to the loss of this majority. In 2004, however, a more unified labor-community mobilization produced dramatic electoral success, with the Democrats taking full control of the state legislature for the first time in forty years as well as winning two previously Republican U.S. House and Senate seats.

This series of contests for state office witnessed the Colorado AFL-CIO progressively taking over leadership and coordination of the political capacity first grown by DALF. With Colorado having been turned into contested terrain, in 2004 the Colorado AFL-CIO could bring together the Coalition for a Better Colorado—a tax-exempt 527 organization that linked organized labor into a coalition with trial lawyers, environmentalists, NARAL Pro-Choice America, and a handful of liberal millionaires to eventually raise $1.6 million. (Tax-exempt 527 political groups conduct "issue advocacy" as apposed to directly working for the election or defeat of a specific candidate; as the infamous example of the Swift Boat Veterans for Truth in 2004 demonstrates, the line between advocacy and working for or against specific candidates is a subject of sharp debate.) As DALF leaders well understood, the 2004 electoral shift represented the beginning rather than the end of building real power within the state.[18] Following the 2004 victory, DALF leaders began discussing the kind of precinct-mobilization structures built in Los Angeles to develop cadres of union members able to act as neighborhood leaders who could mobilize residents to hold city and state elected officials accountable.

Precinct-Level Organization

The U.S. Congress vote to formally abolish "soft money" contributions to political parties has encouraged the explosion of 527-based "independent expenditure" campaigns. The Organization of Los Angeles Workers, detailed in the last chapter, offers one example of how regional power-building leaders can use such expenditures to build long-lasting grassroots organization. The Alliance of Local Leaders for Education, Registration, and Turnout (ALLERT) in South Los Angeles offers another.[19] ALLERT illustrates the difference between the single-shot election efforts often pursued by organized labor and other liberal-progressive groups and projects that build lasting grassroots power.

South Los Angeles is crucial for progressive politics in the city. In an urban region at risk for African American–Latino tension, the historically African American area has become racially mixed. South Los Angeles has the highest concentration of union members. It also offers a potentially large block of voters who tend to be sympathetic to a progressive agenda.

ALLERT's immediate goal, like that of many other independent expenditure projects, is to increase voter registration and turnout in a targeted part of the city. But ALLERT differs from many such efforts both because it is rooted in local organizations and because it aims to build permanent grassroots capacity over time. ALLERT's core partners are all membership-based organizations:

- The anchor, Strategic Concepts in Organizing and Policy Education (SCOPE) and its Action for Grassroots Empowerment and Neighborhood Development Alternatives (AGENDA), were established in 1992 following the Los Angeles riots. SCOPE/AGENDA addresses the problems of poverty and underdevelopment in the inner-city communities of South Los Angeles by increasing residents' capacity to impact public decision making.
- The Community Coalition was formed in 1990 to attack the drug problem through community organizing strategies framed by broad social justice concerns. The coalition network's social service providers maintain an active land use committee that organizes against liquor stores and seedy establishments, and provides support for caregivers of children who have lost their parents to drugs or prison. The organization also trains and organizes students and parents to fight for school reform.
- Service Employees International Union (SEIU) Locals 99, 434B, and 1877 represent school employees, long-term care workers, and building services employees, respectively. Their combined membership reaches in the hundreds of thousands in the greater Los Angeles area and elsewhere.
- In addition to these core partners, ALLERT also involves many area churches in its precinct structure.

Financial contributions from unions and foundations help maintain an office with one staff member, while each partner organization also contributes staffing for specific mobilizations. ALLERT's central resource, however, is the precinct-level team. All partners feed their membership lists into a common database that literally produces color-coded maps of South Los Angeles, plotting out this membership.

These data allow ALLERT to form teams mixing union and community organization members who sign precinct captain pledges and who go through a systematic training program. Where possible, the teams are multiracial. Ideally people walk their own precincts, but they may be assigned to other precincts within an area. The key is not simply that volunteers knock on the targeted doors of nonvoters or occasional voters but that they develop relationships with these local residents. This face-to-face work also allows activists to recruit new volunteers. Phone banks supplement the door-to-door contact.

Unlike single-election efforts, ALLERT builds its grassroots structure over the course of many elections. Adding local candidate elections and ballot measures to the mix presents the project with continual opportunities to mobilize each year. The first six elections that ALLERT organized around occurred in the span of only two years, from July 2002 to March 2004. Two involved Los Angeles City Council races, one a state assembly seat, and the other two the San Fernando Valley secession vote.

ALLERT did not always mobilize in the same parts of South Los Angeles for each election. Indeed, because it is a locally rooted long-term project, ALLERT is able to target different precincts based not only upon the immediate election but also on the logic of building grassroots structure over time. ALLERT's capacity and reach has expanded with each election. For its first effort in 2002, the project covered 113 precincts and contacted 5,532 voters. For the March 2004 primary election it covered 227 precincts and 38,198 voters. During the six mobilizations that span these elections, ALLERT contacted 97,170 voters.

The outreach numbers are precise because ALLERT uses state-of-the art technology—including barcodes on outreach sheets—to record and process each interaction. When combined with mapping technology to identify precinct volunteers, union and community members, and voters and nonvoters, ALLERT is able to organize at a highly sophisticated level.

The 2005 mayoral race won by Antonio Villaraigosa dramatically illustrates ALLERT's accomplishments. This was also the election in which organized labor faced four antiunion state ballot measures promoted by Governor Arnold Schwarzenegger. In 2001, James Hahn beat Villaraigosa by combining white and black support. South Los Angeles was crucial to his win, with roughly two-thirds of voters going his way. The 2005 race tested ALLERT's efforts to build African American and Latino unity. Six hundred volunteers either walked precincts or worked phone banks. They made 71,957 contacts in an election that would see just under half a million voters in the city. In contrast to 2001, South Los Angeles became contested terrain that ultimately produced a majority for Villaraigosa. Election data revealed that turnout among occasional voters was 10.5 percent higher among those contacted by ALLERT than those who were not. New voter turnout was 15 percent higher among those ALLERT had identified and followed up with. While Los Angeles County voted down Measure 75 (to limit political action by public employee unions) by 62 percent, 88 percent of South Los Angeles voted against the unsuccessful proposal.

ALLERT's data go far beyond election-day voter turnout. It has established a database of nearly 150,000 residents educated on the social justice issues key to the core partners. These residents can be mobilized to back public policy reforms and hold officeholders accountable to community concerns.

This electoral organizing also benefits partner organizations directly. Both AGENDA/SCOPE and the Community Coalition have gained participants and members in their programs. SEIU Local 1877, famous for its Justice for Janitors organizing, furthers the connections between its members and the community. Through ALLERT, the school employee members of SEIU Local 99 team up with members of the Community Coalition, which mobilizes school students and parents. Because much of the long-term care work done by its members is in people's homes, SEIU 434B cannot build obvious workplace structures—but ALLERT neighborhood organizing provides a way for the local to activate its members and develop their leadership skills.

There is a lesson in the ALLERT experience even for unions whose members are better concentrated at specific work sites. Because of suburban sprawl and long-distance commuting, attempts by individual unions to mobilize their members as community activists risk suffering dispersal over a wide geographic area. "Labor-neighbor" work is far more effective when organized at a cross-union level.

We should note that these regional grassroots mobilization structures parallel the recent launch and growth of Working America. This new affiliate of the AFL-CIO provides a way for workers who do not have a union at work to join the American labor movement and become involved in labor's political work. Currently active in ten states, Working America uses paid canvassers to knock on targeted nonunion doors in low- and middle-income neighborhoods in both cities and suburbs. The canvassers talk to people about substantive issues—such as rising health care costs or raising the minimum wage—and connect these discussions to concrete upcoming elections, ballot initiatives, worker organizing support, or other grassroots work in the area. According to organizers, canvassers typically talk to between thirty and forty people a night with at least two-thirds of these formally becoming Working America members. Already two million strong in early 2008, the organization anticipated growing to three or four million by the end of that year.[20] The organization's basic goal of building long-term organization that combines electoral, lobbying, and grassroots support work runs parallel to our discussion of regional power building. Indeed, regional Working America chapters are natural allies for regional power-building programs.

Developing Candidates and Holding Them Accountable

When the AFL-CIO called for 2,000 union members to run for public office by the year 2000, the Sweeney administration highlighted the importance for labor of playing a more active role in developing candidates. Traditional postwar labor politics relied on the political system to generate candidates—the labor movement then selected from among this pool whom to endorse in primaries and general elections. This passive approach often leaves organized labor and other progressive groups having to choose between lesser evils.

The existing political system does not naturally generate strong labor champions. Because of the time and financial resources demanded by our nation's candidate-centered election campaigns, the mainstream political system tends to produce candidates who are upscale in their personal backgrounds and their lists of key supporters.

Fostering the political careers of existing progressive candidates and developing pools of new ones poses a set of tasks best organized by a regional labor body such as a central labor council or area labor federation. Since electoral politics is geographically based, a systematic approach to candidate development must be similarly rooted in geographical organization. When regional labor bodies pursue regional power building strategies, their candidate work becomes rooted in long-term plans that allow leaders to target specific individuals and to work with officeholders in systematic ways.

Candidate development presents an ongoing set of tasks that further highlights the limitations of organized labor's current election-by-election focus. By contrast, regional power-building work provides the necessary continuous election, coalition, and policy organizing that allows labor and its allies to develop and interact with existing and would-be candidates on a regular basis.

The power-building work that we have described in this and previous chapters feeds into candidate development. When existing candidates and officeholders participate in civic leadership institutes they are exposed to a progressive regional vision and develop direct relationships with leaders of a regional movement. At the same time, the institutes foster new candidates by not only exposing participants to a vision of regional change but also highlighting the role and functions of public bodies in establishing that future. The field operations and precinct networks described in this chapter provide the basic electoral muscle that frees progressive candidates from having to build a grassroots effort from scratch. These volunteer and lost-timer pools also provide another recruiting ground for would-be candidates. More generally, when a regional labor body plays a leadership role in power building, it is likely to develop the long-term vision and planning that allow for a strategic approach to targeting and developing candidates.

Labor councils that have shifted to regional power-building strategies typically reconsider labor's formal candidate endorsement process. Generally, labor councils and individual unions have relied on candidate questionnaires, often followed by in-person interviews, as the main mechanisms to use in preparing for an official endorsement vote. Power-building labor bodies have instead demanded that candidates sign onto a more specific governing agenda.

In Cleveland, for example, the Cleveland AFL-CIO asked candidates for the 2001 city council race to endorse their Workers' Bill of Rights, which included the right to organize, keeping public services public, and supporting schools and health care. The council endorsed twenty candidates who signed the pledge, eighteen of whom won. Similarly, because of long-term policy work by Working Partnerships USA and the electoral targeting of the SBLC, organized labor in San Jose is able to make endorsements around very concrete policy criteria.

The endorsement process can also serve as a vehicle for candidate education. Several councils require candidates to go through a process in which they learn about key working family issues. For the 2001 local elections in Cleveland, for example, the Cleveland AFL-CIO invited all ten mayoral candidates to attend a Listen Up Forum. Instead of giving stump speeches, candidates listened to union members speak about their issues. The federation worked to get every local to select a member to speak. For example, SEIU 47 had a health care worker talk about health care issues and hospital closures. The mayoral candidates had to listen to the testimonies, and then had two minutes each to respond to the issues by saying what they would do if elected. The affiliate political coordinators did turnout work to make sure their members were in the audience.

Another weakness in traditional labor and progressive politics is the lack of candidate accountability. Having worked to elect good candidates, organized labor and its allies often ask very little in return. As one long-time labor activist put it, many Democratic candidates think in terms of the "one thing" that they need to do for labor in return for labor's electoral support. Certainly few candidates win election with a concrete sense of governing from a systematic labor and progressive perspective. Weak accountability results in part from the failure of traditional election-by-election strategies to build significant ongoing grassroots capacity. Structures with that capacity are needed to mobilize around policy battles that hold office-holders true to election campaign promises.

As we argued in chapter 1, business interests don't simply help individuals win elected office; they also help them govern once in power. Traditional labor and progressive political action, however, has simply sought to win elections rather than govern. Thus, while labor and its allies have developed a capacity to get out the vote, they have rarely articulated a concrete policy agenda, particularly at the local level. Even when they have general ideas on policy reforms, they rarely have the capacity to support that agenda with detailed research, coalition support, and mobilizations for both passage and enforcement.

Thus, policy capacity and deep coalition building are critical for holding candidates accountable once they are elected. The field operations and precinct networks that we have described in this chapter also provide a direct capacity to hold officeholders accountable. Unlike the episodic structures built around national election cycles, this work is rooted at the local level in structures that do not disappear after an election. Thus, activists can mobilize grassroots capacity to demand accountability as officeholders face concrete and crucial policy decisions.

When they are based in permanent regional structures, political operations can also enhance accountability by more actively networking officeholders. The New Right invested heavily in networks that connecteu their state and local champions. Regional power building can do the same. For example, the SBLC is able to draw on the expertise of Working Partnerships USA to hold ongoing public policy education sessions for friendly officeholders. Politicians appreciate the respectful treatment they receive as well as the information shared. This "soft" way of holding candidates accountable helps build strong ongoing relationships and has formed a centerpiece of the council's political program.

The Central Role of Central Labor Councils

In discussing the other two legs of regional power building we pointed to key institutional innovations—the "think-and-act-tank" and the civic leadership institute—that can provide early anchors for building that leg. For aggressive political action, however, the base institutional need lies not in a new creation but in the revival of an existing one: the central labor council (or in some cases, the area labor federation). The natural expression of unionized labor's greater political unity and joint mobilization is leadership by such a body. The examples of seeming exceptions to this experience in fact reinforce the claim. In Los Angeles, ALLERT, for instance, was founded by a coalition of key community and union organizations. The Los Angeles Alliance for a New Economy also grew independently of the Los Angeles County Federation of Labor. But it would be hard to imagine the synergies of work that have propelled power building in the Los Angeles area without the electoral and coalition work led by the labor federation.

Power-building work in New Haven, Connecticut, has developed without a labor council playing a lead role. However, the metropolitan area is relatively small compared to our other cases and activism has enjoyed the target presented by Yale University as a single dominant employer. These conditions meant that political engagement by the Yale unions, as the unions with the greatest capacity in the region, could provide a meaningful third leg around which to pursue a holistic power-building program. Nevertheless, as the regional work continues to develop, power building leaders have looked toward ways to expand the cross-union electoral component through the creation of a 501(c)4 political arm.

Buffalo, New York, demonstrates the limitations of power-building work when a cross-union aggressive political action program has not developed. Buffalo regional labor and community leaders have developed quite innovative programs to reframe the practice of regional economic development and to grow grassroots labor-community coalitions. However, as these programs emerged, the Buffalo AFL-CIO Council and its electoral activity remained quite traditional and relatively weak. Thus, the emerging agendas of high-road development and shared community well-being represent a parallel vision that does not enjoy strong reflection in the halls of elected government. The development of a better-resourced area labor federation in Buffalo—coming out of the state's pioneering New Alliance process (see chapter 7)—therefore hold great promise to address a central gap in regional work.

Preparing for Governance

Regional power building has to create a political movement whose hopes reach beyond placing people in office. As we drew out of our discussion of regime theory in chapter 1, no matter how dedicated or talented the candidate, elected officials are ultimately limited in their ability to enact real change without the organized initiative, support, and accountability demanded by a vibrant and well-organized community. Aggressive political action thus must foster and elect candidates who see their central task as helping to build such an organized community. Ultimately it is the integration of electoral action into a broader program for transforming a region that makes regional power building's political work distinct.

Growing electoral capacity combines with vision building, agenda setting, policy activism, leadership development, and coalition building. Are emerging alternative regional development principles reflected in the candidate selection criteria used by organized labor and other groups? Progressive candidates should expect to govern from the perspective of a broad reform agenda shared by the coalition that helped place them in office. Are potential candidates and officeholders participants in regional leadership development programs? Power building must educate those in elective office to see building such grassroots institutions as core power-building partners as the basic mortar for implementing any kind of serious regional change. Unless union members and others who are mobilized for political campaigns are offered significant long-term changes, the results of their one-shot participation in electoral action will only be long-term disillusionment.

Regional power building ultimately aims to establish a labor-community movement that becomes part of the mainstream. By this we mean that unions, activist groups, elected champions, and progressive reform ideas should be seen by society as familiar elements in the region's daily community and political life. Regional progressive players cannot simply win specific elections or policy reforms but must come to be seen as part of the region's governing fabric. Growing and strengthening such grassroots institutions become a core way to strengthen a region's quality of life.

The Spread of Regional Power Building

6

Understanding the Spread
of Regional Power Building
across the Country

As the regional power-building model emerged within California, would-be organizers elsewhere in the country faced the skepticism of those who argued, "Yes, but that's California." That today we can identify regional power-building projects underway or being attempted in diverse parts of the country demonstrates that the basic model does not depend on conditions particular to one state.[1] Yet, the full-blown model has not emerged from every promising attempt. What can relative success and failure tell us about the conditions necessary to put the model into action? Given these conditions, what can strategic players at the national level do to best foster successful regional power-building programs? This chapter addresses the former question; chapter 7 will take up the latter.

Conditions Fostering Regional Power-Building Work

Four factors appear to be critical in shaping the ability of organizers to successfully pursue regional power-building work: labor leadership, foundation support, peer-to-peer support and regional economic conditions. After introducing each condition we will then explore how they have played out in six regions where leaders have attempted to put into place long-term strategies for building power.

1. *The Emergence of Labor Movement Institutional Leaders.* Every case of active regional power building has grown from central leadership provided by some institution of organized labor. Either a transformed labor council provides leadership, or a partnership among one or more unions with active organizing strategies helps launch the regional work. We are not arguing that community partners are unimportant, but institutional leadership within organized labor is necessary for the regional power-building model to take root. In regions where such labor leadership is not available, regional power building has simply not emerged. There is no example of a regional power-building program that is led only by community players. Despite its decline, organized labor remains the grassroots civic institution with by far the most extensive membership, resource base, and political operations.

2. *Foundation Support.* Because regional power building seeks to intervene in and shape regional economic development decisions the model requires an institutional capacity to engage in focused regional research, creative policy creation, progressive regional leadership development, and staff-supported coalition building. These needs have necessitated the founding of nonprofit organizations like the Los Angeles Alliance for a New Economy (LAANE) and Working Partnerships USA. In smaller regions, budget figures of $100,000–200,000 can support two to four staff members and a viable program. For larger regions, such staffing represents starting levels that must grow. At the top level, such groups as LAANE or Working Partnerships USA have budgets that involve millions of dollars supporting dozens of staffers. All such institutions have relied mainly on foundations for their finances. Regional leaders who cannot raise money to support these necessary institutions will be limited in their ability to pursue the full regional power-building model.

3. *Established Models and the Availability of Peer-to-Peer Support.* Creating innovative strategies from scratch is obviously more difficult than adapting an already established experience to local conditions. In California, regional power building emerged in San Diego and the East Bay Area

in emulation of the pioneering work done in Los Angeles and Silicon Valley. The pioneers provided not only an example but also very direct technical support. The existence of four active regional power-building projects fostered interest elsewhere in the state. The California experiences have in turn provided the model referenced by efforts undertaken elsewhere in the country. The availability of established models and growing peer-to-peer support means that timing is likely to be an important factor as regional projects benefit from what came before.

4. *Regional Economic Conditions.* Emerging first in California, the regional power-building model developed within relatively vibrant economic conditions. Thus, the core strategies focused on steering existing economic growth in more socially and environmentally sustainable directions by redefining regional public policy debates and building capacity among unions and other key grassroots institutions. But what if a region has far less growth? Can power building develop in regions with stagnant or declining economies? Certainly, the policy challenge is much greater as regional organizers need to address more direct strategies for fostering economic growth and/or steer limited economic activity in ways that have to fend off accusations that their regional reforms jeopardize business investment.

The economic context is a far more objective condition that would-be regional power-building leaders have far less control over than the other three, which are more subject to decisions made by actors at the regional, state, and national levels. For this reason we organize our six cases below into two categories. First, we examine the play of the first three factors in the success or weakness of regional work launched in economies with strong economic growth. We will then turn to three regional power-building work attempts in the Rust Belt section of the country in order to take up the question of whether or not the differing economic conditions proved decisive.

Regional Power Building in Growth Economies

Denver, Atlanta, and Seattle offer examples of three efforts to organize regional work in growing economic conditions. Atlanta's economy is representative of corporate investment in the New South. The region boasts the headquarters of fourteen Fortune 500 companies, placing it behind only New York and Houston in this measure of corporate concentration. Already the ninth largest metropolitan region in the United States, the metropolitan area of Atlanta is expected to add another two million people by 2030.[2]

Seattle has successfully promoted itself as a hub of tourism, conventions, logistics, and high technology. The labor force in the Seattle area grew from 1.22 million in 1994 to 1.45 million by 2005, despite the burst of the information technology bubble and the post-9/11 crisis at Boeing and in the hospitality industry.[3]

Denver has been described as a classic growth city with a diversified economy that boasts a higher-than-average portion of professional and managerial jobs. While the regional economy has been impacted by boom and bust cycles over the last several decades, overall the area has grown both economically and demographically. Indeed, the region's population increased by an explosive 49 percent between 1970 and 1990.[4]

All three cases reflect a labor council–led path, yet the context differs among the three cases. Seattle's work occurred in a state with higher union density than California (21 percent compared with 16 percent). Drawing from an affiliate membership base of roughly 150,000, Seattle's King County Labor Council had five staff members in 2005. By contrast, Denver and Atlanta take place in low-density states (9 percent and 7 percent, respectively).[5] Georgia is a right-to-work state while Colorado is a "modified" right-to-work state.[6] The Denver Area Labor Federation drew upon just over 50,000 union members in 2003 and had only two full-time, non-office staffers. Roughly half of the union locals in the Denver area have no full-time staff at all. The Atlanta–North Georgia Labor Council was better positioned at roughly 100,000 affiliate members—one-third of all union members in the state.

Denver

The work begun in metropolitan Denver in the late 1990s represents an early effort to adapt the California model—that of San Jose, in particular—to local conditions.[7] Since we have explored many of the particulars of this work elsewhere in the book, here we will mainly fill in the context. The

Denver Area Labor Federation (DALF) had not been known as a strong activist organization. However, in 1998, a group of reform-minded union leaders, many of whom had been involved in building Jobs with Justice (JwJ) in Colorado, decided to support JwJ staff person Leslie Moody and a reform slate for leadership positions at the federation.[8] Moody had first come to Colorado to work for the Center for Third World Organizing. Under her leadership, Jobs with Justice played a large role in the local Justice for Janitors campaign, hosted Union Summer (a program through which students worked on union campaigns) for two years, built support for the United Farm Worker (UFW) strawberry boycott campaign, and raised funds and awareness around the Detroit newspaper strike, the A. E. Staley strike, and other labor battles with national reach.

In a region with a sparse infrastructure of local progressive groups, a failed 1996 ballot initiative to set a local minimum wage had brought DALF reformers into partnership with the Denver branch of the Association of Community Organizations for Reform Now (ACORN) and several other groups. DALF, ACORN, Communications Workers of America Local 7777, Service Employees International Union (SEIU) Local 105, 9to5 (aka the National Association for Working Women), and several area clergy would go on to spearhead a living wage campaign that secured a Denver ordinance in 2000.[9]

Drawing on direct technical support from the California pioneers, the launch of regional power building in Denver followed the basic model. The DALF established a research, policy development, and coalition support capacity when it founded the Front Range Economic Strategy Center (FRESC) in 2001. In three years, this nonprofit organization grew from one to six staff members and a budget of $450,000 by drawing on a mix of funds that included many of the same national foundations that support the California work; several regional foundations; and contributions from local unions.[10]

In 2003, FRESC and DALF established the Campaign for Responsible Development (CRD). FRESC and DALF targeted the redevelopment of the former Gates Rubber Factory to provide a model for future large public-subsidized projects in Colorado. Building on the Gates win, by 2007 the campaign had taken up two new site-based fights: a community benefits agreement for Denver's Union Station redevelopment and a fight against a rash of evictions involving properties near the new football stadium and along a planned light rail system on Denver's west side. For this later effort, FRESC and DALF teamed up with neighborhood, church, and after-school organizations that participate in the Annie E. Casey Foundation's Strengthening Neighborhoods initiative to fight for affordable housing.

In 2006, Denver become one of three pilot sites chosen by Building Partnerships USA to launch a civic leadership institute modeled after the program in Silicon Valley with FRESC providing the organizing anchor. As detailed in chapter 5, over time DALF has been able to build from its core affiliate supporters a central role for itself in coordinating a more aggressive labor-based political action program that has impacted both regional and state politics. Given that DALF has limited staffing, these electoral efforts would not have been possible without key affiliates internalizing the DALF-led program into their core activities and planning.

Denver regional activism shows our four factors in play. Leadership for regional power building did not simply come from a handful of new labor council leaders isolated from the rest of the labor movement. On the contrary, building power depended upon a coalition of affiliates that saw regional work as part of their core activities. This coalition proved sufficient to establish a viable regional program despite the small size of the area's labor movement and the traditional backwater status of Colorado on the national labor scene. The example of established programs in California helped Denver area leaders articulate what they were attempting to do while also drawing very direct technical support from peer institutions. Although in a state hardly seen as a central location for labor or progressive revival, the California experience had encouraged several national foundations to look toward funding experiments elsewhere. The conservative state's regional economic growth and a relatively close statewide balance of power recommended it as a site of strategic investment.

Atlanta

As the most conservative section of the country, the South is an obvious choice for strategic investment by labor and foundation circles. The Atlanta–North Georgia Labor Council had already established itself as an activist council even before the regional model fully emerged in California.[11] For example, under then president Stewart Acuff, in 1996 the council organized a multiracial coalition to demand union construction work with training and jobs for local residents from the privately funded Atlanta Olympic Games. The coalition represented a deliberate labor effort to connect with the rich legacy and grassroots infrastructure left in the wake of the city's civil rights years. Yet, as with so much labor-community cooperation that typically does not last past the effort at hand, the Olympic coalition did not produce an ongoing labor-community strategy for steering the region's growth or ongoing and expanding job opportunities for the city's low-income communities.[12]

The rapid development of a more holistic power-building strategy after the turn of the millennium reflected the influence of peer-to-peer support as well as fortunate timing. When council head Charlie Fleming took over from Acuff in 2000, he knew about regional power-building experiences through his participation on the AFL-CIO's national Central Labor Council advisory board. He could draw on seasoned national support players including AFL-CIO field mobilization staff, the Partnership for Working Families, and Building Partnerships USA. Cathy Howell, a deputy director for the AFL-CIO Southern Region, explains the connections:

> We were looking at South Florida, Houston, and Atlanta as possibilities [for investing national AFL-CIO support resources]. John Goldstein, then President of the Milwaukee County Labor Council (now National Program Director for the Partnership for Working Families) was enthusiastic about this model [regional power building] for the South, being originally from Florida. Atlanta had a history of an activist council and had just come off organizing a very successful Immigrant Worker Freedom Ride, so Atlanta seemed to have enough community base to really put something together that funders would be interested in.[13]

To facilitate foundation support, Howell introduced Fleming to Ann Bastian of the New World Foundation. Starting with labor's participation in Shirley Franklin's successful 2000 Atlanta mayoral campaign, the Atlanta–North Georgia Labor Council increased its capacity to coordinate union volunteers in neighborhood canvassing, targeted phone bank canvassing, leafleting, putting up signs, and "getting out the vote." By 2006, labor and its allies had built the capacity to have a voice, although not a dominant one, in the affairs of Atlanta's majority African American city council.[14] The labor council had also expanded its electoral work into a new "suburban strategy" to target winnable municipal representation among the metropolitan area's many smaller cities. The 2001 election of Greg Fan—an American Federation of State, County and Municipal Employees local president—to the East Point City Council signified the beginnings of this strategy.

The glue that held regional power-building work together came in 2005 with the founding of the Georgia Strategic Alliance for New Directions and Unified Priorities (STAND UP) as a 501(c)3 nonprofit organization modeled after the California pioneers. The new organization's choice of Deborah Scott as its executive director brought a wealth of political and community connections that built on the labor council's own resources. Married to Lorenzo Scott, an AFL-CIO regional staff person, Deborah Scott's background combined years of protest politics around civil rights, with varied "insider" experience such as work in city government and consulting work around Democratic election campaigns and preparing women to run for office.

One month after Scott went to work, the rapid economic growth experienced by the region produced an immediate opportunity in the form of Atlanta's Beltline Project. The plan for this massive regional development initiative would turn a twenty-two-mile stretch of railroad that circles Atlanta's central city into a commuter and public park corridor that would fuel commercial and residential development for decades. The project promised 30,000 permanent jobs, 48,000 construction jobs, twenty-two miles of public transit, thirty-three miles in bike and walking paths, almost 1,300 acres of new green space, and over 5,600 units of "affordable" housing. Like many large-scale corporate-oriented projects, the Beltline Project did not provide for significant inclusion of voices from either organized labor or low-income communities.

The development plan did need public funding, however, in the form of a Beltline Tax Allocation District estimated to raise $1.7 billion by 2030. With enough power-building political and coalition pieces in place and able to rapidly draw on expertise from established regional projects elsewhere, the Georgia STAND UP and the Atlanta–North Georgia Labor Council quickly drafted and secured an "eleventh hour" amendment for the tax allocation proposal. This provision required that the Beltline Project "reflect through development agreements or funding agreements...certain community benefit principles" such as prevailing wages for workers, first-source hiring, and apprenticeship and preapprenticeship programs.[15] The language also opened the door to integrating additional community benefit principles such as housing affordable to low- (and not just middle-) income groups, space for day care facilities, nonprofit organizations, and so forth.

Taken as an isolated piece of legislation, the amendment's final language offers rather weak commitments. Its main value lies in the opportunity it provides for organizing labor-community coalitions to give it life. Georgia Stand-Up and the Atlanta–North Georgia Labor Council were positioned to serve as community champions helping neighborhoods organize to use the legal rights embedded in the Beltline amendment and Atlanta's system of twenty-four neighborhood planning units. For example, the first community Beltline survey put out by the city's Development Authority was posted on a website and included quite a complex assortment of questions that did not necessarily educate respondents as to the consequences of their survey choices. Georgia STAND UP stepped in and developed a "help sheet" for respondents, which resulted in over three hundred individually completed surveys. It also organized a community input session attended by over forty labor, community, faith, and neighborhood leaders in order to achieve consensus on the survey questions. Advocating for light rail public transit, the Sierra Club was also an active partner with door-knocking efforts, yard signs, and getting people to complete the survey and attend subsequent public hearings.

In 2006, Georgia STAND UP and the labor council piloted an ongoing civic leadership institute. In turn the Georgia STAND-UP Alliance provides monthly meetings through which institute graduates and other grassroots leaders can learn about and organize around issues of economic development and public policy.

Our four factors explain the successful launching of a power building project in a conservative part of the country not known for labor movement strength. A traditionally innovative labor council had sufficient credibility with its affiliates to organize a core of union supporters. The South's political importance helped leaders attract funding. Both the council and Georgia STAND UP drew extensively on outside support. Finally, conditions of regional growth provided ready-made opportunities for pursuing compelling regional policy organizing.

Seattle

Along with those from Atlanta, Los Angeles, and San Jose, Seattle's King County Labor Council (KCLC) ranked among the small number of activist labor councils during the early years of the administration of AFL-CIO president John Sweeney. The famous demonstrations that greeted the World Trade Organization in late 1999 reflected, in part, years of innovative coalition building by the council after Ron Judd was elected executive secretary in 1993. Previously an organizer for International Brotherhood of Electrical Workers Local 46 and president of the Seattle Building and Construction Trades Council, Judd had worked to overcome years of tensions with minority communities through alliances to increase minority and apprenticeship opportunities and union labor on public construction work. He had also been among those labor leaders fostering common ground with environmental organizations.

As we will see, the KCLC did attract resources significant enough to launch several institutional innovations. This work, however, occurred during roughly the same time period (the mid- to late 1990s) as the pioneering work emerging in California. Thus, unlike those in Denver and Atlanta, Seattle leaders were not able to draw upon well-established experiences that offered a clear and coherent set of strategies. When researchers Barbara Byrd and Ian Greer finished their study of the KCLC in early 2005, they identified the development of a long-term regional plan as a challenge facing the council and affiliate leaders. Many innovative pieces had not produced an integrated whole.[16]

The national AFL-CIO's creation of Union Cities in 1997 aided two institutional innovations within the KCLC. It hired Verlene Jones as a full-time Union Cities organizer who helped affiliates build their capacity to turn out members, coordinated an active education program, and promoted coalition-building activities. Reflective of work within the faith community, Jones had served as chair of the Church Council of Greater Seattle's governing board. The key role that the council played in successfully mobilizing support for the 2000 strike at Boeing, the largest white-collar strike in U.S. history, testified to this heightened capacity. At the same time, the KCLC's organizing committee put together an ambitious plan, which the national AFL-CIO funded, called Seattle Union Now (SUN). The project created a council-based "central organizing body" to assist core unions in organizing drives, including SEIU District 925, Teamsters Local 174, the International Alliance of Theatrical Stage Employees Local 15, the International Longshore and Warehouse Union, and Hotel Employees and Restaurant Employees International Local 8.[17] At its height SUN had a director and six staff members, but the project dissolved after three and a half years, and never succeeded in initiating an organizing drive itself. Demands for organizing support from outside the "core unions" dispersed SUN activity while at the same time not involving enough affiliates to build sufficient funding support from inside the regional labor movement.[18]

Prior to these initiatives, the KCLC had brought the local Worker Center under its organizational umbrella in 1995. The organization had been formed by labor and community groups in 1986 to fight plant closures and layoffs in area manufacturing industries. The Worker Center promoted high-skills, high-wage jobs, improved workforce training systems, better delivery of services for dislocated workers, and alliances among labor, community organizations, local governments, and employers. At one point, the center had a staff of seven and a budget of $400,000, including money from public sources and private foundations.

In the course of bringing the organization to the KCLC, Ron Judd won support from the Worker Center's existing funders for a vision of broadening the organization into a vehicle for policy development and research on broader issues of economic and workforce development. The Worker Center has provided such support on economic development issues with the City of Seattle, the Port of Seattle (the authority that manages harbor facilities and the Seattle-Tacoma International Airport) and other public bodies. For example, the port authority has been a focus of direct organizing, community coalition building, and electoral action over commissioners' seats under both Judd and his successor Steve Williamson. The Worker Center played a direct support role in these efforts to secure greater apprenticeship utilization and project labor agreements, the protection of union concession jobs, the establishment of a positive environment for worker organizing, and worker retention, training, and other issues for contracted food service workers.

The Worker Center's activities, however, retained a complex mix of service and more campaign oriented work in comparison to the more exclusive policy and coalition focus found in LAANE, Working Partnerships

USA, and their direct spin-offs. The center's seven staff members left it underresourced relative to the range of work it was called upon to perform. Of this staff, all but the director were limited to working on specific projects for which they were funded.

When Steve Williamson succeeded Judd in 2000 he placed a greater emphasis on the KCLC's electoral program. Hiring a full-time political director in 2001, the council joined the Washington State Labor Council's Labor-Neighbor program, through which union volunteers canvass other union members. In 2001 and 2003 the council led an effort to elect a challenger to the Port of Seattle's governing commission. Hopes for an outright majority on the five-member body, however, were dashed in 2005. Amid split labor endorsements and reduced mobilization, the labor-backed challengers lost and the previously successful 2001 challenger failed to win re-election. In terms of city hall politics, in 2001 the council led a labor effort that delivered the two-thousand-vote margin needed to elect Greg Nickels as mayor. After his election, Nickels publicly took up the call for living wages and project labor agreements, supported contract battles among janitorial, grocery, longshore, and other workers, and vetoed a development subsidy not supported by labor. In 2003, council-supported candidates won a majority on the Seattle City Council.

However, this political work has not integrated with a long-term power building plan around regional development. In addition to the limitations on the Worker Center's ability to dedicate its activities around such work, Seattle activism has faced several other challenges to moving beyond specific campaigns and projects. Over the long term, plans for power building work must encompass the entire Puget Sound region, not simply Seattle. Yet cross-union labor bodies are divided among the KCLC and smaller councils in neighboring Pierce, Snohomish and Kitsap Counties. Furthermore, according to researchers Byrd and Greer, Judd and Williamson acknowledged that the council needed more consistent and strategic participation by the principal officers of affiliated unions, both at the executive board level and in other day-to-day decision making.

Thus, despite favorable economic conditions and an innovative labor council, difficulties connected to our two other factors (peer-to-peer and foundation support) weakened the emergence of a full-blown and integrated power-building model. The early timing of the innovations meant that Seattle leaders could not draw from fully established regional experiences and corresponding technical support. While organizers successfully drew in new resources, these capacities were experimental and funded for activities that only partially aligned with the development of a long-term regional strategy for power. We should note, however, that Seattle remains a region that continues to enjoy labor movement innovation. New council leadership has taken up the ongoing challenge of developing long-term strategies for building regional power and the SEIU, UNITE HERE (a merging of the former Union of Needletrades, Industrial and Textile Employees, or UNITE, with HERE), the United Food and Commercial Workers (UFCW), and the Laborers' International Union of North America helped found (with the leadership of the Church Council of Greater Seattle) a LAANE-type 501(c)3 called Puget Sound Sage.

Regional Power Building in Troubled Economies

Here we examine the play of our four factors in three regions from the Rust Belt section of the country that stretches from the Midwest to the Northeast. Our first case provides a successful adaptation of the California model, while the remaining two cases are examples of the struggle involved in putting the integrated three-legged power building strategy in place. Was the economic context decisive in explaining the limitations of these latter two, or did the other three factors play important roles?

New Haven and Boston

The successful establishment of an ongoing regional power-building project in New Haven reflects our three factors of labor leadership, funding, and peer support but in an economic context quite different from the growing metropolitan areas of Denver, Atlanta, and Seattle.[19] Connecticut provides a stark contrast between its overall high-income levels (relative to those of the other 49 states) and the poverty of its two largest metropolitan regions, Hartford and New Haven. While the overall median household income for the state was $53,935 in 1999, for New Haven households that figure was only $29,604. According to 2004 U.S. Census data for the New Haven School District, nearly one-third of children between the ages of five and seventeen lived in poverty. Hartford is the poorest city in Connecticut, with 31 percent of its residents, and 41 percent of its children, living below the federal poverty level.[20] Since the 1980s, Connecticut has lost 100,000 manufacturing jobs while adding more than 130,000 service sector jobs. A 2001 study has estimated that health care and education had become the two largest employment industries in the state—accounting for 10 percent of all jobs. Both sectors paid median wages below the state average and offered a stark contrast between highly paid professional workers at the top and a large low-wage support workforce.[21]

Power building in New Haven built upon struggles at a single dominant employer: Yale University and its affiliated hospital. One of the wealthiest universities in the world, Yale is New Haven's largest employer, with over 11,000 employees at the university and 7,500 at Yale–New Haven Hospital. Yale's prosperity stands in contrast to the poverty visible in the heavily minority community that surrounds the institution. For decades, Yale has also provoked contentious labor relations with its workers. In the last decade, UNITE HERE locals 34 and 35 have had to engage in civil disobedience and strikes to settle new contracts. District 1199 of the SEIU has attempted to organize additional workers at the hospital, while the Graduate Employees and Students Organization has fought for graduate employee rights and collective bargaining recognition from the university. Given staunch resistance from the elite university administration, all of these struggles have necessitated community outreach and highlighted the need for strong alliances with the poor neighborhoods that surround the university. In 1998, these unions formed a new partnership: the Federation of Hospital and University Employees.

Two years later, the Connecticut Center for a New Economy (CCNE) was founded, modeled directly on the experiences of the Los Angeles Alliance for a New Economy (LAANE). The CCNE defines its mission as conducting research and policy development around issues of economic development and equity, building coalitions to improve the lives of low-wage workers and to support their struggles, and increasing civic engagement in low-income communities. Like the California institutions, support for the CCNE came from specific unions: those involved in the Federation of Hospital and University Employees, with a UNITE HERE community organizer position providing the basis for the CCNE's birth. CCNE President Andrea van der Heever had been active in HERE Local

34 conducting community outreach in the 1980s and '90s. The new organization also incorporated some of the remaining work of the Stamford Organizing Project, a regional organizing effort of the AFL-CIO whose funding was ending.[22] Unlike the California models, the CCNE was founded at the state level, but its first office and active campaigns were in New Haven. (In 2002, the CCNE began work in Hartford with a second office.)

Between 2002 and 2004, the CCNE supported the struggles of unions at Yale while conducting community outreach around the idea of a new "social contract." The CCNE argued that the community and workers needed to establish a new relationship, or social contract, with major employers such as Yale in order to stop the "race to the bottom" and foster family-supporting unionized jobs, affordable housing, access to health care, immigrant rights, and environmental stewardship. Framing research by the CCNE highlighted the contradictions of Connecticut's service economy and Yale's low-wage employment practices. In May 2004, a CCNE convention brought together regional leaders of the various struggles represented by these issues under the framework of a new social contract among employers, government, and the community. Soon thereafter the CCNE seized upon the newly announced Yale–New Haven Hospital's $350 million Cancer Center expansion to put this new social contract idea into practice. The hospital wanted a special development zone from the City of New Haven and public bond financing from the state. This large project, connected to the many labor and community concerns reflected in the social contract and the need for public approval, offered an opportunity to leverage a community benefits agreement.

To organize the community benefits campaign, the CCNE founded a new coalition, Communities Organized for Responsible Development (CORD) in August 2004. The coalition includes twenty-two unions, community, and faith-based organizations as well as hundreds of residents from the neighborhood in which Yale is located. The two-year campaign to secure an agreement with the hospital combined the organizing and bargaining needs of Yale unions with a range of community concerns. The latter included access to jobs, worries about gentrification, local crowding, and traffic and other environmental impacts. CCNE organizing and research also uncovered the significant problem of local resident debt to the Yale–New Haven Hospital—an issue that won national attention. The institution was found to be conducting aggressive medical debt collection, including garnishing wages and placing liens and foreclosing on homes. This behavior seemed all the more grievous because charitable funds earmarked for the bills of poor patients were going unused.

As part of laying the groundwork to develop a clear set of demands, over seventy organizers, including staff from the CCNE and the Yale unions as well as union member volunteers, canvassed the surrounding neighborhood to talk with members of over eight hundred households about their concerns. Although initially Yale–New Haven Hospital did not take the benefits campaign seriously, the campaign gained the support of key elected officials at both the local and state levels. The hospital entered into serious negotiations with the campaign in early 2006, with the mayor's office (which was supportive of a benefits agreement) providing mediation. In March of that year the hospital and the campaign signed a formal accord that included the following community benefits:

- Funds of $1.2 million for affordable housing and economic development.
- A commitment to hire five hundred area residents, and $300,000 a year for a job training and career ladder program so that new hires do not get stuck in the lowest paying jobs.
- A five-year, $100,000-per-year contribution to the city's New Haven Youth Initiative.
- A Citizen's Advisory Committee to review and advise on "free care" medical policies, an annual report on patient financial assistance, and two new medical outreach programs.
- The scaling back of planned new parking spaces, and measures to promote alternative ways for employees to get to work.
- Hospital and campaign members' participation in a city-sponsored comprehensive planning process for the surrounding neighborhood.
- Prohibitions on certain antiunion behavior, and safeguards for workers to engage in a fair secret ballot union election.

Signing the agreement did not end the struggle. In June 2006, local authorities granted all public permits for the Cancer Center's construction, yet during the summer, hospital management stepped up its antiunion campaign. By the end of the year, an independent arbitrator had canceled an SEIU union election due to the hospital's violation of the organizing rights provisions of the community benefits agreement. Since signing the agreement, the CCNE and CORD have pushed the city to establish three related committees: one for long-term planning, a citizen's advisory committee, and another to monitor parking issues. While the alderpersons appointed CORD members and allies to each committee, by early 2007 only one body was meeting. The CCNE and CORD have realized that they need to train their members on these committees to exercise stronger leadership roles.

That the campaign won any agreement at all from the hospital reflects the growth of more aggressive political action by the regional labor movement and its allies. Before 2001, the New Haven labor movement had been minimally involved in local politics; indeed, the central labor council did not endorse municipal candidates. That year CCNE supporters became involved in the state legislative campaign of a woman who had fully participated in a CCNE conference. Since then, the CCNE's social contract organizing has provided a context for growing the electoral work of New Haven's biggest unions—the SEIU and UNITE HERE—as well as a more active central labor council. In 2003, the CCNE and the unions mobilized hundreds of people for a public hearing at which the New Haven Board of Aldermen approved a resolution that raised questions concerning the university's tax-exempt status. That November the only Green Party member of the board, one who had embraced the social contract, successfully beat out a Democratic challenger. In 2005, the Democratic Party (New Haven being a Democratic stronghold) backed challengers to four incumbents who had supported the social contract; only one was successful, however.

The CCNE's efforts in New Haven represent the first stages in a more broadly conceived effort to build a progressive voice in regional economic development decisions. Yale is symbolic of larger opportunities provided by a state economy whose main growth industries are regionally rooted service occupations with a significant portion of low-wage and contingent employment.[23] The CCNE grew and has been sustained, in part, from the activities of unions with ambitions to organize in those same industries. The New Haven work has expanded in other ways as well. The organizing around medical debt grew into the independent Hospital Debt Justice Project and the CCNE actively supports Healthcare4Everyone, a campaign to establish universal public health care in the state. In 2007 the CCNE launched, with the help of Building Partnerships, its first civic leadership institutes in New Haven and Hartford.

In addition to the CCNE's activities, the even more recent growth of regional power-building work in Boston points to a similar set of organizing opportunities provided when stable and growing health care and education sectors have replaced manufacturing as dominant industries.[24] The Boston region enjoyed some vibrant labor-community coalition work, such as a successful Boston–Cambridge–Somerset living wage effort, in the late 1990s and the early years of the new millennium. Efforts to self-consciously develop regional power-building work, however, grew out of a new leadership team at the Greater Boston Labor Council led by the council's executive secretary-treasurer Rich Rogers. In 2004, this team, key affiliates (including building trades and teachers' unions, as well as the UFCW, the SEIU, and UNITE HERE) and such community partners as ACORN, several immigrant groups, and housing and tenants rights organizations launched Community Labor United as a "think-and-act tank."

Starting with former ACORN organizer Lisa Clausen, the new organization had expanded to five full-time, part-time, and contract staff members by 2007. The new organization's framing research fed into its first civic leadership institute in 2006. Its first campaign brought together labor and community groups to win prevailing wages and local hiring on $2.5 million of annual painting work contracted for the Boston Public Schools system. Winning support from the mayor's office, the campaign successfully established a labor-community partnership that uses community organizations to recruit residents who are hired into skilled painting work and preapprenticeships with the International Union of Painters and Allied Trades.

In both New Haven and Boston we see the factors of labor leadership, foundation resources, and peer-to-peer support at play in relatively less-vibrant economic conditions. Both cases witnessed strong union and/ or labor council leadership and successfully attracted foundation support. The examples of pioneering models and concrete peer-to-peer support clearly helped local organizers pursue proven strategic avenues. They did so by adapting the regional power-building model to regional conditions with a development lens focused on locally rooted and growing economic sectors with the potential to deliver a much higher portion of family supporting job opportunities than was previously provided. Yet the economic conditions found in New Haven and Boston are in important ways different from those found in the rest of the Rust Belt. New Haven offers a dominant wealthy employer in a wealthy state; and with its particularly dense concentration of institutions of higher education (and high technology), the Boston area enjoys a certain level of "knowledge economy" energy. Our next two cases offer more classic Rust Belt examples of economic hardship driven by declining manufacturing employment.

Milwaukee

The Milwaukee experiments in regional work developed in tandem with the pioneering work in San Jose and Los Angeles—in some ways even slightly predating such California activism.[25] Yet, despite notable successes and dynamic coalitions this work ultimately did not produce a replicable model. Explaining why this proved the case further illustrates why the regional power-building model explored in this book takes the general form that it does.

Milwaukee activism took place within conditions of economic stress. In the early 1990s, Wisconsin was the only state in the nation to rank in the top ten in both its share of existing firms reporting increased employment and in the survival rate of new firms. Yet, while average real hourly wages fell by 3.2 percent nationwide between 1979 and 1993 Wisconsin's average fell by 8.6 percent. Contributing to this pattern was the dramatic loss of high-paying unionized manufacturing sectors that had been the local economy's strength. During the 1980s and '90s, the urban region of Milwaukee, Racine, and Kenosha lost 96,000 manufacturing jobs. After losing one-third of its manufacturing employment in the 1980s, by the early 1990s Milwaukee would have needed 50,000 new jobs in order to employ everyone looking for work. With almost one-third of new jobs paying under $6 per hour in 1994, Milwaukee ranked just behind Los Angeles and Miami as cities with the greatest level of low-wage job creation.[26]

As in our other cases, key leadership in Milwaukee came from organized labor. The Milwaukee County Labor Council (MCLC), and in particular its then secretary-treasurer Bruce Colburn, played a leading role. Colburn was particularly skilled at bringing together and facilitating relationships among the diverse groups and leaders involved. At the same time the Center on Wisconsin Strategy (an innovative think tank at the University of Wisconsin–Madison) provided the type of applied research that supports regional power building elsewhere. In addition to framing research, the center engaged in a series of detailed analyses of the regional economy. This research helped identify those industries for which the area had a competitive specialization, that were adding jobs, and that provided or had the potential for providing family-supporting wages and benefits. Because researchers surveyed and engaged business leaders, the research also helped forge relationships within such industries. Both the above data and relationships would aid metropolitan Milwaukee work.

Regional experimentation in Milwaukee formed around two major new institutions: The Campaign for a Sustainable Milwaukee (CSM) and Progressive Milwaukee. The former was a broad-based coalition launched as a 501(c)3 nonprofit organization. MCLC leader Bruce Colburn helped lead a yearlong planning process to draft a grassroots plan for Milwaukee's future to undergird long-term alliances of labor and community groups. Unveiled at a 1994 "Community Congress" of three hundred grassroots representatives, the plan—titled *Rebuilding Milwaukee from the Ground Up!*—offered a comprehensive agenda covering jobs and training, credit and banking, education, transportation, and the environment.[27]

The CSM nonprofit subsequently encompassed a formal coalition of more than two hundred community, religious, labor, and business groups. Its efforts focused on four major areas: a sector-based job initiative, living wage activism, job access campaigns, and organizing around regional transportation. The first area, the Milwaukee Jobs Initiative, targeted specific economic sectors—such as construction and manufacturing—that combined three characteristics: regional strength and job growth, the availability of well-paying jobs, and employer difficulty in obtaining entry-level workers. The manufacturing sector in particular also allowed the initiative to link to and build upon the work of the Wisconsin Regional Training Partnership. Staff housed at the CSM helped prepare area residents for entry-level jobs, with specific employers pledged to use the program for hiring. Concluding that to fulfill the foundation's mission of addressing childhood poverty it needed to help parents gain access to decent jobs, the national Annie E. Casey Foundation provided millions of dollars for the eight-year jobs program.

In contrast to the jobs initiative, the CSM's other programs operated mostly through volunteer groups supported by its staff. A living wage task force passed ordinances at the county, city, and school levels. It also sent volunteers into inner-city fast food franchises with flyers comparing wages found at inner-city locations to those paid by the same brand-name franchise in the suburbs. A job access task force overcame historical building trades–minority tensions to forge common efforts to secure union jobs and community apprenticeship opportunities on the publicly funded Wisconsin Convention Center and the new Miller Park baseball stadium. A broad-based transportation task force worked to make transit policy a social justice issue; through its grassroots efforts, a $241 million federal grant for southeastern Wisconsin transportation allocated substantial funds for constructing a light rail system and upgrading regional bus service. However, the state's Republican governor Tommy Thompson and suburban resistance to lines connecting to African American communities eventually scuttled the plans.

The second new institution, Progressive Milwaukee, was a local chapter of the fledgling national New Party. Launched in 1992 with the help of ACORN, the New Party aimed to build a bridge between third-party organizing and the traditional Democratic Party activism of labor and other progressive groups. Most New Party candidates entered local contests, the vast majority of which were nonpartisan. For higher offices, the party hoped to run fusion candidates who would gain votes on both New Party and Democratic Party ballot lines. To this end, the New Party pursued a U.S. Supreme Court decision to strike down the bans on fusion candidates found in most, but not all, states.

Like the electoral operations found in many of our power building cases, Progressive Milwaukee set out to build a neighborhood-by-neighborhood grassroots structure. Allies such as ACORN and the SEIU helped in building this precinct network. Because of such organizing, Progressive Milwaukee did enjoy some electoral success. In the mid-1990s it elected several members to the county board, several to the school board, and had one city councilor change his party affiliation. The New Party chapter in nearby Madison actually won a governing majority on the city council. Both the Milwaukee and Madison chapters also played key roles in passing local living wage ordinances. Progressive Milwaukee, however, was not able to build upon its initial electoral success and in 1997 the national New Party fell into decline following a U.S. Supreme Court decision to uphold state fusion bans.[28]

The Milwaukee work displays many of the strategic elements found in the regional power-building model. It sought to unite a diverse and at times conflicted array of labor and community groups around long-term planning for influencing the regional political economy; it drew on or established staffing capacity to support core research, policy development, and coalition building; it fostered a series of energetic campaigns that translated general goals into concrete demands; and it attempted to support its coalition and policy work with electoral action capable of shifting the political context. The Milwaukee experience also reflects the factors of labor leadership, foundation resources, and economic conditions. It grew out of leadership by key players within organized labor; it supported its work by obtaining foundation funding; and also directly addressed the troubled economic context by deliberately seeking to intervene in those economic sectors that were locally rooted—either due to the geographic-specific nature of the work or because of specific regional advantages.

Yet, both the CSM and Progressive Milwaukee proved unsustainable. Some of the explanation lies in factors specific to these organizations— such as leadership transitions and financial questions—that do not shed light on the larger issues raised by this chapter and are beyond the scope of this study. More important for our purposes, however, are the ways in which the Milwaukee work differed from our regional power-building model. Three differences in particular appear to have weakened the Milwaukee experiments.

The first difference concerns the alignment of funding resources. The CSM was shaped by the multimillion-dollar Annie E. Cassie Foundation grant, which provided the organization's largest single source of funding. These funds were dedicated to the jobs initiative and supported most CSM staff members. While allowing the organization to accomplish the work described above, the funding also posed a potential tension between service work and more political policy activism. The jobs initiative involved intensive one-on-one work with clients and networking area service providers. The job access, living wage, and transit coalitions operated much more as volunteer-driven and -led initiatives supported by CSM staff with other responsibilities. In contrast, LAANE, Working Partnerships USA, and their spin-offs generally draw funding within an overall structure dedicated to policy development, applied research, and coalition support.

The CSM also approached its coalition building differently than our other power building cases. Its starting base was a broad tent of over two hundred organizations brought together by a comprehensive platform for regional public policy. By contrast, the coalition work found in our other regional power-building cases operates at two levels. Individual campaigns often see broad lists of supporting organizations. However, the long-term core regional program is maintained by an alliance of a relatively small core of labor and community partners united by a shared desire to build their grassroots capacity. As researcher David Dobbie has found in examining labor-community coalitions in Pittsburgh, Milwaukee, and Chicago, such a dual-level approach has proven far more sustainable than the kind of broad, inclusive tent attempted by the CSM.[29] In practice, the CSM's broad platform allowed groups to continue to work within their individual core foci. While this could lead to important connections, such as between the African American community and the building trades within the job access task force, it could also allow groups to continue to work in their separate issue "silos" without the kind of transformative issue linking seen among the core players in regional power-building experiences.

Finally, while specific coalition activism included such diverse unions as the building trades, transit workers, and service employees, the CSM did not integrate a core of union locals into the regional agenda to the degree found in our more successful cases. The political dimension in particular shows this limitation. This core part of the power-building model seeks to build greater electoral unity within organized labor's regional political action so that greater union staffing and financial resources flow into coordinated electoral efforts. While an innovative attempt to build a prolabor alternative political voice, Progressive Milwaukee presented a third-party effort that by its nature faced significant difficulty in drawing united labor participation. The Milwaukee County Labor Council never achieved the scale of electoral unity and shared field operations typical of successful regional power-building work.

The ultimate institutional failure of Progressive Milwaukee and the Campaign for a Sustainable Milwaukee did not mean that regional work had come to an end. Indeed, more recent activism in Milwaukee has drawn inspiration and technical support from the regional power-building model, including the community benefits campaign run by the Good Jobs and Livable Neighborhoods Coalition and its 2007 launch of a civic leadership institute.

Cleveland

While Milwaukee represents the most significant regional program in a Rust Belt city to emerge in the early 1990s, Cleveland is the most developed Rust Belt effort to begin in the latter half of the same decade.[30] The decline of a regional economy rooted in unionized manufacturing jobs is, if anything, even more pronounced in metropolitan Cleveland. According to data assembled by Policy Matters Ohio, Cuyahoga County lost 18,000 manufacturing jobs between 2001 and 2003 alone. During the 1990s, union membership in the Cleveland area labor force declined from 15.7 to 10 percent. By 1999, the Cleveland metropolitan area's share of national employment had slipped by 29 percent, its population by 30 percent, and its personal income by 35 percent.[31] In addition, "Greater Cleveland had forfeited about $35 billion in personal income to other regions over the...decade because it couldn't maintain its 1990 share of the nation's population and per capita income."[32] A turn-of-the millennium report from the U.S. Census Bureau recently rated Cleveland as "the nation's poorest big city, putting it ahead of Detroit, Miami and Newark, N.J."[33] As we will see, however, regional work in Cleveland was not simply shaped by its economic context but also (and heavily) by how resources and capacity were gathered and deployed.

As in most of our other cases, initiative came from within the central labor council. In 1996, former Communications Workers of America local president John Ryan won election to head the Cleveland AFL-CIO as part of a reform ticket to rebuild the capacity of the largely moribund organization. In 1987 he had become president of the area's United Way affiliate, the United Labor Agency (ULA). (Nationally, such agencies are the traditional nonprofit arms associated with labor councils; their main focus is on job training and other human services.) Formed in 1972, by the 1980s the ULA had fallen on hard times with a lack of a clear mission and mounting debt; Ryan helped reinvigorate the organization. (As of 2006 the ULA boasted thirty-five staff and a busy agenda.) Prior to his election to the Cleveland AFL-CIO, Ryan had served as a kind of unofficial staff person for the area's active Jobs with Justice (JwJ) chapter. The labor council election was divisive, with Ryan winning 54 percent of the vote. Thus, his initial task was successfully building relationships with affiliates who had not supported him.

Regional activism grew out of three institutional supports. First, Ryan looked toward expanding the scope of the revitalized United Labor Agency's work. While in the ensuing years the ULA has continued its primary service work—including a dislocated worker program for the estimated 62,000 such workers in the region in 2004—it has also served as an incubator and support institution for power building work. In terms of coalitions, for example, it has worked with the building trades unions to establish a preapprenticeship program that guarantees a slot in a union apprenticeship program to those minorities who complete their preapprenticeship training.[34] The ULA also runs a construction program that allows residents who want to renovate and repair their homes to acquire a second mortgage on their house for $15,000; participants are not charged interest, and only have to pay back the loan if they sell the house within thirty years, after this time they do not have to pay. On the political front, the ULA has formed the nonpartisan Greater Cleveland Voter Registration Coalition, which is composed of fifty community organizations targeting voter registration throughout the city's neighborhoods. As ULA director Dave Megenhardt explains, the above kinds of programs serve as a " 'bridge between the community and labor.' "[35]

In 2000, the ULA provided seed money to help the labor council establish Policy Matters Ohio. Within a year, Policy Matters secured a $150,000 grant from the George Gund Foundation, and as of late 2007 it had eight staff members. Unlike the "think-and-act" institutions found elsewhere, Policy Matters Ohio is a more traditional policy think tank and advocacy organization. Part of the reason for this orientation lay in the presence of an active JwJ chapter in Cleveland with some capacity to help build coalitions. The new organization's design and funding also gave it a statewide focus. Policy Matters began with the mission of broadening the debate around economic policy in Ohio, engaging in research that would promote policy decisions benefiting Ohio communities, and providing a voice for workers in state policy debates. While the bulk of the organization's energy now goes toward work at the state level, it has also provided research support for Cleveland's regional work, and its state-level framing reports reflect patterns found in greater Cleveland. It has also pursued Cleveland-specific research, such as two studies assessing the Cleveland living wage ordinance's implementation; one on the earned income tax credit in the county; one looking at the biotechnology industry in northeast Ohio; two on the Cleveland School Voucher Program; and one on day laborers in Cleveland.

As has been true in several power building experiences where key Jobs with Justice staff or leaders go on to labor council leadership, the activities of the Cleveland JwJ chapter waned in the immediate aftermath of John Ryan's election to the Cleveland AFL-CIO in 1996. As part of its revival strategy, in 1997 the JwJ chapter established full-time staff by raising funds from local unions, foundations, and community fund-raising. Jobs with Justice went on to play a central role in the campaign that successfully passed a Cleveland living wage ordinance in 2000 and continues to promote living wage work within the region.

Under Ryan's leadership, the Cleveland AFL-CIO revamped its political program, persuading each member local to assign a political coordinator to work with it. These political coordinators now make collective decisions that they then promote among members within their individual locals. This structure has increased labor's overall mobilization, fostered greater political unity among affiliates, and led to an increase of local unions participating in the federation's political program.

Labor has used its electoral strength to support not only candidates but also ballot issues. In 2001, the Cleveland AFL-CIO worked with the Cleveland Teachers Union and the construction trades to pass a $370 million bond issue for school renovation and repair. The decision posed significant risk, as the bond was both a tough sell to the public and seen as "the mayor's issue" at a time when labor had a rocky relationship with Mayor Michael White. The measure passed, due in part to efforts by 3,000 union volunteers to contact all 42,000 union members in the district. When Mayor White stepped down after twelve years, the Cleveland AFL-CIO successfully negotiated affiliate disagreements over ten would-be candidates to help elect Jane Campbell with 54 percent of the vote. In the same 2001 election cycle, the Cleveland AFL-CIO also asked Cleveland City Council candidates to sign on to a Workers Bill of Rights (which included the right to organize, keeping public services public, and support for schools and health care). The council endorsed twenty candidates who signed the pledge; of those, eighteen won.

While the living wage effort has been the most significant regional public policy campaign, the Cleveland AFL-CIO has also mobilized around state issues. It helped pass a state bill that requires the use of retractable syringes in hospitals and health care facilities in order to reduce "needle-stick" injuries. The bill was a big concern for the SEIU, which represents 15,000 health care workers in the state; for the American Federation of State, County and Municipal Employees, with 9,000 health-care workers; and for the Ohio Nurses Association. It was also a concern for custodians and housekeeping workers who could get syringe pricks while doing laundry. The Democrats had been out of power in the state for fifteen years and as such had a hard time getting their bills passed; the labor mobilization behind the bill was thus significant for successfully passing the law.

Despite a series of noteworthy campaigns and creative capacity building, Cleveland activism has not yet produced a coherent long-term program for building regional power that integrates regional research and policy development, coalition building, and aggressive political action. While labor's growing electoral strength has allowed it to play a more significant role in regional elections, it has less capacity to hold representatives accountable to promises made during the campaign, even among those candidates who signed the Workers' Bill of Rights. Related to this limitation is the lack of emergence of a long-term strategy for intervening in regional economic development. While the living wage effort brought together a vibrant coalition, activists have not been able to translate this experience into active alliances around other public policy issues. Living wage supporters have also struggled to establish aggressive enforcement by the city.

These limitations may reflect the inherent difficulties of organizing in a region whose economy is weak and whose labor movement faces steadily falling membership. However, the living wage campaign focused on economic activity rooted to the geographic area. Why not build other, similar campaigns around regional-based industries? The particular alignment of resources that grew out of creative capacity building in Cleveland does not easily produce such a regional agenda. Cleveland area labor and community work enjoys no institution similar to a LAANE or Working Partnerships USA dedicated to fostering a regional development agenda and organizing coalitions around specific campaigns. While the United Labor Agency has been quite innovative in defining its own work and incubating new institutions, its founding purpose and funding remain rooted in service work. Policy Matters Ohio has provided research support for Cleveland's regional issues, yet its main focus and funding operate at the state level. The Jobs with Justice chapter has had success in " 'labor support work, establishing a Worker's Rights Board, winning the living wage ordinance, organizing big rallies, and building the coalition,' "[36] yet the chapter has struggled with its role and mission. For example, should it operate as a coalition that primarily supports union issues or should it also prioritize campaigns that may not directly benefit unions but build long-term progressive power?

A full assessment of the prospects for regional power building in Cleveland awaits future developments as regional activism continues. Once again we are presented with a case whose origins began early enough in the 1990s that it did not enjoy the examples of a firmly established model and adaptation to different types of regions. Yet this model may continue to offer potential. In 2006, the New Alliance process (see chapter 7) in Ohio merged local labor councils into five area labor federations. At this time, Harriet Applegate took over for John Ryan as the head of the new North Shore AFL-CIO Federation of Labor. Will this new alignment of labor's cross-union resources spur greater regional power-building work? As with Milwaukee, time will tell whether regional organizers can translate a now fully articulated and firmly established regional power-building model to the specific conditions of their struggling industrial region.

Assessing the Spread of Regional Power Building

The experiences of the six cases detailed in this chapter allow us to further articulate the role of our four factors in shaping the spread of regional power building.

Labor Leadership

While a diverse range of groups have become part of regional power-building alliances, our cases exist only due to initiative taken by institutions within the labor movement. Not only must these institutions provide support for launching a regional project but also the work must integrate deeply into each organization's core mission and goals. We can see this aspect most readily in the path where an alliance of unions founds and helps drive a power-building nonprofit—such as in New Haven. But it is also a fundamental need in the central labor council–led path. It is not enough for council officers and staff to allocate their time and energy to regional work. Regional power building is not sustainable over the long term unless the work also becomes deeply integrated into the central activities of a core of council affiliates.

Denver illustrates this point quite well. Even with FRESC's capacity for research and coalition work, with only two full-time staff the Denver Area Labor Federation could not pursue the scale of activities and success it had enjoyed without extensive participation from key affiliates. According to former president Leslie Moody, the transformation has involved locals contributing more resources such as staff time, volunteers, and "lost-timers" and internalizing the council-led power building agenda. In other words, power building campaigns have moved from nice external projects that locals support to internal priorities that become part of the leadership's own strategic planning and resource allocation.[37]

Foundation Support

Foundation support has also been a prerequisite for sustained regional work. While organized labor and other groups have provided seed money and support for "think-and-act" capacity, in the end power-building nonprofits have been run primarily off of foundation funds. Our cases, however, have shown that the question is not simply drawing foundation money but also how the work of the funded institutions is defined. Regional power building draws on a distinct set of capacities ideally housed in a single think-and-act organization. As we have seen, projects that have tried to grow capacity from funding streams and institutional structures not explicitly designed around power building work have struggled with trade-offs in time and energy.

The spread of the regional model to regions outside of California and the establishment of several support institutions testify to the existence of a critical mass of foundations interested in supporting regional power-building work in and of itself.[38] However, dependence on foundations, especially those national in scope, raises questions about the eventual limits of stretching such sources, the geographic (and other) priorities of such foundations, and the need to diversify resource streams as organizers in an increasing number of regions pursue the regional model.

Established Models and Peer-to-Peer Support

Establishing regional power building has clearly become easier over time. Today, organizers can draw upon a proven general model and a growing range of adaptations to differing regional conditions. The first-generation expansion of regional work inside and outside California drew from examples and technical support provided by regional power-building pioneers. Today, the latest-generation programs enjoy peer-to-peer support that includes several support organizations national in scope. Three are worth summarizing here.

The Partnership for Working Families developed as a network of "think-and-act tanks," initially in California and then nationwide. It draws upon experienced power-building groups to offer regional projects a wealth of legal, research, and technical expertise around community benefits and other economic development campaigns as well as support for growing significant regional research capacity. The partnership supports a network of seventeen regional groups—seven in California and ten scattered across the country. The majority of these groups represent the think-and-act tanks so core to most power-building work. Some, however, are central labor bodies pursing community benefits and economic development work that is new for their region.

In 2005, the Los Angeles-based Strategic Concepts in Organizing and Policy Education (SCOPE) and Working Partnerships USA founded Building Partnerships USA, which drew upon San Jose power-building work to develop a curriculum for civic leadership institutes adaptable to regions nationwide. Building Partnerships has supported institute organizing in many of our case cities, including Atlanta, Denver, Connecticut, Milwaukee, and Boston. Building Partnerships' role, however, is not limited to the institutes themselves but also helps groups use education, convenings, and skills training to build their regional alliance and support effective campaigns.

As regional work emerged in California, key AFL-CIO staff who were focused upon the Union Cities initiative realized the significance of this model for revitalizing organized labor's fortunes throughout the country.

Following a series of reorganizations, coordination of this internal AFL-CIO support has a home today in the Field Mobilization Department. The office runs an ongoing leadership institute that brings together regional leadership and staff teams from local labor councils, regional federations, and state federations to develop their planning and organizational skills around a curriculum framed by power-building work and goals. AFL-CIO staff also facilitate the ongoing New Alliance program, which aims to increase the resource capacity and power-building program of regional AFL-CIO bodies. We will explore both programs further in chapter 7.

AFL-CIO staff have also worked closely with the nation's labor educators through the Building Regional Power Research Network, which formed in the early years of the new millennium as a collaboration between the United Association for Labor Education's Task Force on Central Labor Councils and staff at the AFL-CIO's Field Mobilization Department. Its primary work focuses on producing case studies of regional power-building work and AFL-CIO efforts to build capacity within its state and local bodies to pursue the power-building model. These cases have provided much of the source material for this book. Most recently, the network has begun to focus on cross-site research that examines specific challenges and questions involved in growing regional power-building strategies.[39]

Economic Context: Is Regional Power Building's Policy Work a Fair-Weather Endeavor?

The above three factors are all subject to the decisions made by players at the regional and national level. In the next chapter we will address the choices that need to be made by key national actors to support this work in ways that increase opportunities for labor leadership, resources for regional projects, and greater peer-to-peer support. Before taking up this discussion, however, we close this chapter by examining the economic context—the factor that is the least subject to direct influence by decisions of labor and foundation groups.

Our case studies leave the question of economic context unresolved. The two cases of struggling regional work within troubled economies faced difficulties related to our three other factors. These experiences launched at a time before the regional power-building model had become firmly established. While they secured foundation support, the alignment of that support was not dedicated to a regional power-building program in and of itself. Furthermore, although the full-blown model has not crystallized, leaders in both cases continue to pursue power building–related work.

Unfortunately, we have no fully established case of the self-conscious adoption of the regional power-building model in conditions of severe economic strain. The emergence of embryonic regional efforts in places such as Hartford, upstate New York, Pittsburgh, New Jersey, and so forth promise to fully test the adaptability of the model to such contexts. In the meantime, we can make a number of observations that suggest that the economic context may not prove a decisive barrier.

Declining regional contexts do present challenges to some of the policy tools explored in this book. For example, because of the limited growth found in the depressed metropolitan Milwaukee area, the achievement of the Park East community benefits agreement has had to struggle with low investor interest in the development. However, many of the policy tools discussed in the book do fit well with declining economic conditions. For example, in passing ordinances in over one hundred communities, the living wage movement has enjoyed success in many municipalities struggling with tough economic times. Indeed, these very economic difficulties add strength to the argument that limited public dollars must be steered toward promoting quality jobs that lift social well-being rather than poverty-wage jobs that tear down the community. At the same time, extensive research into the impact of living wage laws has demonstrated that fears of driving away business investment are unfounded.[40] Our examples of sectoral strategies in chapter 3 come from regions, such as Milwaukee and Buffalo, that are facing economic decline.

Even for tools such as community benefits agreements, the difference between growing and declining regions may be more in the particulars of how the mechanism is used rather than its overall relevance. For example, in growing regions community benefits campaigns have typically focused on big entertainment/residential projects and scenes of large-scale public investments like the Los Angeles International Airport or Atlanta's Beltway Project. Both types of development reflect the region's growth. By contrast, the Yale–New Haven Hospital campaign focused on investments by employers tied to the region. Even declining regions have employers who must be regionally based because they serve the needs of the region's population. All regional economies have service sectors—such as health care, education, building services, retail, and government sectors—that are rooted locally and operate with or are connected to significant low-wage employment. As the much smaller difference between manufacturing and service wages in a more unionized Europe illustrates, service economy jobs are not inherently of poor quality.[41] Conditions in these industries can be shaped by worker organizing and public policy. It comes as no surprise in this regard that service industry unions have been consistently part of the core regional power-building partners.

Finally, declining economies focus us once again on the importance of thinking regionally as economic decline can involve two separate yet interconnected patterns. The notion of decline can mean the overall weakening of key aspects of a region's economy. For example, many parts of the Rust Belt have experienced significant economic stress due to the drop in manufacturing jobs. However, decline can also refer to the decades-long growth of suburbs at the expense of core cities. Such tensions can be seen in both growing and declining regions. Los Angeles and Detroit both experienced significant crises in their downtowns despite quite different levels of regional prosperity. The two types of decline (inter-regional and regional) are linked, as many suburbs will ultimately share the overall fate of a collapsing inner city while vibrant core cities spark growth for the entire region.

Articulating suburban-urban tensions amid an ultimately shared fate can help identify opportunities for activism even in conditions of regional crisis. Even economically distressed regions will still experience some business and public investments, yet this energy often wastefully goes into the latest exurban sprawl. Regional power building can explore the need to redirect such energy back into core urban areas if the region as a whole is to improve its economic well-being. This opportunity and need has not been entirely lost on mainstream public planning and business circles. Take a city such as Detroit, which is famous for its industrial "ruins" and block upon block of vacant lots (some given over to a vibrant urban gardening movement). At the same time, the metropolitan area's city-suburban split is so stark that research by the Russell Sage Foundation labels the area the most segregated large urban region in the country. Yet the past ten years have seen significant corporate investment in entertainment and upscale condominium and loft development in Detroit's downtown and a corridor leading north to the neighborhood of a continuously expanding Wayne

State University. This urban redevelopment energy may not be as strong as that found in growth regions, but it is real and suffers from all the contradictions common to mainstream development thinking. It primarily benefits wealthier regional residents who want to return to the city to live and enjoy its "new urbanism" or as visitors to enjoy sports and entertainment. Along the same lines, emerging power-building efforts in upstate New York are able to identify viable and active redevelopment efforts open for labor-community intervention, further showing that opportunities exist in every area of the country.

TOWARD A NATIONAL STRATEGY
FOR SPREADING REGIONAL
POWER BUILDING

Imagine that the pioneering regional efforts covered in this book lead to further projects in various parts of the country, that regional power building comes to encompass strong organizing in some thirty or more major urban areas in the Northwest, West, South, Midwest, and Northeast. In some states, this work leads to solid blocks of progressive champions in the state legislature. These champions articulate innovative policy reforms and a vision for the future that have been carefully developed and tested at the regional level. At the same time, all of these regions become ground zero for rebuilding union density and membership-based community organizing. These power building regions in turn provide the basis for labor and its community allies to seriously fight for fundamental change at the national level. They can elect a solid block of members of Congress committed to progressive power; they can articulate a vision and set of policy reforms that have deep resonance within broad sections of the American population; and they have the capacity to move large numbers of people. The nation has thus arrived at a future of battling for national power.

(By this we mean not simply getting out the vote during elections but actually articulating a reform agenda, mounting coordinated campaigns to enact legislation, and fully contesting the Democratic Party's vision and candidates in ways loosely parallel to the way the New Right took over the Republican Party.)

We believe that the scenario above is not utopian vision but a serious possibility if regional power-building work continues to grow as an important part of the broader retooling of the labor and progressive movements in this country. The challenge is to reach a critical mass of regions. Meeting this challenge requires a greater strategic commitment and resources from key national players suggested by the analysis in chapter 6: organized labor and foundations.

Can Regional Power Building Become a Central Strategy in the Fight to Rebuild America's Labor Movement?

While regional power building can potentially provide a crucial mechanism for both increasing union density and transforming organized labor's political influence, it currently operates at the margins rather than at the core of organized labor's debates about its future. Before turning to why this is the case, we first summarize why regional power building should be central to debates over labor's future.

Why Regional Power Building Matters for Rebuilding the Labor Movement

As we explored in the introduction to this book, the labor movement must operate on two levels: in the community and in the workplace. The regional strategies profiled in this book are necessary for reviving labor's fortunes at both levels.

Neither organized labor nor other progressive groups can hope for real national reform without investing in rebuilding America's civic institutions at the regional level. American history reveals that no significant period of progressive reform has taken place without a significant and organized awakening at the grass roots. Labor and its allies must build an independent politics—not in the sense of a third political party but by establishing their own vision of social and economic change, a concrete policy agenda that moves in that direction, and an ongoing capacity to mobilize people at the grass roots. Without such deep political organizing, labor and its allies will remain prisoners of a narrow electoralism in which grassroots mobilizations rise and fall with "key" elections while the overall political process remains dominated and defined by corporate interests.

Rebuilding labor as a community force involves more than politics, however. Historically, organized labor has been resurgent during periods of deep cultural shift in which significant segments of the population come to question elite power and respond to calls for fundamental change. The capacity to support such a social awakening has to be built at the regional level. Furthermore, while organized labor is a necessary part of such a shift, it requires a broader set of community interests also taking ownership and stewardship. Whether or not community allies are able to bring significant clout to labor's campaigns, participating in a broad-based and long-term movement invites a deeper sense of commitment and excitement.

Labor cannot recover union density in American workplaces without the broad political and cultural transformation for which regional power building lays the groundwork. Focused, large-scale, sectoral organizing by more unions is certainly fundamental to rebuilding workplace organization. The track record of the last decade has shown that by building community alliances, seeking all forms of leverage over employers, committing significant resources to operate at sufficient scale, and mobilizing workers to fight on their own behalf, individual unions have been able to grow in their core industries. Such concerted efforts by specific unions, however, have not thus far significantly increased union density overall (or in some cases even within the very industries in which these unions focus).[1]

Operating at the scale needed to organize whole industries is a key part of the answer. We have seen throughout this book how regional power-building work can provide crucial leverage and support for such strategies. It is also true that industrial organizing work needs significant time for success to build on success. However, organized labor as a whole has never grown in America simply based on the additive organizing effort of individual unions. Significant union growth has always been accompanied by a broader social awakening. This surrounding political, social, and cultural context shapes whether specific organizing success translates into a sense of social surge though which organized labor's numbers grow exponentially or remains one isolated and resource-consuming organizing battle after another. Regional power building provides the grassroots vehicle for struggling to reshape this context.

Today, unions often try to organize by "parachuting" staff into areas where they think there may be potential for recruiting union members, but such an approach has often proven frustrating, if not futile. Building progressive civic infrastructure can provide labor an alternative starting point for long-term growth in areas where labor's workplace base is weak or nonexistent.

Notwithstanding many small-scale initiatives, the American labor movement as a whole still has not engaged in a serious broad-based debate about the proper role of central labor bodies and geographic, community-based work in rebuilding organized labor's fortunes. Labor must ask, What is the specific role of an individual union, a coalition of unions, a formal geographic organization like a central labor council or state federation, and organizations based primarily in the community? Regional power building provides a framework for addressing such questions.

It also provides a vehicle for articulating a broad social vision. Organized labor has not debated, let alone achieved, a common social vision for its own and America's future and the process by which it can be realized. Only on the basis of such a vision and process can labor adequately determine the relationship between geographic and sectoral work, between national and regional institutions, or between individual unions and the broader configuration of labor and its allies. Yet for such a vision to be broadly shared and lived on the ground it has to be built where people work and live.

Obstacles to the National Labor Movement's Full Engagement with Regional Power-Building Work

The traditional orthodoxy in the national labor movement is that growing power in industrial sectors is the key to labor's growth. In recent times, organizing to increase "union density" sometimes seems to have become the be-all and end-all of union activity. But the labor movement is unlikely to build power in society—including power at the workplace—unless it also builds power on a geographic basis, in the neighborhoods, towns, and regions where people live and where their political institutions operate. Yet, despite lip service to geographic power building by some national labor leaders, such support has rarely translated into an active push within the nation's major unions to more systematically engage their locals and regional structures in regional work or to fully integrate regional power building into their organizing plans.

The obstacles for full engagement by the national labor movement in regional power-building work can be seen through two lenses: the ultimate limitations of the AFL-CIO's Union Cities and the critical assessments of the work that have been offered by national leaders.

The Limitations of the Union Cities Initiative   Advocates for regional power-building work have to contend with the limitations of the AFL-CIO's Union Cities initiative and the resulting claim, "We tried to rebuild central labor bodies and got nothing new." Indeed, while most power-building central labor bodies became Union Cities, most Union Cities labor councils did not significantly change their overall activities, let alone develop significant power-building work. The problems, however, grow not out of some inherent impossibility of reviving central labor bodies around power-building strategies but out of the limitations of the specific Union Cities initiative. Ultimately, the Union Cities idea suffered from two problems—one in its conception and the other in its execution.

The conceptual difficulty was in many ways a reprise of modern central labor council history. Union Cities presumed that a strong, geographically based, metropolitan labor movement could collectively create political power that would help shape economic development in the interests of workers and the whole community, forcefully support union organizing, and provide mutual support for unions in all of their efforts. Ultimately, national unions would benefit, as some have already. This presumption, however, was not—and today still is not—shared by most of the labor movement. As a result, the transformation of central labor bodies is not integrated into organized labor's struggle either to organize or revamp political action.

This lack of integration reflects questions the labor movement has not adequately addressed: Is organized labor just a workplace institution, or is its community role genuinely important? Is it just a national institution, or is its presence at regional and local levels also essential? National unions concentrate on sectoral, industrial, or labor market power—and with building their own institutions. In contrast, by their very nature, central labor councils focus on geographic power, working to subordinate the rivalries among unions that inevitably erupt. National union leaders often do not like their local unions to engage in activities that they see as excessively independent of the national agenda. They are also typically more concerned with federal elections than with local politics, and they worry that ambitious local labor initiatives will drain time and money from their top concerns.

Too often national leaders do not understand how local and national efforts can be complementary. Few national unions, for example, have traditionally been involved in economic development issues (although this is changing). But defining the nature of economic development that is in the interest of all workers and the community as a whole is an important role for progressive central labor councils. Indeed, it is one of the most effective ways for labor to establish itself as a vehicle for all working people.

At their best, central labor councils become advocates for all workers in a region, both organized and unorganized. This ambition, however, clashes with the tendency of many national unions—and often of their locals as well—to focus simply on their own members. But broad-based advocacy for workers helps unions organize the unorganized and defends union members at the same time. For example, no hotels would be organized in Silicon Valley if it weren't for labor-backed local officials linking workers' rights to organize to publicly supported development projects, but it is also true that if it weren't for janitors organizing in Silicon Valley it would have been harder for the South Bay Labor Council to talk as persuasively about broad issues of growing inequality.

The lack of integration between union organizing and central labor body transformation is not surprising. During the Union Cities experiment, few unions had developed a national organizing strategy and few among those had held a clear concept of how central labor councils fit into their organizing strategy. Certainly the labor movement as a whole has not resolved—nor even thoughtfully debated—the key relationship between building geographic power and doing sectoral organizing.

Making central labor bodies powerful requires building frontline forces of union members and community allies who work together on a full range of issues and build relationships of trust and mutual support. The Union Cities project represented a commitment to rebuild labor's front lines. But the labor movement's overall political work remained focused on immediate electoral victories. Investing in the political capacities of local councils and state federations has not become part of labor's election-by-election mobilizations. For the 2004 and 2006 elections, progressive electoral organizations, many partly funded and staffed by labor unions, frequently relied on short-term employees and eager college volunteers who left no lasting political capacity behind. A movement-building strategy is very different from a strategy to win the next election, but the movement-building ambitions of Union Cities often fell victim to the focus on the next election.

Since central labor council transformation did not figure prominently in either union organizing or political strategies, the Union Cities idea did not have strong and active affiliate advocates in most parts of the country. Only a handful of top national union officials were enthusiastic supporters; many others never took the strategy seriously, even if they didn't oppose it. The union affiliates of the AFL-CIO never really felt that they owned the program, and the AFL-CIO did not have a strategy to generate support among affiliates. Many of the local affiliates that did support the rebuilding of their local labor councils still regarded them as little more than a means for delivering on the agenda of their international union. So central labor council leaders had to engage in a constant struggle to maintain support.

The execution of the Union Cities program also suffered serious limitations. Awareness of the potential for central labor bodies was undermined by a process in which top union officers rarely interacted with central labor council officials. AFL president John Sweeney served as the intermediary and the conversations about Union Cities—one involving Sweeney (with his top staff) and central labor councils, the other involving Sweeney and national union presidents—were kept quite separate. Furthermore, the AFL-CIO wanted to maintain control of the central labor councils, often seeing them as a way to deliver federation programs rather than as independent entities developing their own regional strategies. The typical agendas of many AFL-CIO gatherings of labor council leaders remained crowded with presentations of prepackaged programs that local leaders were expected to implement.

The AFL-CIO's Field Mobilization Department, which was responsible for the Union Cities concept, also lacked a grand vision of what the program could do, especially in developing bottom-up power. There was little long-range planning and all too often staff was inadequately trained, resulting in the blind leading the blind. In addition, since Union Cities was seen as the Field Mobilization Department's program, there was no consensus among department heads—especially within the political department—about the role of the Union Cities strategy.

Union Cities faced obstacles at the regional level as well. Many central labor council leaders had no interest in or talent for the more ambitious program of organizing, grassroots politics, and economic development. Often there was a lack of vision about what could be done locally and a lack of resources to even begin serious program development. While some local union movements have been hotbeds of innovation and eager to share best practices with other regions, the local labor movement can also be the most provincial part of the labor movement, riddled by old rivalries and mainly reacting to initiatives of business and political leaders.

The Union Cities program and its most active central labor councils did begin to bring local leaders together from around the country to create a community of best practices that continues today. This support network has been instrumental in helping spread the power-building model and redefining technical assistance from top-down provision by national "experts" to peer-to-peer learning and support work driven by grassroots needs. Such peer-to-peer technical assistance represents a legacy of Union Cities that has continued to grow both inside and outside the AFL-CIO.

Critical Assessments of Regional Power Building by National Labor Leaders

Few national labor movement leaders write off wholesale the need to foster power regionally or to build and leverage local relationships with community or elected leaders. But all too few can envision the contributions that vibrant regional progressive movements led by reinvigorated central, regional, and state labor bodies can make to the rebound of organized labor and progressive politics in America. Regional power-building work continues to struggle for recognition against several assumptions born in the era of labor's postwar heyday. Three stand out in particular.

First, many labor leaders view central labor councils and other regional labor bodies as lacking in talent and ability. This assumption often proved correct during the postwar decades. Because industrial unionism made cross-union bodies relatively unimportant, most talented and effective leaders looked toward careers elsewhere, not in underresourced and marginal labor councils and state federations. This assumption can no longer be automatically assumed true today. The cases in this book reveal many strong and effective central labor bodies led by dynamic leaders. Expectations make a difference. When regional labor bodies are seen as central vehicles for building a long-term movement for progressive change and labor movement revitalization, they attract and produce talented leaders. Yes, many local labor bodies remain moribund organizations with uninspired leadership. However, our regional power-building cases have fostered a whole new generation of emerging leaders who are taking over the helms of regional labor bodies and looking to head in new directions. Every year greater numbers of these leaders participate in the national support work that we will describe in the next section of this chapter. The challenge is to support this growing interest with sufficient resources to meet the demand.

Second, many national leaders see a trade-off between a coordinated national agenda and "localized" work. Local politics, unions, and labor bodies can be sources of parochial concerns and infighting. Jurisdictional disputes, disagreements over electoral endorsements, conflicting personalities, and other localized concerns can threaten to hijack any kind of coordinated agenda. While the dangers are real, building consensus and managing conflict is what effective cross-union labor leaders do. The task is no different than dealing with similar internal pressures within a local or national union.

Our regional case studies demonstrate that council and federation leaders can handle such tensions. Most of the cases have had to deal with parochial concerns and conflicting personalities and agendas—in some instances quite intense tensions. Yet this has not prevented local leaders from forging effective regional work. Indeed, regional power building counters fragmenting local pressures and fosters greater consensus. It raises the prospect of forward-looking, proactive strategies—ones that can redefine contentious issues. It builds shared capacity and develops coalition-oriented leadership. Most important, regional power building increases the prospect of winning—and nothing encourages unity like success.

It is true that many local labor councils are run by cautious leaders who cultivate their support from a large number of small and relatively passive affiliates. But the most dynamic labor councils pull together the largest and most dynamic locals to form a significant alliance that can jointly exercise significant power in both community and workplace arenas.

There is no trade-off necessary between national program and regional-driven initiative. Despite adapting to local conditions, regional power building has had remarkably similar elements across the country. While these elements are rooted in regional conditions, actions, and successes, they increase local capacity to implement nationally coordinated programs.

The AFL-CIO's Immigrant Worker Freedom Rides, for example, received strong support from our regional power-building cases. And our cases demonstrate that when regional leaders and staff are supported in establishing and growing their electoral capacity in local and state contests they also build capacity for national election campaigns, thus reducing the need to "parachute in" staff from outside. The recent experience of the New Alliance process (discussed in the next section) in Pennsylvania illustrates this point. Pennsylvania is a key battleground state, and the AFL-CIO has traditionally had to bring in staff from elsewhere in order to mount a sufficient mobilization for national elections. The New Alliance reorganization, however, established staffed area labor federations that have demonstrated a growing in-state capacity to move a political program. During the AFL-CIO's spring 2007 mobilization behind the Employee Free Choice Act, for example, Pennsylvania labor's work made it the top in the nation within the AFL-CIO in terms of the number of local government resolutions passed in support of the act.[2]

Finally, many labor leaders do not see a strong connection between regional work and workplace organizing. The possible connection is often seen simply in immediate instrumental terms. Yes, regional power building can forge community relationships and political connections that can be leveraged to support organizing victories. And yes, the organizing numbers it has produced thus far are modest. In part, this reflects the reality that the overall scale of new union organizing remains modest. Since organized labor regards organizing as the province of individual unions, regional power building can only support organizing that unions actually pursue. Greater and more systematic organizing work by more unions would mean more, not less, support from active local and regional labor organizations.

However, regional power building supports organizing at more than simply an instrumental level. As we have argued throughout this book, significantly raising union density in America requires fostering a significant cultural and political shift in society. Historically such a shift has often pre-dated, and certainly has always accompanied, large-scale union growth. In Detroit, for example, Congress of Industrial Organizations member unions grew massively beginning in 1936. Yet the cultural shift in this once solidly antiunion open shop city emerged far earlier. That 65,000 people attended the funeral procession for the five unemployed Hunger Marchers killed by the Ford Motor Company in 1932 revealed the growing preconditions for the union-organizing wave that would sweep the area four years later.

The labor movement cannot rely on "free market" unionism to establish such a social shift. Individual unions organizing individual industries—even on a significant scale—do not guarantee a public perception of orga-nized labor as key to society's future. Indeed, the corporate media generally has demonstrated its sophistication in ignoring worker organizing by de-fining such battles as "not news."

Regional power building establishes labor leaders whose job is to think from the ground up about how to build the labor movement as a recog-nized force for social justice and broad prosperity. All of the power-building elements work toward encouraging this public perception and establishing such a social shift. A strong American labor movement must have an ef-fective organizational layer that not only speaks for the collective interests of individual unions but also establishes a broadly shared social agenda closely intertwined with political change and the reestablishment of fully unionized industries.

We must also keep in mind that the ultimate purpose of organizing unions is to build the power of working people to better their lives through solidarity. While collective bargaining is a central vehicle for establishing such power it is not, nor can it be, the sole source of power. The health care crisis offers a clear example of how collective bargaining alone can-not address a core need of working families. Because the causes of spiral-ing health care costs lie outside the individual firm or industry, collective bargaining can only reset the distribution of costs between employer and worker. Significantly reducing actual costs requires a fundamental restructuring of how health care is delivered in society, including the re-placement of the wasteful private insurance industry with some form of public system similar to those used by the rest of the industrialized world. Similarly, even significant wage gains bargained by low-wage workers do not necessarily translate into either home ownership or residency in the same community as the job if regional land-use policies promote suburban sprawl and upscale development rather than affordable housing and non-gentrifying urban renewal. In short, the labor movement's ultimate goal is to build the power of working people. This task requires both workplace and community organizing.

National Institutional Labor Support for Regional Power Building

Despite the above obstacles, regional power building does enjoy important support within labor that needs to be built upon. Within the national AFL-CIO, the Field Mobilization Department has staff who support regional power building through the transformation of central labor councils and state federations.[3] In the early days of the model, this staff helped to network leaders and encourage peer-to-peer support. Today, two particular AFL-CIO initiatives help to promote regional power-building work.

The first is called the New Alliance initiative. AFL-CIO leadership came to realize that while the Union Cities project had laid out a bold vision for councils to become true movement leaders it had not helped councils address fundamental structural and financial issues that held most back. In 1998, AFL-CIO president John Sweeney appointed fifteen executive council members (from national unions) and one labor council and one state federation representative to the new Committee 2000 that toured the country visiting central labor councils, discovering a vibrant labor movement in the best of them.[4] As a result of the committee's work, the AFL-CIO Executive Council decided in 1999 to launch the New Alliance initiative as an effort to proceed state by state to increase affiliation and support from all unions to the central labor councils and state federations and to reorganize state and local structures to integrate and coordinate plans more effectively.

The New Alliance initiative would bring together, one state at a time, leaders of key unions to rethink and reorganize the structure and program of their state and local labor bodies. For most states, such a process would mark the first reorganization in at least half a century. Within each state, the New Alliance project had four basic goals:

1. Developing a cadre of active and capable council and federation leaders and staff.

2. Increasing the funding and resource capacity of AFL-CIO bodies to support systematic power-building work.
3. Upgrading the program of local, regional, and state bodies to reach for ambitious, long-term goals that support organizing and move from gaining access to officeholders to becoming part of a governing coalition.
4. Increasing coordination among the national, state, and local entities of the AFL-CIO.

New York provided the New Alliance pioneer. Despite its status as the third most unionized state in the nation, New York offered an all too typical picture. When key labor officials toured the state in 1999 they heard tale after tale of labor councils with no full-time staff, few other resources, and little in the way of active programs. Even councils that encompassed relatively large urban areas were trapped in a vicious circle—seen as unimportant institutions by many union leaders, few union locals participated in or paid dues to their local council. In turn, the councils held very limited ambitions that confirmed their marginal status.

To begin the New Alliance process, state leaders and national support staff pulled together a committee of roughly three dozen of New York's top union leaders, reflecting the broad spectrum of the unions in the state. This committee developed a reorganization plan that centered on joining twenty-five of the state's labor councils into five area labor federations. (The large New York City and Long Island councils were not part of this reorganization, although the latter's activities were transformed along New Alliance lines.) Several key elements would allow these new area labor federations to function as power-building regional leaders:

- Their boundaries were drawn to encompass at least 100,000 union members—the minimum felt necessary to provide effective staffing and resources.
- Per-capita dues paid by affiliate unions increased from thirteen cents per member each month to twenty cents.
- State union leaders agreed to push within their organizations for their locals to become fully affiliated with each area labor federation. For example, the Capital District Area Labor Federation (centered around Albany) increased the number of its affiliates from fifteen to forty-seven—thus growing its dues-paying membership base from 30,000 to 71,000 union members.[5]

- The combined increase in resources allowed the area labor federations to establish full-time officers and staff. Overall, the full-time staff of central labor bodies in the state went from 5.5 before the New Alliance to 20 afterward.

Increased union buy-in to these new regional labor bodies happened only because the New Alliance project established a concrete vision for how the area labor federations would play a central role in rebuilding New York's labor movement and thus improve the fortunes of each individual union. Previous interviews with New York labor leaders had identified their practice of "free market unionism." As Jeff Grabelsky characterizes this approach, "Each union leader pursued the particular, and sometime parochial interests, of their own membership with the hope and expectation that, if every other affiliate behaved the same way, the invisible hand of the 'free market trade unionism' would advance the common good of the larger movement."[6]

By contrast, the New Alliance initiative sought to create labor movement leaders. The job of area labor federation officers and staff was to think about building the overall movement. Through participation in their area labor federations, local affiliate leaders would also become movement—and not just workplace—leaders.

Regional power building has provided a reference point for what reorganized and revitalized cross-union regional labor bodies can accomplish. In New York it comes as no surprise, therefore, that newly founded area labor federations have pursued components of regional power-building efforts—especially in the areas of political action and coalition building.[7] Over time, these bodies could potentially develop full-blown power-building programs.

After New York, a New Alliance process took place in nine other states by 2007: Maryland, North Carolina, Colorado, Minnesota, Oregon, Arizona, Pennsylvania, Ohio, and Florida.[8] New York has the distinct advantage, like California, of offering several urban regions that, with reorganization, can produce labor bodies that will encompass at least 100,000 union members. In many other states only one main urban area offers this possibility.

Some states do not have even this. North Carolina is a telling example; the state is the second least unionized in the country—with a union density in 2006 of under 3 percent of workers. The jurisdictional boundary that makes it to over 100,000 members is the state federation of labor. All labor councils and would-be regional bodies have little resources to support staff, and all are staffed entirely by volunteers. The way North Carolina labor leaders have adapted to this situation is to use the state federation as the body for organizing power building–type work. Led by its dynamic new president James Andrews, the North Carolina State AFL-CIO has actively pursued long-term strategic alliances with such community groups as the North Carolina Justice Center, the National Association for the Advancement of Colored People, and the American Association of Retired Persons, of which the last two had not traditionally been close labor allies. These groups have worked together on both traditional "labor" issues—such as raising the minimum wage and protecting workers compensation and health and safety laws—as well as such "community" issues as blocking the move of predatory "payday" lending into the state.[9]

The New Alliance initiative is still a very new process—even among the states that have carried it out—yet the promise is that over time it will create bodies and leaders who are naturally drawn to and capable of organizing full-blown regional power-building work. A recent study of the first two and a half years of New Alliance in Pennsylvania found that the five new area labor federations have increased cross-union political and grassroots capacities not simply on their own but also through their ability to train, inspire, and support greater activity by the all-volunteer labor councils within their jurisdictions.[10]

The second initiative run out of the AFL-CIO Field Mobilization Department is the leadership institute. Each institute gathers teams of state and local AFL-CIO leaders from different parts of the country for two weeklong sessions run six months apart. It brings together leadership teams rather than individual leaders, allowing participants to develop very concrete project plans during the first week of the program. When the whole class reunites six months later, the teams discuss their successes, difficulties, and lessons of implementing their plans. The institute uses regional power building to frame its organizational and leadership skill development. Indeed, case studies derived from examples found in this book are used as part of the curriculum. The yearly institute has attracted enough interest from leadership teams around the country that in 2007 the AFL-CIO decided to expand the program to two institutes per year.

Both the New Alliance initiative and the leadership institute utilize recently developed standards and benchmarks for state and regional labor bodies. On March 3, 2005, the AFL-CIO Executive Council issued a statement titled "Building a Unified Labor Movement: Creating Effective State and Local Labor Councils." The Council aimed to "dramatically improve the performance of our state and local labor organizations" through a program that included the following elements:

- Growing capacity to mobilize union members around issues that affect them in their communities and workplaces. State and central labor bodies "must have the capacity to run effective mobilization programs on a continuing basis, not just during national elections."
- State federations and labor councils must be held to high standards. They must be held accountable for meeting those standards and be fully supported by the AFL-CIO and affiliates when they do.
- The national AFL-CIO should establish, state by state, integrated strategic planning and budgeting systems that provide the resources for carrying out the plans.
- Amalgamation should be pursued in cases where there are too many small and underresourced labor councils not able to implement a viable mobilization program.

The goal was to establish "a unified, effective, and well-resourced mobilization program for politics, legislation, and support for organizing at the national, state, and local levels connecting members where they work and live to local, state, and national issues and campaigns."

Sets of clear standards and benchmarks (one set for state and area federations, the other for central labor councils) guide the mandated planning, resourcing, and accountability. They mix many of the power-building elements discussed in this book with basic organizational development criteria. The state and area federation standards include: political, legislative, and member mobilizing; organizing support programs; community alliances; union affiliation to the state or area body; executive board development; and levels of staffing and volunteers. The central labor council standards are roughly similar; they also come with benchmarks that help define the progress of a labor body through stages of development from "reacting" to "mobilizing," "power building," and "agenda setting." Together the standards and benchmarks allow regional labor leaders to evaluate where they are, where they want to be, and how well they are getting there.

The standards and benchmarks form the basics for the leadership institute agenda. They also form the framework for the strategic planning by state and local bodies mandated by the AFL-CIO Executive Council. The most elaborate implementation has been in California, where state labor leaders used these standards and benchmarks to guide a strategic plan for the state's labor movement.[11] The narrow defeat of Proposition 72 by a margin of 1.8 percent helped push change. State labor leaders made the measure—which would have upheld a state requirement that employers provide health insurance for their employees—a strategic priority. Yet the labor effort contrasted strong examples set by areas with regional power-building work with weak performance in some other parts of the state. Responding to the weakness shown in labor's efforts, in 2005 the California Labor Federation convened a high-level committee of affiliate and central labor body leaders to evaluate the state federation itself, the state's 23 central labor councils, and 1,200 affiliated unions. This strategic planning committee adopted the national AFL-CIO standards and benchmarks to set expectations for the state federation, labor councils, and affiliate unions. The first level of standards and benchmarks implemented were those for labor councils. The idea was to clearly define what such bodies were expected to accomplish, providing them the support needed to meet the standards, and to intervene when the standards were not being met.

This standards and benchmark process led directly to interventions by affiliate leaders in several parts of the state. Orange County offers a good example. Although many union and political strategists had written off this large and influential county, demographic changes—especially a growing Latino population—and a shifting political balance of power offered opportunities to contest this heart of southern California conservatism. Yet the Orange County Central Labor Council (OCLC) had not proven effective, and several of the major unions engaged in organizing in the county were not even part of the council.

On the heels of its statewide planning process, the California Federation of Labor decided to intervene. The federation called a leadership summit of roughly sixty local leaders in April 2006 to discuss the OCLC's problems, including a lack of energy, direction, and coordination. They adopted three proposals: to convene a strategic planning committee of the fourteen leading unions in the county to work with the executive board; to bring back the unions that had disaffiliated and engage their top officials in the OCLC; and to hire as full-time political director the state federation political director for southern California, Tefere Gebre. In a matter of months, Gebre brought the OCLC together so that it went from being among the five worst performing labor councils in the state to being among the top five performers during the 2006 elections.[12] By 2007, the council had changed its bylaws to increase participation, begun hiring more staff, increased involvement of key union leaders, and started discussions of coordinated support of organizing. The revived council was also able to connect with the research and organizing of the Orange County Communities Organized for Responsible Development (OCCORD) launched in 2005 at the initiative of UNITE HERE—a merging of the former Union of Needletrades, Industrial and Textile Employees (UNITE) and the former Hotel Employees and Restaurant Employees International Union (HERE)—as a coalition of unions, faith-based groups, and community organizations. OCCORD has proposed community benefit agreements, such as for a residential and commercial development on fifty acres of city-owned land near the Angel Stadium of Anaheim. The ability of the local labor movement to put into place the initial seeds of an effective power-building program testifies to both the utility of the model and the concrete support offered by more established projects. Even in what had long been considered sterile terrain, the local labor movement has demonstrated that progress on relationship building, organizing, public policy, and politics is not out of the question for Orange County.

This labor-based national support work has proven quite valuable to regional leaders seeking to pursue power-building work. Indeed, the importance of this support routinely comes up in the research interviews for all of the more recent case studies conducted by the Building Regional Power Research Network. The question remains, however, to what extent regional power building and this support work are recognized and prioritized by broad sections of national labor movement leadership, and to what extent they continue to operate at the margins of primary planning and debates. While over time the work has attracted greater national attention, a comparison of resource allocation suggests that appreciation of regional power-building work still has a way to go.

All of this national support work operates on bare-bones resources. For example, the initial AFL-CIO grant that helped expand the North Carolina State AFL-CIO's work was $30,000. A D.C.-based staff of only a few people and four regional staff members are the main support staff for the New Alliance reorganization and state and local strategic planning for the entire country. The Building Regional Power Research Network's annual budget for case study research has been only in thousands of dollars, not tens or hundreds of thousands. These funding levels contrast with the tens of millions of dollars spent by organized labor during election seasons. For the 2004 elections, for example, 527-committee expenditures for the Service Employees International Union (SEIU) reached $48 million, for the International Brotherhood of Electrical Workers $7 million, and for the Laborers International Union of North America $3 million. In 2006, these figures ran $28 million, $5.5 million, and $3.7 million, respectively. The 527 Americans Coming Together (ACT) expended $80 million for the 2004 elections and $7 million in 2006. While the bulk of ACT's funds came from corporate players, such as Peter Lewis and the family of George Soros, organized labor's contributions also reached the hundreds of thousands and even millions, with the SEIU leading the pack at $4 million in 2004.[13]

Ever since the election of John Sweeney to head the AFL-CIO, the call has gone out for internationals and their locals to put up to 30 percent of their resources into organizing. Such a commitment, argue advocates, would allow unions to transform themselves and ultimately their industries. The issue is not simply one of dollar amounts but of making a long-term commitment to workplace organizing and organizational growth.

The labor movement must make a similar long-term commitment to rebuilding its community presence. The regional power-building projects covered in this book have already accomplished a great deal using minimal resources. What might this work look like if the national labor movement took, say, 10 percent of the funds that normally go to single-shot electoral efforts and committed them to long-term regional power building? Such a commitment would expand the resources available to regional efforts exponentially. Expanded support would not only allow existing regional projects to grow and new ones to get off the ground but would also likely result over time in a vast increase in the ability of regional and state labor bodies to implement effective election mobilization campaigns, especially in states that tend to be key battlegrounds for national power. Investing in long-range regional power building also allows organized labor to invest in an area where it is currently weak: the cultivation and development of candidate champions intimately connected to progressive grassroots organizing.

This is not just a question of financial investment. Unless national unions buy into the idea of cross-union power, they will again squander a huge resource that is available for them to activate but that will continue in its often somnolent ways unless national unions are prepared to embrace it. The key question for organized labor should be, What investments, financial and otherwise, have the greatest chance to make a difference? Where could a modest effort have a big effect? Surely power building efforts that create local and regional reforms that could serve as models for national reform are among the most promising.

The debate that led to the group Change to Win splitting from the AFL-CIO, and the split's aftermath, reflects the mixed perspective in which building community power is seen. On the negative side, discussions of regional power-building strategies and even questions about the proper role of cross-union bodies were largely absent from the debate. Labor leaders clashed over the best way to rebuild workplace organization with little reference to the role of geographic power. Similarly, debates over political action proved secondary and mainly revolved around the relative priority of and reliance upon seeking legal reforms to support the right to organize. Certainly there was little discussion of the strengths and limitations of labor's current electoral work or what it means to build real governing power.

Thus, the national labor movement split without ever having really engaged with regional power-building strategies or the reality of power-building central labor bodies. Ironically, however, central labor councils—and, to a lesser extent, state federations—have played a key role in the aftermath of the split. Partly because of the improved practices of many labor councils, local unions in many parts of the country had grown more accustomed to working together locally and were happy with their cooperation. Whatever the reasons for the split at the top, they wanted to remain united at the local level. This was especially true of our regional power-building cases where key local power-building leaders spanned both sides of the national divide.

Eventually the AFL-CIO negotiated an agreement to issue solidarity charters to Change to Win union locals that wanted to remain in their state and local labor federations. Overall this deal has allowed power-building leaders to continue to work together. With the solidarity charters in place the general pattern has been for regional power building to continue to grow. Even before 2005, when most of the key unions were still officially part of the national AFL-CIO, leaders of regional labor bodies had to struggle to build consensus behind power-building strategies and to foster operational buy-in among key union locals. In many cases in which local unions have left and stayed out of power-building central labor councils, the move reflects tensions that predated the national split.

Thus, the national split can be seen as making state and local labor bodies all the more important forums for building labor movement unity. Debates and strategizing over regional power building can offer the context for fostering such consensus and then putting it into concrete shared practice. Certainly, the negotiation of the solidarity charters reflected a level of recognition of the value of central labor bodies. The national split, however, did disrupt national resources precisely at the time when a maturing potential for spreading regional power-building work demands a far greater infusion of resources and energy.

Increasing Foundation Resources

No one axis of activism—be it environment, gender, civic rights, community, faith, antiglobalization, or any other—has the power alone to transform America. Even with all of its corporate money and establishment connections, the New Right had to build alliances of grassroots groups to impact American politics and culture. There can be no decisive progressive change in America without a broad alliance of community-based activism and its integration with a resurgent labor movement.

The cultural shift needed by organized labor is also needed for other progressive concerns. For example, the nation cannot achieve a sustainable environmental future without reestablishing a positive vision of government's role in society. Similarly, the isolated individualism encouraged by the currently dominant corporate culture fosters the growth of right-wing religion in multiple ways. Corporate culture encourages a morality of exclusively personal responsibility while disregarding the need for common responsibility. Its crass secularism provokes a one-dimensional counterresponse. Regional movements that foster values of solidarity and interconnection encourage a cultural shift that moves the perspectives of progressive faith-based groups from the margins to the mainstream.

Progressive grassroots institutions, like unions, grow through periods of social awakening. Creating progressive regions means rebuilding a strong grassroots infrastructure. As we have argued throughout this book, only through vibrant community institutions and groups can progressives truly seek to govern.

We have delved deeply into the labor movement's debates because organized labor is and should provide key resources for supporting regional work. However, as we have seen, the right form of foundation support has also proven critical. Indeed, because of the key role played by local nonprofit "think-and-act tanks," regional power building could not have developed and grown without foundation support. For example, among its list of over two dozen top funders, the Front Range Economic Strategy Center includes such national foundations as the Tides Foundation, the Annie E. Casey Foundation, the Discount Foundation, the Energy Foundation, the Ford Foundation, the Ms. Foundation, the Nathan Cummings Foundation, the Needmor Fund, New World Foundation, the Ottinger Foundation, and the Unitarian Universalist Veatch Program of Shelter Rock. In addition to funding specific regional projects, foundations also fund two of the national support groups mentioned throughout this book: Building Partnerships USA and the Partnership for Working Families.

Foundation interest in regional power building has evolved over time. For the California power building pioneers, their state offered several advantages for finding resources. The state's booming economy was accompanied by the growth of regional philanthropy. The number of in-state funders increased, as did the dramatic size of some of their endowments. The conversion of nonprofit health care providers (Blue Cross/Blue Shield) to for-profit concerns also created new foundations in the process. At the same time the work in California drew interest from a small core of national progressive foundations (the Unitarian Universalist Veatch Program at Shelter Rock, the New World Foundation, the McKay Foundation, the Solidago Foundation, and the French American Charitable Trust, for example). By the mid-1990s the work had also won support from such mainstream groups as the Ford Foundation. By the turn of the new millennium many of these national and regional players had become interested in fostering similar work in other parts of the country. California had, thus, helped pave the way for groups outside of the state to seek foundation support.

Both the regional think-and-act tanks and these two national support organizations have been able to foster viable regional projects across the country, often on shoestring budgets. The amount of progressive foundation money that goes to big national intermediaries dwarfs the budgets of both Building Partnerships USA and the Partnership for Working Families. For example, the Center for Policy Alternatives (CPA) provides an important progressive counterpart to the right-wing American Legislative Exchange Council by networking and supporting progressive state elected officials. In 2003, the CPA's budget exceeded $2 million.[14] Building Partnerships, by contrast, operates with a tenth of this amount.

Institutions such as the Center for Policy Alternatives are important and necessary. However, an equal investment needs to be made at the grassroots level through regional power building if the work with legislators and broad policy reform is to rest on a solid foundation of organized communities. Elected progressive champions have to be backed up with support in order to govern. If this comes only from the national level, progressive elected officials are operating with no legs.

With the national shift having been fostered at the grassroots level, the New Deal era of the second half of the twentieth century ultimately centered progressive change in federal policy and action. As a result, liberal and progressive funding tended to weigh toward Washington, D.C.–based advocacy groups; indeed, such groups often appear the last bastions and vestiges of New Deal traditions. The assault on the New Deal, however, has transferred government responsibility, if not always funding, down to the state and local levels. At a certain level liberal and progressive funding must follow a similar devolution to invest a greater share of resources into regional and grassroots-based groups. Recapturing an era of national change requires first rebuilding strong regional movements for change.

Investments in regional institutions have also paid off directly in support for other regional power-building work across the country. For example, the Los Angeles Alliance for a New Economy drew on its expertise in community benefit organizing to partner with the Washington, D.C.–based Good Jobs First to create a detailed manual on how to organize community benefit campaigns used by groups all over the country. The Partnership for Working Families provides an additional channel for distributing the manual and for providing technical support. Similarly, Working Partnerships USA responded to the widespread interest in its Children's Health

Initiative by producing a written guide on how to pursue such local and regional reforms.

Ramping up the scale of national support, therefore, does not mean establishing large national organizations with numerous staff members. Indeed, it is necessary to rethink what national organizations could do. National intermediaries can serve as "lean and mean" coordinating arms that help facilitate the development of expertise and capacity at the regional level and within broad sections of the country. These intermediaries can cultivate relationships among different groups and help highlight the models and tools developed among different regional projects. They can promote peer exchange, proliferate best practices, and cultivate horizontal practices, including networking across various lines of issue concern and constituency. They can help raise money that is put into the field. And, most important, they can help to facilitate learning across the different regions and parts of the country.

Power building needs to develop at the regional level some of the capacities that have emerged at the national and state levels. It needs regional capacity to train, network, and develop local progressive candidates and officeholders as the Center for Policy Alternatives does at the state level and Wellstone Action does nationally. This means better integration of existing resources and new capacities in different parts of the country.

Building a National Movement: Go Deep, Go Broad

The last century witnessed several waves of grassroots protest that successfully laid the groundwork for historic national change. For half a century, strong national institutions and active government transformed society and established a new social contract in America. The corporate economic restructuring and conservative political and cultural organizing over the past few decades has shredded this social contract.

Today liberals and progressives must return to the grass roots to rebuild the nation's civic infrastructure. Thankfully, the work explored in this book demonstrates that such a bottom-up resurgence is possible. The same potential is revealed by many other innovations that have developed over recent decades but are beyond the scope of this book. We are not arguing that regional power building is a substitute for the many other valuable progressive initiatives around the country; many innovations are necessary to change the nation's path. Rather, we believe that regional power building provides some of the key elements needed for building real national power, elements that naturally synergize with other forms of organizing.

We return to the vision that we painted at the start of this chapter. Imagine that ten to fifteen years from now, in thirty to forty urban areas around the country, labor and community partners, progressive public officials, clergy, and sympathetic academics are part of strong regional movements for progressive change. They have built deep alliances, pursued pioneering progressive policy reforms, fostered growing union density, and articulated a compelling vision of social and economic change. Each of these regional movements has developed extensive horizontal relationships with similar projects in other regions. A well-resourced network of national intermediaries cultivates these relationships and offers mutual support and technical assistance. These thirty or forty coordinated regional movements reach the capacity to contest for governing power in state after state, and networked progressive state caucuses have placed forward-looking policy agendas into broad public debates. Alongside this work, unions have grown and increased their density in core industries. Various forms of community organizing have also turned a corner and are continuing to spread. Connected to regional structures, organized labor and a wide range of progressive groups have matured their capacities to mobilize for national elections and federal policy.

This is an America very different from the America found today. It is an America in which organized labor and progressive vision and reforms are no longer marginalized. It is an America that has returned to an era of social awakening in which the prerogatives of corporate power and privilege are placed in sharp public debate. It is an America in which a broad and integrated progressive movement demonstrates the capacity to seriously contest for governing national power.

We believe that the regional work emerging today can help make such a future—indeed, such an America—possible. But it will happen only if leaders and activists can imagine it and invest in it today. We have written this book as a call for organized labor and progressives to begin to debate the merits of a bottom-up program for contesting national power and to see the regional work emerging today as one building block toward this brighter future.

NOTES

Preface

1. A retired university professor, Nichols was both a Democrat and an open member of the Democratic Socialists of America. During his terms as mayor, Nichols habitually won the distinction of most trusted local figure in the yearly "best of" poll run by the region's free weekly paper, the *Ithaca Times*. David Reynolds worked on Nichols's election campaigns and served on a citizen commission established by Nichols on Ithaca-Cornell relations.

2. David Reynolds, *Democracy Unbound* (Boston: South End Press, 1998), examines the rise of independent grassroots politics (both inside and outside the Democratic Party) during the 1980s and 1990s. David Reynolds with the ACORN Natural Living Wage Resource Center, *Living Wage Campaigns: An Activist's Guide to Building the Movement for Economic Justice,* rev. ed. 2003 (Detroit: Wayne State University/Association of Community Organizations for Reform Now), offers an organizer's handbook for building labor-community coalitions to pass living wage ordinances (see http://www.laborstudies.wayne.edu/research/LivingWage.html). The first part of David Reynolds, *Taking the High Road: Communities Organize for Economic Change* (Armonk, NY: M. E. Sharpe, 2002), examines the lessons of social democracy in Europe for progressive activists in the United States, while the second part examines the experience of grassroots labor-community coalitions in America in the 1990s. The latter theme continues in David B. Reynolds, ed., *Partnering for Change: Unions and Community Groups Build Coalitions for Economic Justice* (Armonk, NY: M. E. Sharpe, 2004).

Introduction

1. Working Partnerships USA, *Children's Health Initiative Workbook* (San Jose, CA: Working Partnerships USA), 20–21.

2. Ibid., 3.

3. Ibid., 35.

4. Ibid., 51.

5. Ibid., 57.

6. Christopher Trenholm, Embry M. Howell, Dana Hughes, and Sean Orzol, *The Santa Clara County Healthy Kids Program: Impacts on Children's Medical, Dental, and Vision Care, Final Report* (Princeton, NJ: Mathematica Policy Research, 2005), 5.

7. Ibid., 38.

8. "Success Story for Kids' Health" (editorial), *San Jose Mercury-News,* August 1, 2001.

9. Ibid.

10. See, for example, Eric Leif Davin, "The Littlest New Deal: SWOC Takes Power in Steeltown, a Possibility of Radicalism in the Late 1930s" (unpublished manuscript, 1989).

1. Thinking Regionally

1. MetroHartford Alliance, "About Us"; retrieved January 8, 2009, from http://www.metro hartford.com/aboutus.aspx?id=96.

2. William R. Barnes and Larry C. Ledebur, *The New Regional Economies: The U.S. Common Market and the Global Economy* (Thousand Oaks, CA: Sage, 1998), 95–98.

3. Dan Luria and Joel Rogers, *Metro Futures: A High-Wage, Low-Waste, Democratic Development Strategy for America's Cities and Inner Suburbs* (MCEDA, 1994), 7.

4. The term *new regionalism* is referenced in Manuel Pastor Jr., Peter Dreier, J. Eugene Grigsby III, and Marta López-Garza, *Regions That Work: How Cities and Suburbs Can Grow Together* (Minneapolis: University of Minnesota Press, 2000).

5. Barnes and Ledebur, *The New Regional Economies,* 65–66.

6. Pastor et al., *Regions That Work,* 4–5.

7. Ibid., 5; includes Saxenian quote.

8. Thanks to David Miller for sharing his database with the authors.

9. Myron Orfield, *American Metro Politics: The New Suburban Reality* (Washington, DC: Brookings Institution Press, 2002); David Rusk, *Inside Game/Outside Game: Winning Strategies for Saving Urban America* (Washington, DC: Brookings Institution Press, 2001).

10. See Orfield, *American Metro Politics,* part 1.

11. For further details see David Reynolds, *Taking the High Road: Communities Organize for Economic Change* (Armonk, NY: M.E. Sharpe, 2002), chap. 11. For Grand Rapids, see *The Sprawling of America Part 1: Inner City Blues,* directed by Christopher M. Cook (Ann Arbor, MI: Great Lakes Television Consortium, 2001).

12. Manuel Pastor Jr., Chris Benner, and Martha Matsuoka, *This Could Be the Start of Something Big: How Social Movements for Regional Equity Are Reshaping Metropolitan America* (Ithaca, NY: Cornell University Press, 2009). Quotes used herein are from a prepublication manuscript, chap. 2.

13. This discussion draws on the classic work of Clarence Stone and his colleagues. See, for example, Clarence Stone and Haywood Sanders, eds., *The Politics of Urban Development* (Lawrence: University Press of Kansas, 1987), 6; and Clarence Stone, *Regime Politics: Governing Atlanta 1946–1988* (Lawrence: University Press of Kansas, 1989), 6.

14. Stone, *Regime Politics,* 6.

15. In addition to the two works cited in note 13, we have also drawn on the summaries provided in Pierre Clavel, *The Progressive City* (New Brunswick, NJ: Rutgers University Press, 1986);

and Pierre Clavel and Wim Wievel, eds., *Harold Washington and the Neighborhoods: Progressive City Government in Chicago 1983–1987* (New Brunswick, NJ: Rutgers University Press, 1991).

16. The California State Legislature, for example, passed paid family leave. Not surprisingly, many of the state's major cities offer significant examples of regional power building—including Los Angeles, San Jose, Oakland, and San Diego. The last speaker of the California State Assembly, Fabian Núñez, had been the political director of the Los Angeles Federation of Labor prior to his election. The national Canadian single-payer health system came into being as a result of the model offered by a left-leaning provincial government formed by the Cooperative Commonwealth Federation (now the New Democratic Party) in Saskatchewan. In the United States, governments at the state level have the authority to enact some form of their own public health insurance.

17. Pastor, Benner, and Matsuoka, *Something Big;* quotes herein are taken from a prepublication manuscript, chap. 2.

18. Ibid.

19. David Montgomery, *Beyond Equality* (New York: Vintage Books, 1967), 160ff. These cross-occupational organizations were initially known as "trades' unions." By the end of the Civil War they were usually called "trades assemblies."

20. Montgomery, *Beyond Equality,* 170.

21. For example, this community presence becomes clear in the city and town case studies undertaken in Leon Fink, *Workingmen's Democracy: The Knights of Labor and American Politics* (Urbana: University of Illinois Press, 1985).

22. Stuart Eimer, "The History of Labor Councils in the Labor Movement: From AFL to New Voice," in *Central Labor Councils and the Revival of American Unionism,* ed. Immanuel Ness and Stuart Eimer (Armonk, NY: M.E. Sharpe, 2001), 7–23.

2. The Model Emerges in California

1. In addition to Amy Dean's knowledge as leader of the South Bay Labor Council during the main time period covered in this chapter, we have also drawn on Barbara Byrd and Nari Rhee, "Building Power in the New Economy: The South Bay Labor Council," *Working USA* 8, no. 2 (2004), http://www.laborstudies.wayne.edu/power/downloads/San_Jose.pdf.

2. Byrd and Rhee, "Building Power" (online version), 3.

3. Ibid.

4. However, the union share of public workers rose from 38.7 percent in 1986 to 57.3 percent in 2006.

5. According to a December 2004 interview with council executive director Phaedra Ellis-Lamkins, the organization had 112 affiliates representing 110,000 union members; Byrd and Rhee, "Building Power," 2. The two biggest affiliates are SEIU Local 715 and the Santa Clara, San Benito Building Trades Council—both with approximately 25,000 members.

6. The building trades actually pulled out of the council during this period.

7. Diana Cohn, interview with the authors, March 2007.

8. Chris Benner, *Shock Absorbers in the Flexible Economy: The Rise of Contingent Employment in Silicon Valley* (San Jose, CA: Working Partnerships USA, 1996).

9. Chris Benner, *Growing Together or Drifting Apart? Working Families and Business in the New Economy* (San Jose, CA: Working Partnerships USA/Economic Policy Institute, 1998).

10. Peter Schrag, *Sacramento Bee.*

11. Jon Eller, interview by Amy Dean, 2005.

12. Byrd and Rhee, "Building Power," 9.

13. Ibid., 19.

14. Ibid., 20.

15. Bill Leininger, interview by Amy Dean, 2005.

16. Byrd and Rhee, "Building Power," 24.

17. Bob Brownstein, interview with the authors, May 2007.

18. "Labor-Backed Candidates Stomp Big Business Boys in Legislative Races," Metro Publishing Inc., 2000 (Silicon Valley).

19. *San Jose Mercury News,* October 27, 2002.

20. *San Jose Mercury News,* November 18, 2002.

21. Byrd and Rhee, "Building Power," 8.

22. Chris Block, interview with the authors, April 2007.

23. While in terms of dollars the tax subsidies were a minor contributing factor, they were important as a symbol to contrast the laxly regulated subsidies with strains on public employees.

24. This did not affect property tax subsidies given via redevelopment authority.

25. *San Jose Mercury News,* November 12, 1998, 10B.

26. *San Jose Mercury News,* May 14, 1998, 8B.

27. The intense controversy over developing this last major area of undeveloped land within the city made relationships with the environmental community—many of whom wanted to block outright its development—complicated. The Greenbelt Alliance turned down an offer by the SBLC to try and get it a seat on the Coyote Specific Plan Task Force.

28. Brownstein interview, May 2007.

29. Byrd and Rhee, "Building Power," 14

30. Ibid.

31. Byrd and Rhee, "Building Power," 12, 13.

32. For example, the small United Electrical union had attempted to organize in the factories in the 1980s and an SEIU Justice for Janitors effort had tried to organize among building service workers.

33. For a more detailed summary of the growth of contingent and temporary work and the subsequent working conditions, see David Reynolds, *Taking the High Road: Communities Organize for Economic Change* (Armonk, NY: M.E. Sharpe, 2002), 212–15.

34. For example, a 1999 survey by the American Management Association found that nearly twice as many firms (36 percent overall) experienced unexpected problems using temps as report unexpected benefits. The top four complaints were workers sent with the wrong qualifications, workers unreliable or absent, temporary worker turnover, and poor values and attitudes. See Reynolds, *Taking the High Road,* 214.

35. The Los Angeles material draws from three main sources: Research conducted by David Reynolds on LAANE, published in Reynolds, *Taking the High Road,* 160–65; Larry Frank and Kent Wong, "Dynamic Political Mobilization: The Los Angeles County Federation of Labor," *Working USA* 8, no. 2 (2004): 155–82; and interviews with several key participants conducted by David Dobbie in July 2008.

36. In 1955, for example, density in the Bay Area was 51 percent, while only 37 percent in metropolitan Los Angeles. See Ruth Milkman and Daisy Rooks, "California Union Membership" in *The State of California Labor* (Los Angeles: University of California Institute for Labor and Employment, 2003), 24.

37. See the Los Angeles Alliance for a New Economy website, http://www.laane.org.

38. *Los Angeles Almanac;* retrieved January 9, 2009 from http://www.laalmanac.com/population/po23a.htm. The U.S. Bureau of Citizenship and Immigration Services estimates more than 2.6 million undocumented immigrants statewide.

39. Walter Julio Nicholls, "Forging a 'New' Organizational Infrastructure for Los Angeles' Progressive Community," *International Journal of Urban and Regional Research* 27, no. 4 (2003), 892.

40. Ibid., 890.

41. See LAANE, *The Other Los Angeles: The Working Poor in the City of the Twenty-First Century* (Los Angeles: Los Angeles Alliance for a New Economy, 2000); Shea Cunningham, Jessica Goodheart, Paul More, Melanie Myers, and David Runsten, *Taking Care of Business? An Evaluation of the Los Angeles Business Team* (Los Angeles: Los Angeles Alliance for a New Economy, 1999); and UCLA Labor Center and Los Angeles Alliance for a New Economy, *Who Benefits from Redevelopment in Los Angeles? An Evaluation of Commercial Development Activities in the 1990s* (Los Angeles: Los Angeles Alliance for a New Economy, 1999). These and other reports are available from LAANE's website at http://www.laane.org.

42. Julian Gross with Greg LeRoy and Madeline Janis-Aparicio, *Community Benefits Agreements: Making Development Projects Accountable;* retrieved January 9, 2009, from http://www.communitybenefits.org/downloads/CBA%20Handbook%202005%20final.pdf.

43. Los Angeles County map of supervisor districts, 2007, http://www.laalmanac.com/government/gl01b.htm.

44. The living wage campaign attempted to pass a zone-based ordinance covering all business in the city's public-supported coastal zone. Large hotel and restaurant interests fought the measure—first by attempting to pass a far weaker city ordinance that would exclude zonal coverage, and then by funding a successful ballot drive to repeal the city council–passed zone ordinance. For more details see David Reynolds, *Living Wage Campaigns: An Activist's Guide to Building the Movement for Economic Justice,* available at www.laborstudies.wayne.edu/research/LivingWage.html.

45. By 2003 HERE had gone from representing roughly one out of five airport workers in its bargaining jurisdiction before the living wage to four out of five. The SEIU moved from representing one in ten workers within its jurisdiction to representing more than half.

46. While SCOPE was still developing the alliance, it launched a campaign to organize similar statewide groups in five other states—Alabama, Kentucky, Mississippi, New Mexico, and New York. With California, they constituted the beginnings of the national Pushback Network, which was designed to build leaders and educate voters on national issues. In each state, organizing follows a similar model: developing leaders with education about analyzing social power, developing public policy campaigns, and effectively mobilizing voters.

47. Nicholls, "Forging a 'New' Organizational Infrastructure," 889.

48. We should note that the leading employer, the Swedish-based Securitas, had already agreed to neutrality in negotiations with the SEIU.

49. *San Diego Union-Tribune,* May 5, 2003.

50. U.S. attorneys charged three prolabor council members with corruption linked to campaign contributions from the owner of a strip club. One of these officials died, one was convicted, and the third was convicted but then cleared on some counts and ordered to have a new trial on two others. Though unions were not implicated in the legal charges, they were tarnished by association and their majority in the council became slimmer and less reliable.

51. In 2004, labor backed incumbent Republican mayor Dick Murphy over a more conservative Republican candidate until late in the game when Democrat Donna Frye, an environmental activist who labor had helped elect to the city council, announced a write-in candidacy. Most unions then backed Frye, who would have won if 4,400 of the ballots cast for her had not been invalidated because voters did not fill in a bubble next to her name as they wrote her in. When Murphy resigned a year later, Frye ran again but did not win the support of the municipal unions and lost to police chief Jerry Sanders.

52. For example, the SDICLC helped win a project labor agreement covering construction of a new San Diego Padres ballpark, but lost a fight to win a labor-friendly agreement for new SeaWorld construction in 2002. In 2004 it mobilized support for the large grocery strike and a downtown San Diego janitor strike.

53. Jim DuPont, interview, April 2007.

54. For example, in 2007 EBASE led a fight to reinstate and protect a group of twenty-one immigrant workers at an Emeryville hotel. The workers had been demanding that their employer, Woodfin Suites, abide by the living wage ordinance. The hotel managers began pressuring around thirty veteran workers about their documentation, including work authorization papers and Social Security "no match" letters, eventually dismissing twenty-one workers shortly before Christmas 2006.

55. Sharon Cornu, interview, April 2007.

56. The Alameda Labor Council AFL-CIO also sees its political and community work as a way of helping workers organize, such as 2007 campaigns by unions organizing bakery, health care, trucking, grocery, and telecommunications workers.

57. From 2003 to 2006, for example, the Living Wage Coalition won passage of ordinances in three cities: Sebastopol, Sonoma, and Petaluma. In coalition with environmentalists and housing advocates, NEWS won approval of developer fees for an affordable housing trust fund in Sonoma County and five cities, starting with Petaluma in 2003. Much of that work was supported by research reports prepared by NEWS and commissioned from researchers at the University of California–Berkeley's Labor Center. NEWS and its offshoots also supported organizing drives by home health-care workers, hospital janitors, garbage collectors, nursing home workers, and others. The Living Wage Coalition and the North Bay Labor Council played major roles in winning a living wage and card check neutrality agreement for the Petaluma Sheraton hotel, which led to the workers successfully organizing as part of UNITE HERE.

58. The agreement provides for local hiring, union contractors, affordable housing, green building materials, and living wages for any SMART contractors of lessees. It was part of a campaign for transit-oriented development that complements the effects of urban growth boundaries established for every one of the eight major cities in Sonoma County in the 1960s. In 2006, voters narrowly turned down a ballot initiative (which required a two-thirds vote in both Marin and Sonoma counties) for a sales tax increase to finance expansion of light rail across both counties, but NEWS board chair and founder Martin Bennett is confident that simply better mobilization of Latino voters can guarantee victory in the future.

59. The law also mandates a "minimum health spending requirement" for medium to large businesses. Advocates argued that the law would provide coverage for many, if not all, of the estimated 82,000 uninsured city residents after it took effect in stages during 2007 and 2008.

3. Developing a Regional Policy Agenda

1. Louise Auerhahn and Bob Brownstein, *The Economic Effects of Immigration in Santa Clara County and California* (San Jose, CA: Working Partnerships USA, 2004).

2. For more details, see David Reynolds and Jen Kern, *Living Wage Campaigns: An Activist's Guide to Building the Movement for Economic Justice,* rev. ed. (Washington, DC: Association of Community Organizations for Reform Now, 2003), chap. 8; and Stephanie Luce, *Fighting for a Living Wage* (Ithaca, NY: Cornell University Press, 2004) chaps. 6–10.

3. For more details see Reynolds and Kern, *Living Wage Campaigns,* chap. 9; and Luce, *Fighting for a Living Wage.*

4. *Yale Don't Lien on Me: The Attack on Homeownership by the Yale–New Haven Health System and Yale School of Medicine* (CCNE, 2003); *Uncharitable Care: Yale–New Haven Hospital's Charity Care and Collection Practices* (CCNE, 2003); and *Coming to a Town Near You? Charity and Collections at Bridgeport Hospital, Member of Yale–New Haven Health* (CCNE, 2003).

5. New World Foundation, "Building the New Majority" (New York: New World Foundation, 2005).

6. We use the term *free market* to denote an ideology. We should note that actual practice hardly follows Adam Smith's market ideal. When given a chance, private firms will naturally seek

to out-compete their competition and establish dominance rather than open markets. How many business leaders have called for public or private intervention to bring more competitors into their industry in order to establish the proper conditions for a "free market"? For an example of a critique of free-market ideology that separates theory from practice, see David Korten *When Corporations Rule the World* (San Francisco: Berrett-Koehler, 2001), esp. chap. 5.

7. Bill Quinn, *How Wal-Mart Is Destroying America* (Berkeley, CA: Ten Speed Press, 1998), chap. 3.

8. Shea Cunningham, Jessica Goodheart, Paul More, Melanie Myers, and David Runsten, *Taking Care of Business? An Evaluation of the Los Angeles Business Team* (Los Angeles: Los Angeles Alliance for a New Economy, 1999); UCLA Labor Center and Los Angeles Alliance for a New Economy, *Who Benefits From Redevelopment in Los Angeles? An Evaluation of Commercial Development Activities in the 1990s* (Los Angeles: Los Angeles Alliance for a New Economy, 1999). These and other reports are available from LAANE's website at http://www.laane.org.

9. Manuel Pastor Jr., Peter Dreier, J. Eugene Grigsby III, and Marta López-Garza, *Regions that Work: How Cities and Suburbs Can Grow Together* (Minneapolis: University of Minnesota Press, 2000).

10. Greg LeRoy and Tyson Slocum, *Economic Development in Minnesota: High Subsidies, Low Wages, Absent Standards* (Washington, DC: Good Jobs First, 1999), 1.

11. Larry Ledebur and Douglas Woodward, 1990, quoted in Greg LeRoy, *No More Candy Store* (Washington, DC: Good Jobs First, 1997), 7.

12. LeRoy and Slocum, *Economic Development in Minnesota,* 4.

13. Chris Benner, *Shock Absorbers in the Flexible Economy: The Rise of Contingent Employment in Silicon Valley* (San Jose, CA: Working Partnerships USA, 1996). Chris Benner, *Growing Together or Drifting Apart? Working Families and Business in the New Economy* (San Jose, CA: Working Partnerships USA/Economic Policy Institute, 1998).

14. Louise Auerhahn, Bob Brownstein, Brian Darrow, and Phaedra Ellis-Lamkins, *Life in the Valley Economy: Silicon Valley Progress Report 2007* (San Jose, CA: Working Partnerships USA, 2007).

15. Enrico A. Marcelli and Pascale M. Joassart, *Prosperity and Poverty in the New Economy: A Report on the Social and Economic Status of Working People in San Diego County* (San Diego, CA: Center for Policy Initiatives, 1998).

16. Enrico Marcelli and Pascale Joassart, *Planning for Shared Prosperity or Growing Inequality? An In-Depth Look at San Diego's Leading Industry Clusters* (San Diego, CA: Center for Policy Initiatives, 1998).

17. Tony Robinson, *The Denver Atlas: A Region in Living Color* (Denver: Front Range Economic Strategy Center, 2006).

18. Because the living wage movement has been relatively well documented we will not explore it further here. For more information, see David Reynolds *Taking the High Road: Communities Organize for Economic Change* (Armonk, NY: M.E. Sharpe, 2002) chap. 7; and Reynolds and Kern, *Living Wage Campaigns.*

19. See the Good Jobs First website at http://www.goodjobsfirst.org.

20. Part of the land that is owned by the City of Milwaukee is under review for development and is not covered by the county CBA.

21. For an explanation and critique of mainstream sectoral strategies with examples from Los Angeles, see Pastor et al., *Regions That Work.*

22. For greater detail, see Reynolds, *Taking the High Road,* chap. 8.

23. See below for further discussion of high road and low road development.

24. *San Jose Mercury News,* May 31, 2000, p. 7B.

25. For a more detailed discussion of high road–low road framework see Reynolds, *Taking the High Road,* esp. the introduction.

26. Ian Greer and Lou Jean Fleron, *Labor and Urban Crisis in Buffalo, New York: Building a High Road Infrastructure;* retrieved January 9, 2009, from http://www.laborstudies.wayne.edu/power/downloads/Buffalo.pdf.

27. Ibid., 4.

4. Deep Coalitions

1. Jeremy Brecher and Tim Costello, *Building Bridges: The Emerging Grassroots Coalition of Labor and Community* (New York: Monthly Review Press, 1990); David B. Reynolds, ed., *Partnering for Change: Unions and Community Groups Build Coalitions for Economic Justice* (Armonk, NY: M.E. Sharpe, 2004).

2. Shalini Bhargava, Bob Brownstein, Amy Dean, and Sarah Zimmerman, *Everyone's Valley: Inclusion and Affordable Housing in Silicon Valley* (San Jose, CA: Working Partnerships USA, 2001).

3. Amanda Tattersall, "There Is Power in Coalition: A Framework for Assessing How and When Union-Community Coalitions Are Effective and Enhance Union Power," *Labour and Industry* 16, no. 2 (2005).

4. San Jose ACORN and the South Bay Labor Council memorandum of understanding, quoted in Steve Kest, "ACORN's Experience Working with Labor," in Reynolds, ed., *Partnering for Change,* 32.

5. Louise Simmons and Stephanie Luce, "Community Benefits Agreements: Lessons from New Haven," *Working USA* 12, no. 1 (2009).

6. Jerry Butkiewicz, interview, May 2006.

7. Under "just in time" production systems, manufacturers do not warehouse large stockpiles of parts but instead rely upon close relationships with supplier firms to deliver parts "just in time" as they are needed for production. When worker organizing at a supplier threatens to disrupt parts production it can draw pressure from the customer company to force the supplier's management to resolve the organizing dispute.

8. In Colorado, the AFL-CIO has a constitutional structure in which the Denver Area Labor Federation receives its budget from the state federation. Thus, when the UFCW left the state organization this move automatically stopped their financial support for DALF. The UFCW represented one-fourth of the affiliated base.

9. Stephanie Luce and Mark Nelson, "The Cleveland AFL-CIO," April 2005, unpublished manuscript available at http://powerbuilding.wayne.edu.

10. Kate Bronfenbrenner, "It Takes More Than House Calls: Organizing to Win with a Comprehensive Union-Building Strategy," *Organizing to Win,* Kate Bronfenbrenner, Sheldon Friedman, Richard Hurd, Rudy Oswald, and Ronald Seeber, eds., 19–36 (Ithaca, NY: Cornell University Press/ILR Press, 1998).

11. Marc Linder, *Wars of Attrition: Vietnam, the Business Roundtable, and the Decline of Construction Unions,* 2nd ed. (Iowa City, IA: Fanpihua Press, 2000).

12. Robert P. Hunter, "Union Racial Discrimination Is Alive and Well" (September 8, 1997); retrieved February 2003 from http://www.mackinac.org/article.aspx?ID=325.

13. Immanuel Ness, *Immigrants, Unions, and the New U.S. Labor Market* (Philadelphia: Temple University Press, 2005), chap. 2.

14. New World Foundation, "Building the New Majority" (New York: New World Foundation, 2005).

15. The inclusion of a lost-time provision in union contracts, which allows the union to buy out the time of workers who are on leave from their job to work with their union, has been another cornerstone in the development of labor's political power.

16. Tracy Zeluff, interview with the authors, July 24, 2004.

17. Eliseo Medina, quoted in Larry Frank and Kent Wong, "Dynamic Political Mobilization: The Los Angeles County Federation of Labor," *Working USA* 8, no. 2 (2004): 164.

18. Frank and Wong, "Dynamic Political Mobilization," 165.

19. Tom Karson, "Confronting Houston's Demographic Shift: The Harris County AFL-CIO," *Working USA* 8, no. 2 (2004): 213.

20. In its pamphlet "Building the New Majority," 12, the New World Foundation argues that the current distribution of progressive political funding is seriously out of balance—having focused on national efforts and one-shot "parachute" operations that leave little in the way of long-term civic structure behind after the targeted election.

21. Kim Bobo, "Religion-Labor Partnerships," in Reynolds, ed. *Partnering for Change,* 21.

22. Ibid., 21.

23. Barbara Byrd and Nari Rhee, "Building Power in the New Economy: The South Bay Labor Council," *Working USA* 8, no. 2 (2004).

24. Fred Rose, *Coalitions across the Class Divide: Lessons from the Labor, Peace, and Environmental Movements* (Ithaca, NY: Cornell University Press, 2000).

25. Byrd and Rhee, "Building Power in the New Economy," 147.

26. Ibid.

5. From Access to Governance

1. We offer a critique of the U.S. election process that is quite common among left-leaning scholars and activists. For more detailed examples (from two political science works), see Howard Reiter, *Parties and Elections in Corporate America* (White Plains, NY: Longman, 1992); and Michael Parenti, *Democracy for the Few,* 7th ed. (New York: St. Martin's Press, 2002).

2. As the voting-rights scandals of the 2000 and 2004 national elections illustrate, with accusations of tens of thousands of voters disenfranchised, the right to vote is still contested terrain.

3. In 1976 the average campaign for the U.S. House of Representatives spent $87,000; by 2000 that figured jumped to $840,000.

4. Generally speaking, the United States has no system of public financing that would displace corporate money. According to U.S. Supreme Court standards, the ability to make electoral campaign contributions is considered a form of "free speech" protected by the First Amendment. The only exceptions to this pattern are the "clean election" laws passed in such states as Arizona, Maine, Massachusetts, and Vermont, under which serious candidates for state offices who voluntarily forgo private campaign contributions have their campaigns funded by the state and at competitive levels. See David Reynolds, *Democracy Unbound: Progressive Challenges to the Two-Party System* (Boston: South End Press, 1997), 286–87.

5. The Center's database is accessible at http://www.opensecrets.org.

6. For examples, see the data provided by Free Press at http://www.freepress.net/resources.

7. For a full discussion of these and other mechanisms, see Reynolds, *Democracy Unbound,* chap. 9.

8. For more on the substantial democratic mobilization that infused the populist and socialist crusades see Reynolds, *Democracy Unbound,* chap. 1.

9. These national turnout numbers are measures from the pool of citizens eligible to vote rather than the overall voting-age population. See the United States Election Project at George Mason University, http://elections.gmu.edu.

10. Keystone Research Center, quoted in Holly Sklar, "Booming Economic Inequality, Falling Voter Turnout," *Z Magazine,* March 2000; retrieved January 10, 2009, from http://www.zmag.org/zmag/viewArticle/13272.

11. Reynolds, *Democracy Unbound,* chap 2. See also Frances Fox Piven and Richard Cloward, *Why Americans Don't Vote: And Why Politicians Want It That Way* (New York: Pantheon, 1988), chaps. 2–3.

12. Reynolds, *Democracy Unbound,* chap. 2.

13. A 2006 survey of SEIU members who were registered Republicans in Pennsylvania, Minnesota, Michigan, and Oregon by Harstad Strategic Research titled "SEIU Republican 4-State Member Survey—September 2006."

14. E. E. Schattschneider *The Semi Sovereign People: A Realist's View of Democracy in America* (Harcourt Brace College, 1975), 100–101.

15. While the pro–Proposition 226 campaign tried to frame the issues as dues money going to candidates that members did not support, by national law no union dues can be given as candidate campaign contributions. To raise money to support candidates, unions must establish political action committees that seek *voluntary* member contributions.

16. Reynolds worked with District 2 of the United Steelworkers in 2000 and 2002, the Monroe County AFL-CIO in 2000, AFSCME Council 25 in 2000, the United Auto Workers Region 1A in 2004, and SEIU 517M in 2006–7.

17. This information comes from AFL-CIO materials, including "Union Member Vote Drove Shift in Balance of Power," press release, November 8, 2006; and "AFL-CIO General Board Approves Union Member Education and Mobilization Around Politics," press release, May 22, 2002.

18. Indeed, in the year following the Democratic takeover the Colorado legislature seemed to pass no major piece of prolabor legislation.

19. Many of the details on ALLERT come from SCOPE president Anthony Thigpenn, "Building a Precinct Structure Election by Election," presentation at the Building Partnerships USA convention in Chicago, April 25, 2006.

20. Figures come from various Working America staff and canvassers' "Working America" presentation to the United Association for Labor Education 2008 Conference, Minneapolis, April 2008. Although members are encouraged to pay five dollars in dues, they need only to officially sign onto the membership list to join the organization.

6. Understanding the Spread of Regional Power Building

1. We should note that there are California-specific factors that help explain why the model first emerged in this particular state. Scale, for example, is one such factor. At 36.5 million people, California has by far the largest state population in the country. Business leaders, politicians, and the media frequently describe the state's economy as among the top ten in the world. Thus, institutional scales and capacity can support innovation. For example, in attempting to build regional labor bodies capable of supporting sufficient full-time staff, national AFL-CIO New Alliance organizers (see chapter 7) have looked toward a union membership base of at least 100,000. At best, most states have one large urban area with such potential. California, despite entering the 1990s with only midrange levels of union density, is one of the few states to have a number of large metropolitan areas that offer a member capacity of over 100,000. Thus, the principle innovating labor councils all started with significant full-time staffing levels comparable only to the nation's largest and most union-dense metropolitan areas. Other California-factors are also identifiable: that the state is far from national union and AFL-CIO headquarters provides a space for innovation and encourages mutual assistance among local unions; and California has also been at the forefront of regional business thinking within the "new economy."

2. Kevin Hart, "ARC Projects Huge Growth for Outlying Counties," *Atlanta Journal-Constitution,* November 12, 2006.

3. Source: U.S. Department of Labor monthly reports for Seattle–Bellevue–Everett.

4. Paul Lewis, *Shaping Suburbia: How Political Institutions Organize Urban Development* (Pittsburgh: University of Pittsburgh Press, 1996), chap. 4.

5. Barry T. Hirsch and David A. McPherson, *Union Membership and Earnings Data Book: Compilations from the Current Population Survey* (Washington, DC: Bureau of National Affairs, 1999).

6. Right-to-work laws render a union security or similar provision in a collective bargaining contract illegal. These provisions require workers to join the union or pay a union representation fee. Right-to-work laws require the union to represent all workers within the boundaries of the bargaining units, however—whether individuals join the union or not. In Colorado, union representation elections are won with the standard "50 percent plus 1" vote, but a union must prevail in a second election with 75 percent of the vote in order to bargain a union security clause. Right-to-work legislation has been proposed in nearly every legislative session for decades.

7. The Denver material comes primarily from Stephanie Luce and Mark Nelson, "Starting down the Road to Power: The Denver Area Labor Federation," *Working USA* 8, no. 2 (2004). A February 2006 updated version, with revisions by David Reynolds, is available at http://www.laborstudies.wayne.edu/power/downloads/Denvernew.pdf.

8. Support and initiative for the leadership change included leaders from the Service Employees International Union, the Communication Workers of America, the Newspaper Guild, the United Food and Commercial Workers, and the International Brotherhood of Electrical Workers.

9. At one time the DALF's website also named Save Our Section 8 Housing Coalition, Atlantis/ADAPT, Rights for All People, and the Alliance for Retired Americans among the core groups that it works with.

10. A full list of FRESC funders is available at www.fresc.org/docs/About%20Us/FRESC%20Funders.htm.

11. The Atlanta material herein is drawn from Tom Karson, "Atlanta: Local Initiative Combines with National Support," *Working USA* 10, no. 1 (2007): 27–47.

12. Ibid., 30.

13. Ibid., 32.

14. In 2006, the city council included such labor-community champions as Joyce Sheppard, a Communications Workers of America member with thirty years at Bell South, and Carla Smith, who has been active with the organization South Atlanta Neighborhood Development.

15. Karson, "Atlanta," 33.

16. Barbara Byrd and Ian Greer, "The King County Labor Council: Building a Union City on the Pacific Rim" (unpublished manuscript); available at http://www.laborstudies.wayne.edu/power/full.html by clicking on the "Seattle" link. The discussion herein uses this research as its primary source.

17. Ibid., 18.

18. Multiunion organizing projects generally have been tricky to establish and maintain. Larry Frank and Kent Wong, "Dynamic Political Mobilization: The Los Angeles County Federation of Labor," *Working USA* 8, no. 2 (2004), note the Los Angeles County Federation of Labor's failure to sustain an organizing director position to support multiunion organizing. Janice Fine, "Contemporary Community Unionism: Some Lessons from Baltimore and Stamford," in *Partnering for Change: Unions and Community Groups Build Coalitions for Economic Justice,* ed. David B. Reynolds, 165–89 (Armonk, NY: M.E. Sharpe, 2004), explores the gains but ultimate limitations of the multiunion project in Stamford, Connecticut.

19. The New Haven material herein comes from Louise Simmons and Stephanie Luce, "Community Benefits Agreements: Lessons from New Haven," *Working USA* 12, no. 1 (forthcoming); and interviews conducted for authors in May 2007.

20. These figures are cited in Simmons and Luce, forthcoming.

21. Connecticut Center for a New Economy, *Good Jobs, Strong Communities: Creating a High-Wage Future for Connecticut* (New Haven: Connecticut Center for a New Economy, 2001).

22. For more on the Stamford Organizing Project see Fine, "Contemporary Community Unionism."

23. According to CCNE research, in addition to health care and education, Connecticut's other top-growing industries include business services, amusement and recreation, and social services.

24. Boston is a relatively vibrant "recovered" manufacturing city in comparison to Cleveland or Milwaukee. Our point here is to use the city's particular strengths in health care and education to highlight the power-building organizing possibilities that these sectors can offer.

25. This section draws from David Reynolds, *Taking the High Road: Communities Organize for Economic Change* (Armonk, NY: M.E. Sharpe, 2002), chap. 8; and David Dobbie, "More Than the Sum of Their Parts: Labor-Community Coalitions in the Rust Belt," PhD diss., University of Michigan School of Social Work, 2008.

26. Reynolds, *Taking the High Road,* 173–74.

27. Campaign for a Sustainable Milwaukee, *Rebuilding Milwaukee from the Ground Up!* (Milwaukee, WI: Campaign for a Sustainable Milwaukee, 1994).

28. Core staffing for the New Party transferred to the Working Families Party in New York (one of the few states to allow fusion candidates), which has met with some success and whose organizing has spread to neighboring Connecticut.

29. See Dobbie, "More Than the Sum of Their Parts," chap. 2.

30. The Cleveland case herein drawn from Stephanie Luce and Mark Nelson, "The Cleveland AFL-CIO" (unpublished manuscript); available at http://www.laborstudies.wayne.edu/power/full.html by clicking on the "Cleveland" link.

31. Ibid., 1–2.

32. "Quiet Crisis: Income Lost," *Cleveland Plain Dealer,* October 17, 2004; available at www.cleveland.com/quietcrisis/index.ssf?/quietcrisis/more/081201lost.html.

33. Tony Dejak, "Cleveland Ranked Nation's Poorest City," *USA Today,* October 17, 2004, available at www.usatoday.com/news/nation/2004-09-23-cleveland-poor_x.htm.

34. The program comes in the wake of the Fannie M. Lewis Cleveland Resident Employment Law passed by the Cleveland City Council in June 2003 to encourage construction contractors to hire locally.

35. Dave Megenhardt, quoted in Luce and Nelson, "The Cleveland AFL-CIO," 6.

36. Michael Charney of the Cleveland Teachers Union, quoted in Luce and Nelson, "The Cleveland AFL-CIO," 16.

37. Leslie Moody, interview with David Reynolds, May 2005. In 2007 Moody had stepped down from the DALF to become director of the Partnership for Working Families.

38. The New World Foundation has attempted to raise greater awareness of power building work among the foundation world in general. Drawing parallels to the investments of the New Right in civic education and mobilization, the foundation argues for greater funding for what it calls "new majority structures." The foundation's "Building the New Majority" pamphlet identifies many of the nonprofits that we have covered here as examples of these structures. The foundation has established its own $3 million annual fund to help support these structures and calls on other funders similarly to expand their support for such work. See New World Foundation, "Building the New Majority" (New York: New World Foundation, 2005).

39. Using modest funds provided by the AFL-CIO, labor educators had, by 2007, written up detailed case studies of Los Angeles, San Jose, Denver, Houston, Seattle, Cleveland, Atlanta, North Carolina, and New York's New Alliance. New case studies of Boston, New Haven, Pennsylvania, and California strategizing were in the works. The network posts each case study on its website (http://www.powerbuilding.wayne.edu), and many have been published in the journal *Working USA.* The network also produces shorter pieces for training use and has developed a one-session training module to introduce power-building strategies.

40. See David Reynolds and Jen Kern, *Living Wage Campaigns: An Activist's Guide to Building the Movement for Economic Justice,* rev. ed. (Washington, DC: Association of Community Organizations for Reform Now, 2003), chap. 7, as well as the articles found in *Economic Development Quarterly* 19, no. 1 (2005) debating this subject.

41. See, for example, Richard Freeman, ed., *Working Under Different Rules* (New York: Russell Sage Foundation, 1994).

7. Toward a National Strategy

1. Richard Hurd, "The Failure of Organizing: The New Unity Partnership and the Future of the Labor Movement," *Working USA* 8, no. 1 (2004): 5–26.

2. See Sean Flaherty, "Building Regional Capacity: The New Alliance Process in Pennsylvania," *Working USA* 12, no. 1 (2009): 45–56.

3. The old Field Mobilization Department used to house staff that supported regional power building by labor council and state federation transformation. Sometime around 2005, these staff were reconstituted as the Office of State and Local Affiliates. By 2007 this was moved back into Field Mobilization.

4. The committee deliberated for a year about the successes and failures of the central labor councils. But there was no widespread conversation among union leaders at different levels about strategy. While at least several national union presidents were favorably impressed by what they saw in the more dynamic councils, the international unions as a whole did not adopt new plans for how to work more concretely with central labor councils.

5. Jeff Grabelsky, "A New Alliance in New York State: A Progress Report on the Labor Movement's Restructuring, Capacity Building and Programmatic Work," *Working USA* 10, no. 1 (2007): 15.

6. Ibid., 12.

7. For a fuller description, see Grabelsky, "A New Alliance."

8. For a fuller commentary on the New Alliance experience from two figures who played a key role at the national AFL-CIO level see Bruce Colburn, Scott Reynolds, and David Reynolds, "Commentary: Reflections on New Alliance across the Country," *Working USA* 10, no. 1 (2007): 133–39.

9. For a full case study of North Carolina, see Monica Bielski Boris and Randall G. Wright, "North Carolina AFL-CIO: How a Small State Federation Builds Political and Legislative Power without Money or Numbers," *Working USA* 10, no. 1 (2007): 47–76.

10. Flaherty, "Building Regional Capacity."

11. This overview is taken from Jeff Grabelsky, "Building Labor's Power in California: Raising Standards and Expanding Capacity among Central Labor Councils, the State Labor Federation, and Union Affiliates," *Working USA* 12, no. 1 (2009): 17–44.

12. According to the state labor federation's standards of voter identification, communication with members, and planning.

13. All funding data are from the Open Secrets website, http://www.opensecrets.org, maintained by the Center for Responsible Politics.

14. Figures from the Center for Policy Alternatives' 2003 Annual Report, available at http://www.stateaction.org.

INDEX

Note: Page numbers followed by letters *f* and *t* refer to figures and tables, respectively.

3Com Corporation, 118
9to5 (National Association for Working Women), 191
501(c)3 organizations, 42
527 organizations, 174–78
Academics: adjunct faculty, 100; alliances with, 68–69, 96, 123
ACORN. *See* Association of Community Organizations for Reform Now
ACT. *See* Americans Coming Together
Action for Grassroots Empowerment and Neighborhood Development Alternatives (AGENDA), 59, 67, 175, 177
Acuff, Stewart, 35, 192, 193
Advertising strategies, in elections, 161
Affordable housing: as economic development issue, 91, 92; labor-business partnership on, 118; San Jose campaigns, 45, 53, 128–29; San Marcos campaign, 73; Sonoma County campaigns, 252n57
AFL. *See* AFL-CIO; American Federation of Labor
AFL-CIO: and central labor councils, 227; Change to Win split from, 16, 34, 140, 240–41; Common Sense Economics program, 36; Field Mobilization Department, 36, 217, 227–28, 232, 235, 259n3; focus on national politics, 37–38; Immigrant Worker Freedom Rides, 75–76, 150, 230; leadership institute, 235, 237; New Alliance program, 217, 230, 232–35, 239, 256n1; Sweeney's campaign for presidency of, 35; Union Cities program, 36–38, 196, 216, 225–28, 232
African Americans: relations with Latinos, 67, 150, 176; tensions with immigrant workers, 149; in urban growth regimes, 30

AFSCME. *See* American Federation of State, County, and Municipal Employees
AGENDA. *See* Action for Grassroots Empowerment and Neighborhood Development Alternatives
Aggressive political action, 12–13, 169–81. *See also* Political work
Airport workers, organizing of: in East Bay area, 75; in Los Angeles, 69–70, 97, 110
Alameda County AFL-CIO, 76, 77
Albuquerque, New Mexico, 25
Alliance of Local Leaders for Education, Registration, and Turnout (ALLERT), 68, 150, 171, 174–77, 181
American Association of Retired Persons, 235
American Federation of Labor (AFL): creation of, 34; policies of, 16–17. *See also* AFL-CIO
American Federation of State, County, and Municipal Employees (AFSCME), 166, 213
American Leadership Forum, 118, 153
American Legislative Exchange Council, 243
American Postal Workers Union, 72
Americans Coming Together (ACT), 239
Andrews, James, 141, 235
Annie E. Casey Foundation, 192, 206, 208, 242
Applegate, Harriet, 214
Aron, Melanie, 153
Asian-Pacific Environmental Network, 76
Association of Community Organizations for Reform Now (ACORN), 10, 142, 143, 151; in Denver, 191; in East Bay area, 76; and New Party, 207; in San Francisco, 79; and South Bay Labor Council (SBLC), 45, 53, 132–33
Atlanta, Georgia: Beltline Project in, 105, 194–95; civic leadership institute in, 81, 158, 195; economy of, 189–90; regional power building in, 81, 192–95
Atlanta—North Georgia Labor Council, 192–95; affiliate members of, 190

Barnes, William, 22
Bass, Karen, 64, 68
Bastian, Ann, 193
Bay Area Organizing Committee, 79
Bay Area Rapid Transit system, 54
Believe in Buffalo—Niagara campaign, 122
Beltline Project (Atlanta, Georgia), 105, 194–95
Benhamou, Eric, 118–19
Bennett, Martin, 252n58

Block, Chris, 50
Blue Cross/Blue Shield, 242
Blueprint Project (Connecticut), 82
Bobo, Kim, 151, 152
Boeing, 2000 strike at, 196
Boston, Massachusetts: building trades–minority cooperation in, 145; civic leadership institute in, 133, 141, 158, 204; economic conditions in, 205; regional power building in, 81, 135, 204; school refurbishing campaign in, 93, 133–34
Bridge builders, 154
Bronfenbrenner, Kate, 143
Brown, Lee, 149
Brownstein, Bob, 49
Buffalo, New York: gap in regional work in, 182; high-road cooperation in, 122–23; sectoral development strategies in, 115; unionization in, 123
Buffalo AFL-CIO Council, 182
Building Partnerships USA, 96, 154, 192, 195, 216, 242, 243
Building Regional Power Research Network, 217, 238, 239, 258n39
Building trades unions: coalitions with, 54, 141; innovation by, 138; and minority groups, 140, 144–45
Business: and electoral process, 160–61; and governance, 7, 11, 28–30; high-road vs. low-road strategies of, 120, 121–22; and leadership development, 153; regional focus of, 21–24, 26–27; restructuring of, 24; success of, vs. social well-being, 89, 99; tactical alliances with, 116–23
Business tax subsidies. *See* Public subsidies
Bustamante, Chava, 119
Butkiewicz, Jerry, 72, 137
Byrd, Barbara, 48, 153, 196, 198, 249n5

California: East Bay area, 74–77; North Bay area, 78–79; Proposition 72 in, 237; Proposition 187 in, 138; Proposition 209 in, 120; Proposition 226 in, 165–67; Proposition 227 in, 154; regional power building in, 39–80, 256n1; San Diego, 72–74, 137, 251n51; San Francisco, 54, 79–80; Santa Monica, 66, 136, 251n44. *See also* Los Angeles; San Jose; Silicon Valley
California Labor Federation, 237
California Partnerships, 78

California State Alliance, 67
Campaign for a Sustainable Milwaukee (CSM), 206–7, 208, 209
Campaign for Clean and Safe Ports (Los Angeles), 92–93, 128t
Campaign for Responsible Development (Denver), 111, 191
Campbell, Jane, 212
Canada, single-payer health system in, 249n16
Candidate accountability, 180–81
Candidate development, 178–80; civic leadership institutes and, 49, 179
Capital District Area Labor Federation, 233
Catholic Charities, 74
CBAs. *See* Community benefits agreements
CCNE. *See* Connecticut Center for a New Economy
Center for Policy Alternatives (CPA), 243, 244
Center for Third World Organizing, 191
Center on Policy Initiatives (CPI), 73, 95, 97, 106
Center on Wisconsin Strategy (COWS), 115, 206
Central Labor Council Advisory Committee, xvii, 35–36
Central labor councils, 9; Committee 2000 on, 232, 259n4; decline of, 34–35; early role of, 33; and economic development, 226; and electoral mobilization, 172–74; first formal convention of, 36; and governance, 50; innovation by, 35, 38; leadership role of, 71, 81; leaders of, 140–42, 229; national labor leaders' assumptions about, 228–29; national support for, 236; vs. national unions, 34, 225–26; nonprofits founded by, 95, 188; and political action, 171–72, 181–82; proper role of, 224; and regional power building, 9–10, 38; reorganizing for increased effectiveness, 233–34; standards and benchmarks for, 236–37; Sweeney's campaign and, 35; and Union Cities program, 36–38, 225, 227–28, 232. *See also specific councils*
Central New York Labor Federation, 82
Champions Network, 122–23
Change to Win federation, 16, 34, 140, 240–41
Charities Housing Development Corporation, 50
Chavez, Cindy, 154
Cherokee Denver LLC, 110, 111
CHI. *See* Children's Health Initiative

Chicago, Illinois: immigrant rights marches in, 146; labor movement in, xvi–xvii
Chicago Trades Assembly, 33
Chicano Federation, 74
Children's Health Initiative (CHI), 4, 45, 91–92; replication of, 6, 243–44; success of, 5–6
CIM Group, 54
CIO. *See* Congress of Industrial Organizations
Cisco Systems, 51
Civic leadership institutes, 153–58; in Atlanta, 81, 158, 195; in Boston, 133, 141, 158, 204; and candidate development, 49, 179; in Connecticut, 82; curriculum for, 155–56, 155t, 216; in Denver, 146, 149, 158, 192; framing research and, 107; in Los Angeles, 68–69; relationship building in, 157; in San Jose, 46–47, 49, 55, 153, 154, 156; in Syracuse, 81; think-and-act tanks and, 98, 107; and worker organizing, 55
Clausen, Lisa, 204
Clergy and Laity United for Economic Justice (CLUE), 66, 152
Cleveland, Ohio: economic conditions in, 210; regional activism in, 210–14; Workers' Bill of Rights in, 179, 212, 213
Cleveland AFL-CIO, 141, 171–72, 179–80, 210, 212–13
Clinica Romero, 147
Clinton, Bill, 104
CLU. *See* Community Labor United
CLUE. *See* Clergy and Laity United for Economic Justice
Coalition building: and candidate accountability, 180–81; common agenda and, 88; community benefits agreements and, 109; with community groups, 6, 45–46, 129, 130t, 142–43; in Connecticut, 127t; dual-level approach to, 209; in East Bay area, 76; with employer groups, 116–23; with immigrant groups, 133, 137–38, 146–51, 154; with interfaith groups, 66, 135, 151–53; living wage campaigns and, 108, 127–28; in Los Angeles, 59–60, 62, 65–69, 128t, 175–76; majority, requirements for, 10; with minority groups, 120–21, 143–51, 196; in North Bay area, 78–79; in North Carolina, 235; regional power building and, 10–11, 44–47, 126; in San Diego, 74; in San Francisco, 79–80; in San Jose, 4, 44–47, 137; social vision and, 45–46; strategic, 128–36;

Coalition building *(continued)*
  think-and-act tanks and, 94–95, 96, 97;
  three-layer framework for, 134–35, 134f;
  among unions, 137–38, 141
Coalition for a Better Colorado, 174
Coalition for a Better Inglewood, 110
Coalition for a Better Sonoma County, 79
Coalition for a New Century, 66
Coalition for Clean and Safe Ports (Los
  Angeles), 66
Coalition for Economic Justice (Buffalo, New
  York), 123
Coalition for Humane Immigrant Rights of
  Los Angeles, 60, 147
Coalition for Immigrant and Refugee Rights
  (San Francisco), 79
Coastal Alliance United for a Sustainable
  Economy (Ventura County), 95
Cohen, Donald, 73
Cohn, Diana, 42
Colburn, Bruce, 35, 205, 206
Collective bargaining, limitations of, 231
Colorado: labor movement and electoral pol-
  itics in, 170; political landscape in, 173;
  United Food and Commercial Workers
  (UFCW) in, 139–40, 254n8. *See also* Denver
Colorado AFL-CIO, 174
Commercial Redevelopment Agency (Los
  Angeles), 62
Committee 2000, 232, 259n4
Common Sense Economics, 36
Communication Workers of America, 173;
  Local 7777, 191
Communities Organized for Responsible De-
  velopment (CORD), 201, 203
Community activism: use of term, 16. *See also*
  Community groups; Grassroots organizing
Community benefits agreements (CBAs),
  109–13; in Atlanta, 194–95; in Denver, 81,
  110–12; in East Bay area, 75; economic
  context and, 218; in Los Angeles, 62, 70,
  109–10, 243; manual for, 243; in Milwaukee,
  112–13, 218; in New Haven, 201–2; in Or-
  ange County, 238; in San Jose, 53–54, 121;
  in San Marcos, 73; in Sonoma County, 79
Community Blueprint Project (San Jose), 3, 58
Community Coalition (Los Angeles), 176, 177
Community colleges: creation of, xvi; funding
  for, 93
Community development regionalism, 31

Community groups: coalitions with, 6, 45–46,
  129, 130t, 142–43; free-market orientation
  and exclusion of, 99; support for, 2; types
  of, 142–43. *See also* Grassroots organizing;
  specific groups
Community Labor United (CLU), 81, 95,
  133–34, 135, 141, 145, 204
Community Scholars Program, 68
Congress of Industrial Organizations (CIO):
  changes in strategy in 1930s, 16–18; and
  local labor councils, 34. *See also* AFL-CIO
Connecticut: coalition building in, 127t; economic conditions in, 199–200, 205; regional
  power building in, 82, 135–36, 181, 200–204
Connecticut Center for a New Economy
  (CCNE), 82, 95–96, 200–204; community
  organizing by, 135–36; creation of, 200–201;
  medical debt work of, 97–98, 201–2, 203;
  mission of, 200; three layers of group
  outreach by, 134–35, 134f
Conservative social vision, 124
Conservative sociopolitical context, regional
  power building in, 72, 74
Construction industry. *See* Building trades
  unions
Contingent employment: in Los Angeles
  County, 59; in Silicon Valley, 43, 56–57;
  Working Partnerships' research on, 56–57
Contra Costa County, California: central labor
  council in, 77; political climate in, 76
Contreras, Miguel, 61, 63, 64, 69, 71
CORD. *See* Communities Organized for
  Responsible Development
Cornell University, xviii, 123
Cornu, Sharon, 77
Corporate tax subsidies. *See* Public subsidies
Corporations. *See* Business
Costco, 121
County governments, limits on, 26
COWS. *See* Center on Wisconsin Strategy
CPA. *See* Center for Policy Alternatives
Craft union model, 138–39
CSM. *See* Campaign for a Sustainable
  Milwaukee
Cultural shift, regional power building and,
  230–31, 241

DALF. *See* Denver Area Labor Federation
Dalrymple, John, 77
Databases, use in campaigns, 136, 177

Davidoff, Al, xviii

Davis, Grey, 78

Dean, Amy, xv–xviii; and Central Labor Council Advisory Committee, xvii, 35; and civil leadership institutes, 154; and coalition building, 119; and regional power building, 39; and South Bay Labor Council, xvii, 41, 49, 71, 137

Dean, Howard, 159

Deep coalitions, 10–11. *See also* Coalition building

Dellums, Ron, 77

Democracy, filtered, 161

Democratic Party, 7; CIO unions and, 17; labor's role in primaries of, 49; Latinos and, 65

Denver, Colorado: civic leadership institute in, 146, 149, 158, 192; community benefits agreements in, 81, 110–12; economy of, 190; Gates Rubber Factory redevelopment in, 106, 110, 191; regional power building in, 81, 190–92; research agenda in, 106–7; think-and-act tank in, 81, 95

Denver Area Labor Federation (DALF), 81, 172–74, 191–92; budget of, 254n8; staff of, 190, 215

Detroit, Michigan, 219–20; empowerment zone in, 104; union growth in, 231

Diaz, Manny, 49

Discount Foundation, 242

Dobbie, David, 209

Donahue, Tom, 35.

Door-to-door campaigns. *See* Grassroots organizing

Dreier, Peter, 23, 103

DuPont, Jim, 75

Durazo, María Elena, 60, 65–66, 71, 146

East Bay area, California, 74–77

East Bay Area Alliance for a Sustainable Economy (EBASE), 75–76, 77, 95

East Bay Asian Youth Center, 76

Economic conditions, and regional power building, 189, 217–20

Economic development: affordable housing and, 91, 92; central labor councils and, 226; community benefits agreements and, 109–13; current mainstream approaches to, limitations of, 99–105; health care access and, 91; immigrant rights and, 93; land use and, 91; living wage campaigns and, 108;

progressive perspective on, 43–44, 90–94, 99; recession of 2008 and, xi–xii; regional focus of, 21–24; regional power building and, 70, 73, 89–90; research reframing, 105–7; secretive policies of, 104–5; sectoral development strategies, 113–16; subsidy accountability campaigns and, 108–9; transportation policy and, 91, 92–93; worker organizing and, 93–94

Economic Development Group (Buffalo, New York), 115, 122–23

The Economic Effects of Immigration in Santa Clara County and California (report), 93

Economic regions: definition of, 22–23; municipal fragmentation undermining, 25

Education: framing research used for, 107; isolated individualism and, 100; organizing opportunities in, 204; of political candidates, 179–80; as regional economic development issue, 91. *See also* Civic leadership institutes

Electoral mobilization/politics: in 1996, 37; in 2004, 168, 174; in 2006, 167–68; business and, 160–61; candidate development, 49, 178–80; crossing racial lines in, 146; in Democratic primaries, 49; in Denver, 81; field operations for, 172–74; fragmentation among unions, 170–71; funding for, vs. funding for regional power building, 238–39; increasingly effective, 167–68; issue mobilization and, 167, 168; labor movement and, 1, 160; living wage issue and, 52; in Los Angeles, 63–65, 67–68, 175–77; low voter turnout and, 162–63, 163t; in Milwaukee, 207; people-to-people, 165–67; precinct-level organization, 174–78; in San Diego, 73–74; in San Jose, 48–50; in Seattle, 198; short-term vs. power-building, 37–38, 48, 159, 168, 227; technology used in, 136, 176; traditional methods of, limitations of, 164–65, 168–69; unified endorsement process, 48, 169, 171–72

Electoral process, limitations of, 160–64

Eller, Jon, 45

Ellis-Lamkins, Phaedra, 71, 249n5

Emeryville, California: IKEA store in, 76; Woodfin Suites in, 252n54

Employee Free Choice Act, 230

Employee Rights Center (San Diego), 73

Endorsement unity, regional, 48, 169, 171–72

Energy Foundation, 242
Entrepreneurship, individual, limitations of, 100–101
Environmental organizations, coalitions with, 195, 196
Ethnic chambers of commerce, partnerships with, 120–21

Faith community: coalitions with, 66, 135, 151–53; networks in, 143
Faith in Action educational meetings, 47
Fan, Greg, 194
Federation of Hospital and University Employees, 200
Ferrer, Maria, 154
Field Mobilization Department, AFL-CIO, 36, 217, 227–28, 232, 235, 259n3
Figueroa Corridor Coalition for Economic Justice, 62
Filtered democracy, 161
Fleming, Charlie, 193
Flint Alliance, 17
Ford Foundation, 242
Ford Motor Company, 231
Foundation support, 42, 98–99; established models and, 192; increasing, 242–44; and sustained regional work, 188, 215–16; for Working Partnerships USA, 42, 133
Frank, Larry, 69, 147
Franklin, Shirley, 193
Freedom Academy, 75–76
Free market, use of term, 252n6
Free-market framework, limitations of, 99–105
Free market unionism, 234
French American Charitable Trust, 242
Front Range Economic Strategy Center (FRESC), 81, 95, 96, 191–92, 215; funding for, 242; reports by, 106–7
Frye, Donna, 251n51
Funding: imbalances in, 255n20; for regional power building vs. election work, 238–39. *See also* Foundation support

Gamaliel Foundation, 10, 112–13, 135, 143, 152
Garden Alliance for a New Economy (GANE), 82–83
Gates Rubber Factory redevelopment (Denver), 106, 110, 191
Gebre, Tefere, 238
General Motors, 15, 17–18

George Gund Foundation, 211
Georgia Strategic Alliance for New Directions and Unified Priorities (STAND UP), 81, 95, 194–95
Goldstein, John, 193
Gonzalez, Ron, 4, 53, 119
Good Jobs and Livable Neighborhoods Coalition (Milwaukee), 112, 210
Good Jobs First, 51, 62, 96, 103, 109, 243
Governance: business/elite interests and, 7, 11, 28–30; coalition building and, 10; labor councils' involvement in, 50, 70–71; labor's role in, 182–83, 233; regime theory of, 27–30; regional, fragmentation of, 25–27; regional, moving toward new regime of, 30–31; social vision and, 8
Grabelsky, Jeff, 234
Grand Rapids, Michigan, 26
Granholm, Jennifer, 100
Grassroots organizing, 2, 12, 16, 18, 165–67, 174–78; "independent expenditure" campaigns, 174–75; Knights of Labor and, 33; in Los Angeles, 59, 176–77; need for ongoing capacity for, 14, 223; in New Haven, 136, 202; regional thinking and, 32; in San Jose, 5, 53
Great Depression, 16
Greater Boston Labor Council, 81, 134, 135, 141, 204
Greater Cleveland Voter Registration Coalition, 211
Greer, Ian, 196, 198
Gregory, Terry, 49
Grigsby, J. Eugene, 23, 103
Grillo, Mary, 73
Growing Together or Drifting Apart? Working Families and Business in the New Economy (report), 43–44
Growth coalitions, 29–30, 99

Hahn, James, 63–64, 67, 150, 171, 176
Hammer, Matt, 4, 46
Hammer, Susan, 52, 53
Harris County AFL-CIO Council, 148–49
Hartford, Connecticut, 199–200
Health Access Plan (San Francisco), 79
Healthcare4Everyone, 203
Health care access: crisis of, 231; as economic development issue, 91; and medical debt problem, 97–98, 201–2, 203; and organizing

opportunities, 204; in San Francisco, 79; in San Jose, 2–7, 91–92; state governments and, 249n16; trade unions' position on, 3

Health care workers, organizing of: in Cleveland, 213; in Los Angeles, 69, 138, 177

Healthy Kids program, 5–7, 45, 91–92

HERE. *See* Hotel Employees and Restaurant Employees International Union; UNITE HERE

Hermandad Mexicana National, 147

Hickenlooper, John, 173

Hospital Debt Justice Project, 203

Hotel Employees and Restaurant Employees International Union (HERE): and Children's Health Initiative, 6; Local 8, 197; Local 11, 59, 60, 147; Local 2850, 75, 76; in San Francisco, 79. *See also* UNITE HERE

Hotel workers, organizing of: in East Bay area, 75; in Los Angeles, 70, 152; in North Bay area, 252n57; in Santa Monica, 136

Housing. *See* Affordable housing

Housing for All coalition, 45, 128–29

Houston, Texas, labor-immigrant alliances in, 148–49

Howell, Cathy, 193

Hunter, Robert, 145

IFC. *See* Interfaith Council on Race, Religion, Economic and Social Justice

IKEA, 76

Illinois. *See* Chicago

Immigrant rights: 2003 Freedom Rides, 75–76, 150, 230; 2006 marches for, 146; EBASE and, 75–76, 252n54; as economic development issue, 93

Immigrants: African Americans and, 149; building trades unions and, 140; coalitions with, 133, 137–38, 146–51, 154; and labor movement, xv–xvi, 65; in Los Angeles County, 59; in San Diego, 73; in urban growth regimes, 30

Individualism: and conservative social vision, 124; and political candidates, 161; and public policy, 100–101

Industrial Areas Foundation, 79, 143

Inequality: high-tech boom and, 44; in Los Angeles County, 59; in San Diego, 73; in Silicon Valley, 44; trend toward, 7, 8

Innovation: in California, 256n1; by central labor councils, 35, 38; and consensus,

tension between, 140–41; in political work, 159

Integrative policy agendas, 88–89

Intel, 51

Interfaith Committee for Worker Justice, 74, 148

Interfaith Council (IFC) on Race, Religion, Economic and Social Justice, 46, 152–53

Interfaith Worker Justice, 10, 135, 151, 152

International Alliance of Theatrical Stage Employees Local 15, 197

International Brotherhood of Electrical Workers: funding for, 239; Local 46, 196

International Ladies Garment Workers Union, xvi

International Longshore and Warehouse Union, 197

International Union of Painters and Allied Trades: and Boston school refurbishing campaign, 93, 134, 145, 158; in Milwaukee Good Jobs and Livable Neighborhoods Coalition, 112; Proposition 226 and, 166

Jackson, Jesse, 70

Jackson, Luther, 153

Janis, Madeline, 70, 110

Jobs: public subsidies and quality of, 73, 102, 103, 104; quantity vs. quality of, 43, 101, 104; in service economy, 219. *See also* Contingent employment

Jobs with a Future initiative, 114–15

Jobs with Justice (JwJ): and central labor councils, 141–42; in Cleveland, 211, 212, 214; in Colorado, 191

Joint Venture—Silicon Valley Network, 21, 40, 43, 117

Jones, Verlene, 196

Judd, Ron, 35, 196, 197, 198

Justice and Equality in the Workplace Partnership, 148

Justice for Janitors: in Colorado, 191; in Los Angeles, 69, 138, 177; in San Jose, 43, 119

JwJ. *See* Jobs with Justice

Kest, Steve, 132

Keystone Research Center, 162

King County Labor Council (KCLC), 190, 196

Kirkland, Lane, 35, 36

Knights of Labor, 33–34

Kucinich, Dennis, 162
Kydd, Andrea, 133

LAANE. *See* Los Angeles Alliance for a New Economy
Labor/Community Leadership Institute (San Jose), 46–47, 49, 55, 153, 154, 156
Laborers International Union of North America, 239
Labor movement: building unity in, 12, 137–38, 170–72; coalitions among unions, 137–38, 141; decline of, xi, xii, 7; differences among unions, 136–40; dual organizing required by, 12, 18, 177–78, 222, 232; and electoral politics, 1, 160; free-market orientation and exclusion of, 99; and free market unionism, 234; goals of, xvi, 232; immigrants and, xv–xvi, 65; local institutions and, 9–10; rebirth in 1930s, 15, 16–18; and regionalism, 32–38; and regional power building, obstacles to full engagement with, 224–28; regional power building and revitalization of, xii, 222–24; social role of, xvi, 1–2; social vision required for revitalization of, 8, 9, 14, 224; in urban growth regimes, 30. *See also* Central labor councils; National unions; Regional power building; Worker organizing; *specific unions*
LACRA. *See* Los Angeles Community Redevelopment Agency
Land use: as economic development issue, 91. *See also* Community benefits agreements
Latinos: African Americans and, 67, 150, 176; coalitions with, 147–50; in Los Angeles, 65–66, 133, 135, 147–48; political power potential of, 146–47; in urban growth regimes, 30
Leadership: accountability of, 180–81; of central labor councils, 71, 81, 140–42, 229; and regional power building, 71, 188, 192, 214–15
Leadership development programs: AFL-CIO, 235, 237; business and, 153; first Spanish-language, 68; Immigrant Workers Freedom Ride (2003) and, 75–76; New Alliance and, 232, 234; think-and-act tanks and, 98; UCLA and, 68–69. *See also* Candidate development; Civic leadership institutes
League of Women Voters, 50
Ledebur, Larry, 22, 103

Lee, Barbara, 76
Leininger, Bill, 47
LeRoy, Greg, 51, 62
Lewis, Peter, 239
Life in the Valley Economy: Silicon Valley Progress Report 2007 (report), 106
Living wage campaigns/ordinances, 108, 127; in Cleveland, 212, 213; and coalition building, 108, 127–28; in East Bay area, 75; economic context and, 218; in Los Angeles, 61, 66, 70, 97, 136, 152; in Milwaukee, 207; in San Diego, 73; in San Francisco, 79; in San Jose, 52–53, 120; in Santa Monica, 66, 136, 251n44; and union organizing, 55–56
Living Wage Coalition of Sonoma County, 78–79, 252n57
Local government: limits on, 27; regime theory of, 28–30. *See also* Regional governance
Local labor councils. *See* Central labor councils
López-Garza, Marta, 23, 103
Los Angeles, California: Campaign for Clean and Safe Ports in, 92–93, 128t; coalition building in, 59–60, 62, 65–69, 128t, 175–76; community benefits agreements in, 62, 70, 109–10, 243; electoral politics in, 63–65, 67–68, 175–77; fragmentation of public policy in, 25; health care worker organizing in, 69, 138; hotel worker organizing in, 70, 152; independent expenditure campaigns in, 174–77; interfaith alliance in, 152; Justice for Janitors campaigns in, 69, 138, 177; labor-Latino alliance in, 65–66, 133, 135, 147–48; living wage campaigns in, 61, 66, 97, 136, 152; mayoral elections in, 63–64, 65, 67, 150, 171, 176–77; Measure 75 in, 177; public subsidies in, 102; regional power building in, 39, 58–71; South, 174–77; Staples Center development in, 109
Los Angeles Alliance for a New Economy (LAANE), 59, 95, 181; Accountable Development Project of, 109; board of directors of, 60; and coalition building, 66; and community benefits agreements, 62, 70, 109–10, 243; EBASE compared with, 75, 76; and interfaith alliance, 152; and living wage campaigns, 61, 66, 97, 136, 152; public subsidy research by, 102; and regional economic development, 70; research and policy development by, 60–62, 71, 96; staff of, 61, 95;

and worker organizing, 66, 70; and worker-retention ordinance, 61
Los Angeles Apollo Alliance, 68
Los Angeles Business Team, 62
Los Angeles City Council, 64
Los Angeles Community Redevelopment Agency (LACRA), 70, 110
Los Angeles County Board of Supervisors, 64
Los Angeles County Federation of Labor: and coalition building, 65–66, 181; and community college funding, 93; and electoral mobilization, 63–64, 181; and interfaith alliance, 152; leadership role of, 71; and regional power building, 59; transformation of, 61, 62; and worker organizing, 69
Los Angeles International Airport: community benefits agreement at, 110; worker organizing at, 69–70, 97
Los Angeles Metropolitan Alliance, 67
Luce, Stephanie, 141
Lucy, William, 35
Ludlow, Martin, 64, 68, 70
Luria, Dan, 22

Mackinaw Center, 145
Madison, Wisconsin, 114–15
Maersk, 92
Maldonado, Maritza, 2
Mares, Don, 173
Martinez, Marty, 64
Mathematica Policy Research, 5
Mayoral contests: in Atlanta, 193; in Los Angeles, 63–64, 65, 67, 150, 171, 176–77; in San Diego, 251n51
Mayor's Office of Immigrant and Refugee Affairs (MOIRA), 149
McKay Foundation, 242
MCLC. *See* Milwaukee County Labor Council
McMillan, MaryBe, 141
Measure 75 (Los Angeles County), 177
Media: electoral coverage by, 160–61; framing research and, 107; Spanish-language television, 147–48
Medical debt campaign (New Haven), 97–98, 201–2, 203
Medina, Eliseo, 147, 148
Megenhardt, Dave, 211
Mehrens, Dereka, 45
MetroHartford Alliance (Connecticut), 21

Metropolitan Advisory Committee Project (San Diego), 74
Mexican-American Advisory Committee (San Diego), 74
Mexican American Legal Defense and Education Fund, 148
Michigan: Detroit, 104, 219–20, 231; fragmentation of public policy in, 25; Grand Rapids, 26; Reagan Democrats in, 164–65; worker-to-worker organizing in, 167
Miller, David, 25
Milwaukee, Wisconsin: community benefits agreements in, 112–13, 218; economic conditions in, 205; experiments in regional work in, 205–10; worker training in, 114–15
Milwaukee County Labor Council (MCLC), 205, 209
Milwaukee Innercity Congregations Allied for Hope, 112
Milwaukee Jobs Initiative, 206
Minnesota, tax revenue sharing program in, 26
Minority groups: and Boston school refurbishing campaign, 93, 145; building trades unions and, 140, 144–45; coalitions with, 143–51, 196; ethnic chambers of commerce, 120–21; and political power structure, 145–46. *See also* African Americans; Immigrants; Latinos
MOIRA. *See* Mayor's Office of Immigrant and Refugee Affairs
Montgomery, David, 33
Moody, Leslie, 191, 215
MoveOn.org, 159
Moyski, Steve, 111
Ms. Foundation, 242
Murphy, Dick, 251n51
Murphy, Frank, 18

NARAL Pro-Choice America, 174
Nathan Cummings Foundation, 133, 242
National Association for the Advancement of Colored People, 235
National Association for Working Women, 191
National unions: and central labor councils, 34, 225–26, 228–29, 236; first efforts to form, 33; role of, need to rethink, 244; and worker organizing, 69. *See also specific unions*

Needmor Fund, 242
Neighborhood Community Institute (San Jose), 47
Neighborhood Development Alternatives (Los Angeles), 156
Nelson, Mark, 141
New Alliance program, 217, 230, 232–35, 239, 256n1
New Deal, 17, 243
New Economy Working Solutions (NEWS), 78, 79, 95, 252n57
New Haven, Connecticut: economic conditions in, 199, 205; regional power building in, 82, 135–36, 181, 200–204
New Jersey, regional power building in, 82–83
New Party, 207, 208, 258n28
New Right, 124, 181, 222, 241, 258n38
NEWS. *See* New Economy Working Solutions
New Voices campaign, 35, 36
New World Foundation, 98–99, 193, 242, 255n20, 258n38
New York State: New Alliance in, 233–34; regional power building in, 82. *See also* Buffalo
Nicholls, Walter Julio, 59–60
Nichols, Ben, xix
Nickels, Greg, 198
Nonprofit organizations: 501(c)3, 42; 527-based, 174; capacity provided by, 71; central labor councils and, 95, 188. *See also* Think-and-act tanks
North American Free Trade Agreement, 164
North Bay area, California, 78–79
North Bay Labor Council, 78
North Carolina: regional power building in, 235; unionization levels in, 234–35
North Carolina State AFL-CIO, 235
North Shore AFL-CIO Federation of Labor, 214. *See also* Cleveland AFL-CIO
Núñez, Fabian, 64, 249n16

Oakland, California, 76
Oakland International Airport, 75
Ohio. *See* Cleveland
Ohio Nurses Association, 213
OLAW. *See* Organization for Los Angeles Workers
Orange County Central Labor Council (OCLC), 237–38

Orange County Communities Organized for Responsible Development (OCCORD), 238
Oregon, regional governing structures in, 26
Orfield, Myron, 25, 26
Organization for Los Angeles Workers (OLAW), 65, 135, 147, 174
Ottinger Foundation, 242

Pacific Institute for Community Organizing (PICO), 45, 76, 143
PACT. *See* People Acting in Community Together
Pandori, David, 53
Partnerships for Working Families, 78, 82, 95, 96, 216, 242, 243
Pastor, Manuel, 23, 24, 31–32, 60, 103
Paulson, Tim, 80
Peer-to-peer support: and regional power building, 189, 192, 193, 216–17; Union Cities and, 228
Pennsylvania: New Alliance program in, 230, 235; regional power building in, 82; steel industry organizing in, 18
People Acting in Community Together (PACT), 2–6, 45–46
People-to-people politics. *See* Grassroots organizing
PICO. *See* Pacific Institute for Community Organizing
Pittsburgh UNITED, 82
Plumbers, Steamfitters and Refrigeration Fitters Local 393, 154
Policy action centers. *See* Think-and-act tanks
Policy development, 11–12, 94–99; and candidate accountability, 180–81; in East Bay area, 77; integrative agendas and, 88–89; in Los Angeles, 59, 60–62; in San Diego, 73; in San Jose, 41–44; think-and-act tanks and, 104–8
Policy Matters Ohio, 95, 210, 211–12, 214
Policy reform regionalism, 31–32
Political parties: and American electoral system, 161; "soft money" contributions to, 174. *See also* Democratic Party; Republican Party
Political work: aggressive regional, 12–13, 169–81; candidate accountability, 180–81; candidate development, 178–80; central labor councils and, 171–72, 181–82; in East Bay area, 77; field operations, 172–74;

fragmentation among unions, 170–71; and governance, 182–83; innovation in, 159; in Los Angeles, 62–65; national focus of, 37–38; need for unity in, 170–72; people-to-people, 165–67; power-building vs. traditional, 48, 159; precinct-level organization, 174–78; rethinking of, 164–69; in San Diego, 73–74; in San Jose, 47–50; social vision and, 48. *See also* Electoral mobilization; Grassroots organizing

Poverty, mainstream vs. progressive approaches to, 101

Preminger, Steve, 118–19

Progressive Milwaukee, 206, 207, 208, 209

Proposition 72 (California), 237

Proposition 187 (California), 138

Proposition 209 (California), 120

Proposition 226 (California), 165–67

Proposition 227 (California), 154

Public policy: fragmentation among tools for, 105. *See also* Policy development

Public subsidies, 102–4; accountability campaigns, 50–52, 108–9; and community benefits agreements, 111; growth of, 103; ineffectiveness of, 103–4; lax standards for, 102, 104; and quality of jobs, 73, 102, 103, 104

Puget Sound Sage, 199

Pushback Network, 251n46

Racism, 144, 145, 149

Reagan, Ronald, 165

Reagan Democrats, 164–65

Recession of 2008, xi–xii

Regime theory, 27–30

Regional governance: fragmentation of, 25–27; regime theory of, 27–30; toward new regime of, 30–31

Regionalism: business, 21–24, 26–27; community development, 31; labor movement, 32–38; policy reform, 31–32; social movement, 32

Regional power building: and AFL-CIO leadership institute, 235; approach to business, 116–23; in Atlanta, 81, 192–95; in Boston, 81, 135, 204; central labor councils and, 9–10, 38; Change to Win split and, 240–41; in Cleveland, 210–14; conditions fostering, 187–89, 256n1; in conservative socio-political context, 72, 74; and cultural shift,

230–31, 241; in Denver, 81, 190–92; in East Bay area, 74–77; economic conditions and, 189, 217–20; and economic development, 70, 73, 89–90; foundation support and, 188, 215–16, 242–44; funding for, vs. funding for electoral mobilization, 238–39; importance of, 13–14; and integrative policy agendas, 88–89; investing in, 238–40; and labor movement revitalization, xii, 222–24; leadership and, 71, 188, 192, 214–15; in Los Angeles, 39, 58–71; in Milwaukee, 205–10; national institutional labor support for, 232–41; national labor leaders' critical assessment of, 228–32; national strategy for, 221–22, 244–45; in New Haven, 82, 135–36; in New Jersey, 82–83; in New York State, 82, 233–34; in North Bay area, 78–79; in North Carolina, 235; obstacles to labor's full engagement with, 224–28; in Orange County, 238; origins of, xvii, 39; peer-to-peer support and, 189, 192, 193, 216–17; in Pittsburgh, 82; and progressive governance regimes, 30–31; research and, 41–44, 94, 96–97; in San Diego, 72–74; in San Francisco, 79–80; in San Jose, 39, 41–50; in Seattle, 196–99; and sectoral development work, 113–16; and social vision, 71, 124–25; struggle for recognition, 228; sustainability of, 71–72; three legs of, 10–13, 41–50, 87; ultimate goal of, 30; and worker organizing, 56, 69–70, 138–39, 230–31. *See also* Coalition building; Policy development; Political work

Regional Power Building Research Project, xix

Renters' rights: as regional economic development issue, 92; San Jose campaign for, 129

Republican Party: anti-immigrant attacks of 1990s, 65; and conservative social vision, 124; New Right, 124, 181, 222, 241, 258n38

Research: Center on Policy Initiatives (CPI) and, 73; and economic development reframing, 105–7; Los Angeles Alliance for a New Economy (LAANE) and, 59, 60–62; New Economy Working Solutions (NEWS) and, 78; and regional power building, 41–44, 94, 96–97; Working Partnerships USA and, 43–44, 53–57, 105–6

Reuther, Walter, xv, xvi

Reynolds, David, xviii–xix, 154, 162, 167

Rhee, Nari, 48, 153, 249n5

Right-to-work laws, 190, 257n6
Rogers, Joel, 22
Rogers, Rich, 204
Rose, Fred, 154
Rusk, David, 25
Russell Sage Foundation, 219
Ryan, John, 95, 141, 171, 210–11, 212, 214

SAJE. *See* Strategic Actions for a Just
    Economy
Salas, Angelica, 60
Sam's Club, 121
Sanchez, Orlando, 149
Sanders, Bernie, 162
Sanders, Jerry, 251n51
San Diego, California: disunity of labor
    unions in, 137; mayoral contests in, 251n51;
    political climate in, 72, 74; regional power
    building in, 72–74
San Diego—Imperial Counties Labor Council
    (SDICLC), 72–74, 137
San Diego United Way, 72
SANE. *See* Syracuse Alliance for a New
    Economy
San Francisco, California: Bay Area Rapid
    Transit system, 54; labor movement in,
    79–80
San Francisco Labor Council, 79, 80
San Jose, California, 40; children's health care
    campaign in, 2–7, 91–92; civic leadership
    institute in, 46–47, 49, 55, 153, 154, 156;
    community benefits agreements in, 53–54,
    121; interfaith alliance in, 152–53; Justice
    for Janitors campaign in, 43, 119; labor-
    ACORN partnership in, 45, 53, 132–33;
    labor-business partnerships in, 116–21; liv-
    ing wage campaigns in, 52–53, 120; regional
    power building in, 39, 41–50. *See also* South
    Bay Labor Council (SBLC)
San Jose City Council, 47, 50, 154
San Jose State University, Labor/Community
    Leadership Institute, 46–47, 49, 55, 153,
    154, 156
Santa Clara, San Benito Building Trades
    Council, 249n5
Santa Clara Family Health Plan, 4, 5
Santa Clara Valley. *See* Silicon Valley
Santa Monica, California, 66, 136, 251n44
Santa Monicans for Responsible Tourism
    (SMART), 66, 136

Santa Rosa City Council, 79
Sawyer, Rick, 137
Saxenian, Annalee, 24
SBLC. *See* South Bay Labor Council
Schattschneider, E. E., 164
School employees, organizing of, 177
Schrag, Peter, 44
Schwarzenegger, Arnold, 176
SCOPE. *See* Strategic Concepts in Organizing
    and Policy Education
Scott, Deborah, 194
Scott, Lorenzo, 194
SDICLC. *See* San Diego—Imperial Counties
    Labor Council
Seattle, Washington: 1999 World Trade
    Organization protests in, 126, 196; economy
    of, 190; regional power building in, 196–99;
    unionization in, 190; United Food and
    Commercial Workers (UFCW) in, 139
Seattle Building and Construction Trades
    Council, 196
Seattle Union Now (SUN), 196–97
Sectoral development planning, 113–16
SEIU. *See* Service Employees International
    Union
Service economy jobs, quality of, 219
Service Employees International Union
    (SEIU): and Children's Health Initiative, 6;
    District 925, 197; District 1199, 200; fund-
    ing for, 239; and immigrant groups, 137;
    Justice for Janitors campaign of, 43, 138,
    177; living wage ordinances and organiz-
    ing by, 55; Local 47, 180; Local 99, 148, 175,
    177; Local 105, 149, 191; Local 434B, 175,
    177; Local 707, 78; Local 715, 51, 56, 249n5;
    Local 1877, 147, 175, 177; in Los Angeles,
    69–70; in Milwaukee, 112
Shaw, Richard, 148
Sheet Metal Workers International Associa-
    tion, 166
Sheppard, Joyce, 257n14
Shock Absorbers in the Flexible Economy
    (report), 43
Sierra Club, 195
Silicon Valley, California, 2–3, 40; coalitions
    with technology companies in, 116–17;
    labor movement in, xvii; progressive per-
    spective on economy of, 43–44, 106, 107;
    regional power building in, 40–58. *See also*
    San Jose

Silicon Valley Leaders Group, 40
Silicon Valley Manufacturing Group (SVMG), 54, 117
Sillen, Robert, 5
Small businesses, coalitions with, 120–21
SMART. *See* Santa Monicans for Responsible Tourism
Smith, Adam, 252n6
Smith, Carla, 257n14
Smith, Sabrina, 60
Social contract, need for new, 8, 201, 244
Social movement regionalism, 32
Social vision: alternative, regional power building and, 71, 124–25; and coalition building, 45–46; and Healthy Kids program, 6–7; and labor movement revitalization, 8, 9, 14, 224; and labor's rebirth in 1930s, 16, 18; of New Right, 124; and political work, 48
Social well-being, vs. business success, 89, 99
SOL. *See* Strengthening Our Lives
Solidago Foundation, 42, 242
Solis, Hilda, 64
Sonoma County Accountable Development Coalition, 78, 79
Sonoma County Clergy and Laity United for Economic Justice, 78
Soros, George, 239
South Bay Labor Council (SBLC), 40–58; and ACORN, 45, 53, 132–33; aggressive political action by, 47–50; Amy Dean at, xvii, 41; and business tax subsidies campaign, 50–52; and children's health care campaign, 2, 4; coalition building by, 44–47, 137; and community benefits agreements, 53–54; and Community Blueprint Project, 58; and electoral mobilization, 48–49; and employer groups, 116–18, 120; endorsements by, 48, 172, 179; and faith community, 153; foundation support and expansion of, 42; Housing for All campaign of, 45, 128–29; leadership role of, 6, 71; and living wage campaign, 52–53, 120; power of, 49; public policy education sessions of, 181; and public transit issues, 54–55; research and policy development capacity of, 41–44; and worker organizing, 55–56
Stamford Organizing Project, 201
Stanford University, 56
Stone, Clarence, 27, 248n13

Strategic Actions for a Just Economy (SAJE), 59, 62, 68, 109
Strategic Concepts in Organizing and Policy Education (SCOPE), 10, 32, 66–68, 175, 251n46; and Building Partnerships USA, 216; and civic leadership institutes, 156; and electoral organizing, 177; and LAANE, 60
Strengthening Neighborhoods initiative, 192
Strengthening Our Lives (SOL), 65
Subsidies. *See* Public subsidies
SUN. *See* Seattle Union Now
SVMG. *See* Silicon Valley Manufacturing Group
Sweeney, John, 159, 164, 165, 196, 239; and central labor councils, 35; and Committee 2000, 232; and electoral politics, 164, 165; and regional power building, xvii; and Union Cities program, 227
Swift Boat Veterans for Truth, 174
Syracuse Alliance for a New Economy (SANE), 82

Tattersall, Amanda, 129
Tax subsidies. *See* Public subsidies
Team San Jose, 56
Teamsters: Local 174, 197; Proposition 226 and, 166
Technology, use in electoral mobilization, 136, 176
Technology companies: coalitions with, 116–17; craft union model and, 138–39
Temporary agencies: exploitative practices of, 57. *See also* Contingent employment
Tenants' rights. *See* Renters' rights
Texas, labor-immigrant alliances in, 148–49
Thigpenn, Anthony, 66
Think-and-act tanks, 11–12, 94–99, 188; acting role of, 97–98, 107–16; in Boston, 81; and civic leadership institutes, 98; coalition building by, 94–95, 96, 97; in Connecticut, 82, 95–96; in Denver, 81, 95; in East Bay area, 75–76, 77, 95; framing research by, 105–7; funding for, 42, 98–99, 242–44; key role of, 242; network of, 216; in North Bay area, 78, 79; and policy development, 104–8; in San Diego, 73, 95; in San Francisco, need for, 80; thinking role of, 94, 96–97. *See also* Los Angeles Alliance for a New Economy (LAANE); Working Partnerships USA (WPUSA)

This Could Be the Start of Something Big (Pastor, Benner, and Matsuoka), 31–32
Thompson, Tommy, 207
TIDC. *See* Tourism Industry Development Council
Tides Foundation, 242
Tompkins-Cortland Labor Council, xix
Torrico, Alberto, 77
Tourism Industry Development Council (TIDC), 60–61
Transportation policy: Campaign for Clean and Safe Ports (Los Angeles), 92–93, 128t; Contra Costa County Labor Council and, 77; labor-business partnership on, 117; as regional economic development issue, 91, 92–93; in Sonoma County, 252n58; South Bay Labor Council (SBLC) and, 54–55; in Wisconsin, 207

UCLA. *See* University of California—Los Angeles
UFCW. *See* United Food and Commercial Workers
ULA. *See* United Labor Agency
Union Cities, 36–38, 196; limitations of, 225–28, 232; and peer-to-peer support, 228; and regional power building, 216
Union Summer, 191
Unitarian Universalist Veatch Program of Shelter Rock, 242
United Association for Labor Education, 217
United Association of Plumbers and Pipefitters, 138, 154
United Auto Workers: and 1936 GM strike, 17; Local 2300, xviii–xix; president of, xv
United Brotherhood of Carpenters and Joiners of America, 166
United Farm Workers (UFW), 191
United Food and Commercial Workers (UFCW): in Colorado, 139–40, 254n8; in Contra Costa County, 77; in Seattle, 139
United Labor Agency (ULA), 95, 210, 211, 213–14
United Transportation Union, 70
United Way, 74
UNITE HERE: and immigrant groups, 137; living wage ordinances and organizing by, 56; Local 2850, 75, 76; Locals 34 and 35, 200; and Los Angeles International Airport

workers, 69–70; in Orange County, 238; in Santa Monica, 136
University of California—Berkeley Labor Center, 252n57
University of California—Los Angeles (UCLA): Center for Health Policy Research, 4; Center for Labor Research and Education, 59, 60, 68–69; Urban Planning Department, 68–69
University of California—Santa Cruz, 96
University of Wisconsin—Madison, Center on Wisconsin Strategy, 96, 206
Univision (channel 34), 147–48
Urban regimes, 28–30
Urban Strategies Council, 76

Van der Heever, Andrea, 200
Villaraigosa, Antonio, 63–70, 150, 171, 176
Voss, Ed, 49
Voter turnout, 162–63, 163t. *See also* Electoral mobilization

Wal-Mart: campaigns against, 77, 92, 110; low-road strategies of, 121; pressures on suppliers, 100; public subsidies to, 102
Washington, Harold, xvi
Washington State. *See* Seattle
Washington State Labor Council, 198
Wayne State University, 220
Wellstone, Paul, 162
Wellstone Action, 244
West, Tony, 49
White, Michael, 212
Williams, Lloyd, 138, 154
Williamson, Steve, 197, 198
Wilson, Pete, 166
Wisconsin: community benefits agreements in, 112–13, 218; experiments in regional work in, 205–10; sectoral development strategies in, 114–15
Wisconsin Regional Training Partnership (WRTP), 114–15, 206
Wolsey, Lynn, 78
Wong, Kent, 60, 147
Wood, Jim, 63
Woodward, Douglas, 104
Worker Center (Seattle), 197–98
Worker organizing: contingent work as barrier to, 56; as economic development issue,

93–94; "just in time" production systems and, 139, 254n7; Los Angeles Alliance for a New Economy (LAANE) and, 66; rebuilding of, 223; regional power building and, 56, 69–70, 138–39, 230–31; social shift required for, 230–31; South Bay Labor Council (SBLC) and, 55–56; think-and-act tanks and, 97; worker-to-worker, 17, 165, 167

Workers' Bill of Rights (Cleveland), 179, 212, 213

Worker training: inadequacy of, 102; sectoral development strategies and, 114–15

Working America, 177–78, 256n20

Working Families Party, 258n28

Working Partnerships USA (WPUSA), 42–43, 95; academic connections of, 96; affordable housing research by, 53, 128; and Building Partnerships USA, 216; business alliances of, 118–19; capacity provided by, 71; and children's health care campaign, 2–6; and Community Blueprint Project, 58; as community leader, 6; on contingent employment, 56–57; creation of, 42; endorsements of political candidates by, 179; experimental staffing service created by, 57; foundation support for, 42, 133; framing research by, 43–44, 105–6; on health care reform, 243–44; on immigration and economic development, 93; LAANE compared with, 61, 62; and Labor/Community Leadership Institute, 46–47; and living wage campaign, 120; and media attention, 107; public policy education sessions of, 181; support to local unions, 42–43; transit system analysis by, 54

World Trade Organization, 1999 protests against, 126, 196

Wortham, Dale, 148

WPUSA. *See* Working Partnerships USA

WRTP. *See* Wisconsin Regional Training Partnership

Yale—New Haven Hospital campaign, 82, 91, 97–98, 136, 200–202

Yale University, 200; unions at, 82, 136, 181, 201

Young Workers United, 79